"This is the most important work our schools need to do ... Santoyo is the master. Without a doubt, Paul's expertise ha ... student achievement gains. His insights have provided our school leadership and, more importantly, our teachers with the skills to use the data to improve their instruction and ensure all of our students are successful."

—Jennifer Niles, founder and head of school, E.L. Haynes Public Charter
School, Washington, D.C.

Driven by Data is much more than a compilation of chronicles about schools that have made outstanding progress. Paul Bambrick-Santoyo's work not only shares the results, but actually tells the story of *how* the results were achieved. This invaluable book is indeed a desk reference for any instructional leader seeking a concrete, data-driven solution to problems in his or her school or district."

—Jarvis T. Sanford, managing director, The Academy for Urban School Leadership

"*Driven by Data* is an inspiring and encouraging manifesto of how schools can make significant student learning gains by using data-driven instruction. Paul provides the proof and the tools that guarantee high expectations and rigor in any school's daily routine. This model should be replicated everywhere across the country."

—Turon Ivy, former director of Chicago International
Charter School, Bucktown Campus

"Every leader who is accountable to increase student achievement should read Paul Bambrick-Santoyo's book, *Driven by Data*. I have been fortunate enough to have worked with Paul prior to becoming a principal, and learned from him how to best implement his theories on how to assess, analyze, and respond to student data."

—Sean Conley, principal,
The Morrell Park Elementary/Middle
School, Baltimore, Maryland

"There are many books on the topic of data-driven instruction, but Paul provides a true road map for approaching this important work. The book is all inclusive: research-based strategies, instructions for the practitioner, and evidence of success."

—Tiffany Hardrick, co-founder and principal, Miller-McCoy Academy for
Mathematics and Business

DRIVEN BY DATA

A Practical Guide to Improve Instruction

Paul Bambrick-Santoyo

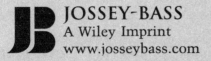

JOSSEY-BASS
A Wiley Imprint
www.josseybass.com

Published by Jossey-Bass
A Wiley Imprint
989 Market Street, San Francisco, CA 94103-1741—www.josseybass.com

NORTH ★ STAR

Uncommon Schools
EXCELLENCE ⟩ NORTH ★ STAR ⟨ COLLEGIATE ⟩ TRUE NORTH ⟨ PREPARATORY ⟩

Poem by Carl Sandburg on page 18 courtesy of Houghton Mifflin Harcourt Publishing Company: "Chicago Poet" in CORNHUSKERS by Carl Sandburg, copyright 1918 by Holt, Rinehart, and Winston, and renewed 1946 by Carl Sandburg, reproduced by permission of Houghton Mifflin Harcourt Publishing Company.

Jossey-Bass books and products are available through most bookstores. To contact Jossey-Bass directly call our Customer Care Department within the U.S. at 800-956-7739, outside the U.S. at 317-572-3986, or fax 317-572-4002.

Jossey-Bass also publishes its books in a variety of electronic formats. Some content that appears in print may not be available in electronic books.

Library of Congress Cataloging-in-Publication Data
Bambrick-Santoyo, Paul, 1972-
  Driven by data : a practical guide to improve instruction / Paul Bambrick-Santoyo.
  p. cm.
  Includes index.
  ISBN 978-0-470-54874-5 (paper/cd-rom)
  1. Education–United States–Data processing–Case studies. 2. Educational tests and measurements–United States–Case studies. 3. Educational assessment–United States–Case studies. 4. School improvement programs–United States–Case studies. 5. School management and organization–United States–Case studies.
I. Title.
  LB1028.43.B35 2010
  371.27'1–dc22

                                                                            2009046005

Printed in the United States of America
FIRST EDITION

PB Printing   10

Contents

Contents of the CD-ROM

Assessment

Elementary Interim Assessment Calendar
Middle School Interim Assessment Calendar
High School Assessment Calendar
Interim Assessment Review Checklist
Student Assessment Reflection Template: Williamsburg Collegiate
   Charter School
Literacy Sample Assessments: Fifth Grade
Math Sample Assessments: Middle School
Algebra Sample Assessment: High School

Analysis

North Star Assessment Analysis Sheet and Instructional Plan Template:
   Elementary
Assessment Analysis Instructional Plan Template: Middle School and
   High School
ECS Assessment Analysis Sheet and Instructional Plan Sample
Data-Driven Analysis Meetings: Leading Effective Assessment Analysis
   Meetings
Results Grids
   Sample Results Grid: Third Grade Literacy
   Sample Results Grid: Fifth Grade Literacy
   Sample Results Grid: Middle School Math
   Sample Results Grid: High School Math

Action

Action Planning Worksheet
Increasing Rigor Throughout the Lesson: Data-Driven Classroom
 Best Practices
Results Meeting Protocol

Culture

Entry Plan for Data-Driven Instruction: New School Start-Up
Entry Plan for Data-Driven Instruction: New Principal in Existing School
Implementation Calendar

Case Studies

Douglass Street School Case
Entry Plan Case Studies
Entry Plan Case Studies Highlighted for Presenters
Data-Driven Instruction Failed
 Springsteen School Case: Elementary Narrative
 Springsteen School Case: Elementary State Test Data
 Springsteen School Case: Elementary STANFORD 9 and TN Data
 Springsteen School Case: Middle School Narrative
 Springsteen School Case: Middle School State Test Data
 Springsteen School Case: Middle School STANFORD 9 and TN Data

PowerPoint Presentations

Comprehensive Leadership Workshop
Entry Plan Leadership Workshop
Mid-Year Follow-Up Workshop
Teacher Training Workshop

Data-Driven Implementation Rubric

About the Author

Paul **Bambrick-Santoyo** has spent seven years at North Star, and during that time the network has seen dramatic increases in performance in student achievement, reaching 90/90/90 status (90 percent free or reduced lunch, 90 percent students of color, 90 percent proficient on state assessments) in almost every category and grade level, making North Star one of the highest-achieving urban schools in New Jersey. Bambrick-Santoyo is currently a managing director of Uncommon Schools, uniting North Star to a community of some of the highest-achieving urban schools in the country. In that work he is currently managing the expansion of North Star into a network of three elementary schools, three middle schools, and a high school by 2011. He has trained more than 1,800 school leaders nationwide in his work at Uncommon Schools and as the data-driven instruction faculty member for New Leaders for New Schools, the leading national urban school leadership training program. Prior to joining North Star, he worked for six years in a bilingual school in Mexico City, where he founded the International Baccalaureate program at the middle school level, led significant gains in English test score results, and was named Teacher of the Year in 1999. He earned a B.A. in social justice from Duke University (1994) and his M.Ed. in school administration via New Leaders for New Schools from the City University of New York—Baruch College (2003).

To all school leaders, teachers, and staff—that we may build

schools that guarantee the highest levels of learning for every child;

our children most certainly deserve them.

Acknowledgments

The ideas in *Driven by Data* were formed and shaped through work with thousands of schools across the country. Each interaction with a school leader—and each opportunity to give a workshop—helped sharpen the focus of the model presented here and allowed it to be tested in a wide variety of environments. All those who put it to the test and gave me feedback along the way had a profound influence on the end product.

First and foremost, Dan Rauch was just a college student with no prior experience when he immersed himself into the work of forming this book with me. With a tremendous talent for grasping the data-driven model, and a brilliance for putting thoughts into writing, he shaped the initial drafts of many of the chapters in this book. His footprint remains embedded here, and it is a sure sign of the future success that will come to him in any field he chooses.

When it came to finding probing thought partners for the ideas in this book, none were more present than Kim Marshall and Mark Murphy. In their respective work as principals and leaders of principals, they gained invaluable insight into what worked—and what didn't—in schools nationwide. From Kim's multipage feedback letters after workshops to Mark's pre-workshop planning meetings, their guidance as friends and colleagues helped make sure this work was accessible and usable for all school leaders.

Every story has a beginning, and this one occurred when James Verrilli and I traveled to Amistad Academy in New Haven, Connecticut, to see this "new world" of data-driven instruction. A person of utter integrity, Jamey remained steadfast in the implementation of this model, even when we had no real certainty that we would succeed. I wish everyone gets the chance to work with someone as inspiring and humble as Jamey. Behind the scenes, Jamey's co-founder Norman Atkins planted the seed: he was willing to entrust his legacy to me and gave me a perfectly formed launching pad to grow as a learner and a leader. His mentorship was fundamental to the leader I have become today.

Honing this to perfection were the school leaders at North Star and Uncommon Schools, some of whom are highlighted in the success stories in this book. Julie Jackson, Jesse Rector, Mike Mann, Shana Pyatt, and Juliann Harris put this work to the test every day in our North Star schools. John King, Doug Lemov, Brett Peiser, and Evan Rudall brought their own expertise in the areas of planning, instruction, culture, and operations, and they integrated the data-driven model within our larger framework for school excellence.

The real heroes of this book are all the school leaders who have launched this work successfully and are transforming urban education nationwide. Only twenty of those school leaders were able to be highlighted in this book's success stories, but there are so many more!

While the school leaders are the heroes of the book, the heroes of my heart are my wife and children. Ana, Maria, and Nicolas were all quite young during the formation of this book, and they endured many an afternoon of me writing on the computer or staring thoughtfully off into space! Gaby stood by me through it all, supporting me in my weakest moments and providing me daily inspiration of how to love and listen.

Thank you to each and every one of you who have had an impact in the field. With your help, we will improve and reshape education nationwide.

Foreword

If you've ever taught in an American public school, you know the drill. The principal alerts you to her upcoming annual trip to "observe" your class. You sweat the preparation of what you hope is your best lesson. She jots notes in the back of your room. Your kids muster their least disruptive behavior, perhaps on account of the rare presence of two additional humongous eyeballs on their necks.

A few weeks later (if all goes well, not a few months later), there's the post-observation conference. The principal slides a standard-issue form across her desk. She's rated you "satisfactory" in most of the boxes, "needs improvement" in a few. Should you dispute the recommendations in the space allotted on the bottom of the template or smile and pledge to do better? Best-case scenario: the principal supports you, knows her stuff, and shares helpful feedback on your craft—for example, how you can be more engaging in your delivery. More typically, she encourages you to pick up the pace so that you can "cover" the required curriculum by year's end or urges you to "integrate technology" per the district mandate to modernize. You sign your review, close your classroom door, and resume teaching, relieved you won't have to relive these rituals for another year. As both professional development and accountability, this has been our education system's losing playbook for as long as the oldest teachers you can remember can *themselves* remember.

Now comes Paul Bambrick-Santoyo—a brilliant instructional leader and trainer of principals—charging onto the field like a middle linebacker with the game-changing volume you're holding in your hands, *Driven by Data*. Mr. Bambrick—as he's known to students—has the instructional equivalent of linebacker eyes. His peripheral vision catches all the subtle teacher moves in any one lesson, and he's peripatetic, ranging widely across a school, weaving in and out of classrooms. Gone are the set-piece annual observations. But what's really significant here—in light of the broken observational paradigm—is that Bambrick has trained his eyes on *the students* as much as the teachers. The first question provoked by his work is ontological, the schooling equivalent of the fabled tree-forest conundrum:

If there's teaching going on, but the students aren't learning, is it really teaching?

I first met Bambrick in the late summer of 2002 when he arrived at North Star Academy. Five years earlier, I had co-founded and then co-led North Star with one of the greatest teachers and principals of our generation, James Verrilli. It was one of New Jersey's very first charter public schools, located in the city of Newark, a troubled district that had been taken over by the state. We'd begun with seventy-two fifth and sixth graders, picked from a random lottery, 90 percent of whom were eligible for a subsidized lunch, 99 percent of them black or Latino, and who scored—on average—worse than their Newark peers on the state test. North Star was immediately successful at generating huge demand from low-income families, creating an electric student culture that was celebrated in the media and copied by countless other schools, and posting initial test state results that were well above the district average.

Bambrick had been sent to us by an organization with which I'd been involved—New Leaders for New Schools—as the principalship equivalent of a medical resident. He was supposed to spend the year with us and learn how to be a school leader. Had he been born a century ago, my hunch is that Bambrick would have been a priest. Instead he's tethered his humble but deep commitment to social justice—most manifest in two years of Jesuit Community Service as a campus minister in Mobile, Alabama—to the work of closing the achievement gap, one of the most pressing issues of our day. At the same time, he generated a strong sense of academic rigor and the value of high educational expectations and standards during six years as an AP English teacher, basketball coach, and assistant principal at an International Baccalaureate high school in Mexico City, where his wife is from and where he started his family. A 1994 graduate of Duke University, Bambrick is a chronically curious student of how humans learn and a habitual problem solver. He found in North Star a school committed to innovation and excellence.

At North Star and literally hundreds of other schools, I'd watched teachers *covering* an ambitious geometry curriculum, the *Diary of Anne Frank,* an entire earth science textbook; observed teachers standing in front of the classroom *covering* World Wars I and II, or assigning students to write e-mails on laptops to pen pals in Australia. But what math, science, reading, writing, and history had the students really learned? What portion of the intended skills and covered knowledge had lodged in their brains? Where did the lessons fail to meet their mark? Who wasn't getting what?

Many strong teachers know the answers to these questions because they constantly "check for understanding" throughout their classes, and the very best adjust their instruction to meet the learning objectives. But it's hard even for the best teachers, and nearly impossible for novices, to track student progress in an organized, effective way in real time. Novice teachers are, after all, learning to teach, but are they teaching to learn? It's a well-worn convention for teachers to give weekly quizzes or unit tests, which should ostensibly address our core problem, except when those assessments—as is so often the case in the vast majority of schools—lack alignment with the meaningful standards for which students are meant to gain mastery.

As a result, for decades American public schools have given students passing marks, promoted them to the next grade, and then (in the summer) received state test scores showing an alarming number of those promoted students lack basic proficiency, much less mastery, of the concepts they were supposed to learn. Come the fall, even when enterprising teachers use those state test results to inform their instruction, it's already too late. Students have moved on to new teachers and teachers have moved on to new students. Such a vicious cycle tragically harms precisely those children who need the greatest attention: those who come into the lowest-performing public schools with the weakest skills and the most challenging social and economic circumstances. Without the ability to diagnose and support their progress toward meeting college-prep learning standards on a systematic basis, too many adults consign too many of our children to a destiny based on their demography.

About the same time Bambrick started at North Star, another young leader named Doug McCurry had begun to build data systems to track student learning at Amistad Academy, a high-performing charter school serving low-income students in New Haven, Connecticut. Every six weeks, Amistad administered "Curriculum-Based Measurements"—aligned with the state standards—to track student progress. One day I watched as McCurry's team, teacher by teacher, came to see him armed with data on which students had learned which state standards. They used the data to diagnose, for example, which individual students were struggling with multiplying fractions.

To me, it looked like McCurry had created the school equivalent of what data-driven leaders had done to revolutionize public service, business, politics, and sports. In the mid-1990s, for instance, New York City Police Chief William Bratton armed precinct captains and officers with fast data so that they could deploy resources effectively to fight crime. At about the same time, Oakland A's General Manager Billy Beane armed his scouts with new metrics to find productive, undervalued baseball players.

Not long after, I encouraged my colleagues to spend time watching McCurry's data meetings in New Haven. Bambrick did that—and he also went to school on the whole subject. He looked at how the public schools in Brazosport, Texas, and other districts had been quietly doing similar work over the preceding decade. He led a team of teachers in writing a set of interim assessments aligned with the New Jersey state standards; used the assessments to push our program toward increasing levels of college-ready rigor and expectation for all students; designed an effective spreadsheet system for tracking student progress; and, along with co-leader and co-founder James Verrilli, changed the culture of the school so that our leaders and teachers gathered around data to drive student learning. Our teachers began to engage and own responsibility for upping the rigor of student learning, re-teaching failed lessons, analyzing errors in understanding, and creating better assessment tools. Their meetings moved from the sad convention of post-observation conferences to data meetings in which they fought as tenaciously for student achievement gains in their classrooms as Bratton's police officers battled crime on New York City streets.

Changing the mind-set of teachers and the culture of a school so that team members are enthusiastic about assessment; this is precisely what takes a very good school like North Star and makes it great. Bambrick and Verrilli made that happen. Within two years of his first day on the job, Bambrick replaced me—and within three he'd become the managing director of the burgeoning network of North Star Academies, which in the fall of 2010 will be three middle schools, two elementary schools, and a growing high school. At the same time, North Star helped birth and is a part of a growing charter management organization, Uncommon Schools, a network that will eventually include more than thirty schools and twelve thousand students in Newark, New York City, and upstate New York.

Meanwhile, the idea of data-driven instruction has also caught on in a larger educational universe, and Bambrick has become a pathfinder on the entire subject, having trained more than one thousand principals serving a half-million children in cities all over the country. The results can be seen not only in the twenty case studies in this book but in schools and classrooms nationwide.

As it happens, leaders and teachers often arrive at his sessions highly skeptical about an overtested culture. They imagine that data-driven instruction is an elaborate stratagem for promoting "test prep." They often show up because under the accountability pressure generated by federal No Child Left Behind law, they are desperate to find a magic formula to improve their state test results and avoid public censure. At the highest conceptual level, NCLB—despite all of its faults—has indeed focused educators on accountability for student achievement in low-income communities. If NCLB gets them through the door, Bambrick is waiting for them on the other side with meaningful strategies and ideas that are at the heart of this wonderfully accessible and practical book. What's most remarkable about his training—and it's captured in this book—is that Bambrick gets the adults to "live the learning." Instead of lecturing or hectoring his audience, he creates a highly energetic learning environment where his audience does the heavy intellectual work. I hope his *next* book is on this subject!

In the meantime, we're fortunate that he has codified his work in *this* book. Data-driven instruction is not a panacea. But—developed and used in the way that Bambrick describes—we have here one of the more important tools to ensure that America's classrooms are not simply filled with teaching but are assuredly alive with learning, growth, and meaningful achievement for all students.

October 2009   Norman Atkins

Norman Atkins *is the founder and CEO of Teacher U; the founder, former CEO, and board chair of Uncommon Schools; the co-founder and former co-director of North Star Academy; and the former co-executive director of the Robin Hood Foundation.*

Preface

This book can be used in many ways. It is divided into two parts: the practical framework for effective data-driven instruction (Part One) followed by the professional development activities needed to build the framework (Part Two).

I strongly recommend that you do not jump to Part Two (the professional development materials) without first reading Part One. Part One explains many of the pedagogical choices made in Part Two and can help you avoid the common pitfalls that have ensnared schools struggling to implement data-driven instruction effectively. Also noteworthy is the Application section at the end of Chapters One through Four. This section offers concrete first steps targeted to three audiences: teachers, school-based leaders (principals, coaches, instructional leaders, and the like), and multicampus or district-level leaders. In this way, you should be able to apply the concepts in Part One directly to your role in your school community.

If you're not yet sure if this framework will work for you, please start by reading some of the case studies dispersed throughout the book (use the Contents to identify the location of each one). The sheer quantity of these stories—describing success in such a wide variety of contexts—should show the flexibility and universality of this approach. In each case, the key drivers implemented are highlighted so that you can see the connection between theory and practice.

The Appendix includes the highest-leverage, most highly recommended support materials that are mentioned throughout the book. The accompanying CD-ROM provides those materials and others needed to deliver effective professional and leadership development on the topic of data-driven instruction. Please use anything and everything that is useful for your school.

Introduction

What Is This All About?

Rafael Munoz did not see a bright future in front of him during elementary school in Newark, New Jersey.[1] He had been an undisciplined student who was suspended multiple times and fell just short on academic measures of proficiency. By his own admission, he was at risk of not graduating from high school. However, things turned around in middle school. Munoz made dramatic gains in achievement, scoring well above proficiency on state assessments and in the 90th percentile on a national norm-referenced assessment. Such remarkable gains merited an interview with U.S. Secretary of Education Arne Duncan in June 2009. When Duncan asked him what was the difference, he responded:

> "In elementary school, I didn't know what I was doing. It didn't seem to matter whether I came to school or not. I didn't see the point, and I was frustrated trying to learn. When I changed to the middle school, however, teachers began working with me on my areas of weakness. They supported me in my learning, and I could see the direction of where I was headed. For the first time, I had a sense of purpose."

Munoz's experience is not an isolated one. He is one of a growing number of students nationwide who are benefiting from the successful implementation of best practices that increase student achievement. More specifically, he attended a school that had systematically implemented a data-driven instructional model to increase learning.

By now, the outlines of the story have been highlighted across the covers of education magazines nationwide: a school adopts a new model of instruction using data-driven methods and in a few short years achieves remarkable results. In this context, "data-driven instruction" has become one of the most widely discussed concepts in education. It has also been among the most misunderstood. For some, a data-driven school is simply one that conforms to the dictates of No Child Left Behind legislation. For others, it is any school in which assessments are used. More ominously, some consider data-driven schools to be those that ride roughshod over genuine learning in a mindless quest to "teach the test." With so many conflicting definitions to choose from, it is often tempting for school leaders to adopt a this-too-shall-pass approach and avoid data altogether.

This would be a mistake. The proper use of data-centered methods in education isn't an empty platitude and isn't a matter of mindlessly teaching to the test—it's a clearly defined and incredibly effective pathway to academic excellence. Rather than make vague assertions, *Driven by Data* lays out the specific measures needed to create a data-driven culture and, in doing so, achieve remarkable results. If this book is ambitious in its claims, it is because the facts are on its side. When correctly applied, data-driven instruction has led to dramatic gains in student performance nationwide.

Consider the North Star Academy and the Greater Newark Charter Schools, two public middle schools in Newark, New Jersey. The schools had much in common: both had randomly selected student populations drawn from Newark's Central Ward, a neighborhood in which 90 percent of students qualify for free or reduced lunch and 85 percent are African American. Through diligent work, both schools created strong academic cultures in which students could thrive academically and behaviorally. Yet despite having fostered an effective environment for learning, both schools had been struggling to eliminate the achievement gap. At North Star, students outperformed the local district but tested below their suburban peers. At Greater Newark, the challenges of school start-up trumped rigor: in state math tests, only 7 percent of eighth-grade students achieved even basic proficiency.

Against this backdrop, both schools adopted the model of data-driven instruction outlined in this book. Figure I.1 shows what happened next. Table I.1 gives the numbers in detail.

In just four years, each school made tremendous gains in student achievement, outstripping the district average by at least thirty points on each assessment, and surpassing the statewide average in almost every category. These gains are not just number-crunching: they represent tens and hundreds of additional students reaching proficiency, which opens the doors for those students for future

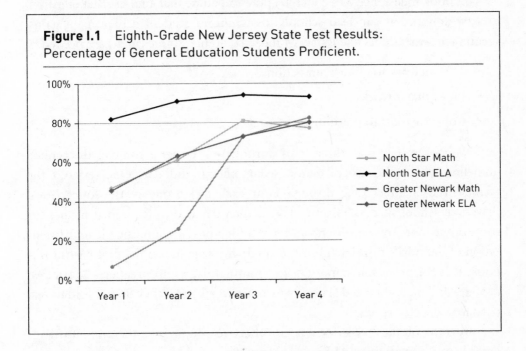

Figure I.1   Eighth-Grade New Jersey State Test Results: Percentage of General Education Students Proficient.

Table I.1   Eighth-Grade New Jersey State Test Results (Detail)

School	Subject	Year 1	Year 2	Year 3	Year 4	Gain	District Average	State Average
North Star	Math	47%	61%	81%	77%	+30	41%	71%
	Literacy	82%	91%	94%	93%	+11	54%	82%
Greater Newark	Math	7%	26%	73%	82%	+75	41%	71%
	Literacy	46%	63%	73%	80%	+34	54%	82%

Source: New Jersey School Report Cards, 2003–2006 for North Star Academy Charter School of Newark; 2004–2007 for Greater Newark Academy Charter School.

opportunities and creates far greater likelihood of success in college and life beyond.

How did two schools with such different beginnings end up with such tremendous student achievement? They focused on the core drivers that matter, separating themselves from schools that didn't.

While the narrative is compelling, it is not yet common. Unfortunately, for every school that succeeds with data-driven instruction, many more fall short and, despite years of intense effort, fail. Why?

This book is designed as a concrete, practical guide that answers that question, and by doing so it can lead schools to significant student achievement gains, creating more students like Rafael Munoz. To do that, three things are needed:

• A framework to guide your actions

• Proof that it works

• Concrete tools to put it into practice

This book provides all three. This introduction presents some of the general guidelines about the use of data-based methods, and Part One sets out the framework. Chapters One through Four each tackle one of the four critical drivers of school success. Chapter Five is then devoted to focused strategies for some of the more frequently encountered difficulties surrounding the implementation of data-driven instruction. If a single message unites the first part of this book, it is the profound importance of putting plans into practice: the subtlest analyses and most nuanced action reports are worthless if they do not lead to real change in the classroom.

Part Two of the book focuses on effective training in the framework of data-driven instruction. Although many factors shape a school's ability to turn data-driven instruction from educational theory to concrete reality, none are as fundamentally important as effective leadership and teacher training. If school leaders and teachers are not taught how to use data in their schools and classrooms, then they—as too many before them—will fail. Chapter Six provides the pedagogical framework that was used in designing these adult learning activities. The *Living the Learning model* it describes is applicable to all sorts of professional development sessions, but here it is directly applied to the work of teaching adults about data-driven instruction. After establishing these basic guidelines, the remainder of the book contains extensive workshop materials for teaching data-driven instruction to leaders and teachers in a variety of contexts.

This book was not created in a theoretical laboratory; it comes from the experience of working with more than a thousand schools across the country. To illustrate its impact, I have highlighted a cross-section of twenty of those schools that have used our model to achieve impressive results. These schools come from every region of the country, from Oakland to Chicago to New York to New Orleans, and they range from district schools to charter schools, from schools who (before implementation) had only 7 percent of students proficient on state exams to schools who launched the framework from the first year of opening the school. They each journeyed upward on the ladder of student achievement, moving from poor results to good or from good to great. More than anything, they show that when a school makes student learning the ultimate test of teaching, teaching improves to produce better learning. Teaching and learning, then, walk hand in hand.

It is my hope that with the framework, training methods, and school success stories outlined in this book, school leaders will finally be able to receive and lead the comprehensive training they need to make data truly work for them.

THE FRAMEWORK: WHAT DOES IT MEAN TO BE DATA-DRIVEN?

Data-driven instruction is the philosophy that schools should constantly focus on one simple question: are our students learning? Using data-based methods, these schools break from the traditional emphasis on what teachers ostensibly taught in favor of a clear-eyed, fact-based focus on what students actually learned. In doing so, they create a powerful paradigm to drive academic excellence. Although each such school is unique, effective data-driven instruction is almost always premised on just a few fundamental building blocks, shown in the box.

Each of the four principles is fundamental to effective data-driven instruction, and the next four chapters will examine them in much greater detail. For now, though, another question is more pressing: With so few fundamental factors, why

> ## The Four Key Principles
>
> - *Assessment:* Create rigorous interim assessments that provide meaningful data.
> - *Analysis:* Examine the results of assessments to identify the causes of both strengths and shortcomings.
> - *Action:* Teach effectively what students most need to learn
> - *Culture:* Create an environment in which data-driven instruction can survive and thrive.

haven't more schools succeeded? After all, almost every school in the country has assessments, does some sort of analysis, teaches (and thus acts), and has a culture.

The simple answer is that, in most cases, schools have made mistakes. On face, this statement isn't terribly helpful; after all, *every* school makes at least some mistakes. When it comes to data-driven instruction, however, the *type* of mistake that a school makes goes a long way toward determining whether or not it will succeed.

THE EIGHT MISTAKES THAT MATTER

In general, the schools that implement data-driven instruction effectively are those that avoid a set of eight particularly perilous pitfalls:

- Inferior interim assessments
- Secretive interim assessments
- Infrequent assessments
- Curriculum-assessment disconnect
- Delayed results
- Separation of teaching and analysis
- Ineffective follow-up
- Not making time for data

Inferior Interim Assessments

Interim assessment of students is the lifeblood of data-driven instruction. Without well-thought-out and carefully written tests, effective analysis of student strengths and weaknesses is impossible. Unfortunately, many schools employ inferior interim assessments that suffer from serious shortcomings: they set bars that are too low, fail to align to end-goal tests, and neglect open-ended response sections. Effective data-driven instruction is impossible unless schools invest in creating or acquiring excellent interim assessments.

Inferior Assessments: A Tale of Caution

Before the advent of state testing at every level from third to eighth grade, most states only tested students in fourth and eighth grades. To bridge the gap and assess performance, one middle school chose to use a nationally normed standardized test in sixth and seventh grade to measure performance. The teachers prepared their students intensely to do well on that national assessment, and their students excelled, scoring over the 80th national percentile. Basking in their results, the school leaders were confident that the students would do equally well on the eighth-grade state test. They were quite shocked when the students performed notably worse, with only half of the students scoring proficient. What went wrong? The state test was far more rigorous and challenging than the nationally normed assessment: it required more writing, critical thinking, and sophisticated problem solving. No matter how hard the school had worked toward excelling on the nationally normed assessment, the bar was so low that students were not prepared to excel in a more challenging environment. Inferior assessments undermined their progress from the very beginning.

Data-Driven Success Story

Fort Worthington Elementary: Big on Building Rigor

The Results

Maryland State Assessment (MSA): Percentage at or Above Proficiency,
Third Through Fifth Grade

Subject	English and Language Arts			Mathematics		
Year/Grade	3	4	5	3	4	5
2005–06	49%	50%	42%	44%	43%	44%
2006–07	55%	62%	55%	74%	71%	74%
2007–08	**88%**	**92%**	**86%**	**86%**	**88%**	**86%**
Two-year gains	+39	+42	+44	+42	+45	+42

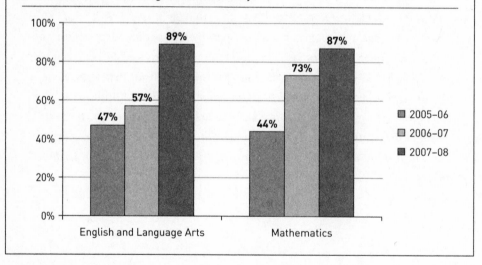

Figure I.2 Maryland State Assessment: Averages of Third Through Fifth Grades at Fort Worthington Elementary.

Met or exceeded statewide average at every grade level.
Eliminated the achievement gap for African American students.

The Story

When Shaylin Todd started at Fort Worthington Elementary School, teachers were not making an impact with the student body, which was 85 percent free or reduced lunch and 98 percent African American. Todd had attended all three data-driven workshops presented in this book prior to beginning the principalship (see Chapter Twelve and the Appendix), and she immediately began putting it all to work.

In the first year (2006–07), Todd focused on training her leadership team how to implement interim assessments and lead effective assessment analysis meetings every six weeks. She changed the instructional calendar to add more professional development time for teachers, which she used consistently to examine student data. She built a culture of public accountability: data boards were established throughout the building that included attendance data, SMART goals, interim assessment results, and student reading levels. She created professional learning communities devoted to looking at this data to determine what the teachers needed to do better on a daily basis. When teachers identified an area that was causing them difficulty as teachers (for example, teaching effective fluency techniques), Todd responded by offering professional development aimed at building capacity in those areas. Math saw dramatic gains in that year, yet reading improved more slowly.

In 2007–08, Todd and her leadership team took a closer look at their Open Court reading interim assessments, comparing them to the Maryland State Assessments (MSA). They noticed that the Open Court unit tests functioned primarily with literal comprehension questions, which matched the type of instruction that Todd was seeing in her teachers' classrooms. Yet the MSA had significantly higher levels of critical and interpretive comprehension. So Todd led the leadership team to identify the areas that lacked sufficient rigor, and they charged the strongest teachers on each grade-level team to rewrite the questions to build up the rigor of the assessments. Todd then built an even more effective re-teaching plan: she used the Assessment Analysis Template (see the CD-ROM) to identify needs for whole-group instruction, small-group re-teaching, and individual support. Teachers added "MSA Vitamins" (mini-assessments) and a Saturday school for students who were right on the cusp of reaching proficiency. All the hard work at Fort Worthington Elementary paid off: scores skyrocketed, obliterating the achievement gap and setting new standards for achievement in Baltimore City.

Secretive Interim Assessments

If interim assessments drive rigor, then teachers and schools must know the end goal before they can work toward it. Unfortunately, most schools and districts prefer to be inflexible and secretive. They have many reasons for this approach. For one, it costs money to develop new assessments, so it's easy to believe (questionably) that you cannot reuse an interim assessment if people can get a look at it and that it's economically unviable to release interim assessments. Imagine setting off on a trip without a map; not revealing the interim assessments in advance is like getting a map after you're already lost.

Infrequent Assessments

For interim assessments to work they need to be just that: interim. If students aren't regularly assessed you have no way to track progress through the year and no way to identify problems in time to correct them. An assessment given once every three or four months cannot provide the data needed to make a difference.

Curriculum-Assessment Disconnect

It is tempting to view curriculum design as separate from interim assessment creation—but that's an extremely dangerous move. This is one of the more common mistakes made in implementing data-driven instruction. If the curriculum scope and sequence do not precisely match the standards on the interim assessments, then teachers will be teaching one thing and assessing something else altogether. Then any assessment results gathered have no bearing on what actually happens in the classroom. Furthermore, if curriculum and assessment are disconnected, then teachers will (rightly) complain that the tests are unfair and that they should not be accountable for student performance, which will make the implementation of data-driven instruction all the more difficult.

Delayed Results

Even the most nuanced assessment is worthless if it isn't graded and analyzed in a timely manner. The prompt scoring of results may seem to be a menial housekeeping task, but it is absolutely essential if schools are to make meaningful adjustments during the year. Every day that passes between the assessment and analysis of results is another day in which teachers present new material without correcting errors.

Separation of Teaching and Analysis

When implementing data-driven instruction, many schools leave the task of assessment analysis to school leaders on a *data team.* Although this strategy stems from a well-intentioned desire to let teachers teach, it invariably leads to failure. Data-driven instruction succeeds only when it is truly teacher-owned, meaning teachers must personally analyze their own classes' data. Only when teachers feel that data-driven instruction is *theirs* will fundamental improvements begin to occur.

Ineffective Follow-Up

What happens after teachers have analyzed their results? In all too many school districts, the answer is a vague and nebulous commitment to take action that is generally ignored. This is a critical shortcoming. Districts and schools that do not create a clear, simple system to implement specific plans at a specific time won't be able to make real change at the level of the classroom.

Not Making Time for Data

Finally, school calendars must reflect the reality of data-driven instruction by assigning structured, scheduled time for assessment, analysis, and follow-up. School years are busy, and if data-driven instruction is not explicitly embedded within the calendar it will be overlooked and ignored—and ineffective. The same is true for school leaders. Data-driven instruction will not be implemented effectively if the leaders do not embrace the process and make it a priority in their own scheduling. We must all practice what we preach!

ROADSIDE DISTRACTIONS: FALSE DRIVERS

Fortunately, although these mistakes can pose serious problems, none of them are unavoidable. By vigilantly guarding against these particular dangers, savvy school leaders can go a long way toward achieving success. Beyond the eight pitfalls, however, there is another, more subtle source of error in data-driven schools: focusing on false drivers.

As their name suggests, *false drivers* are factors that appear to be causes of school success but are actually surface changes that don't influence results. Though they may appear as pathways to excellence, they are instead more like roadside distractions. By mistaking these factors for root causes, school leaders waste tremendous resources on things that have little to do with actually improving their school. Many well-intentioned data-driven school leaders have failed because they have emphasized false drivers while overlooking other, more necessary changes. Of these false paths, these three are the most commonly traveled:

- The pursuit of total buy-in
- Reliance on poorly implemented "professional learning communities"
- Year-end assessment analysis

The Pursuit of Total Buy-In

Any leader who thinks that an initiative requires complete buy-in before beginning will fail. Initiatives mean change, and teachers and school leaders are wary of change until it demonstrates results. Time and effort invested in making people love an unproven idea are almost always wasted. Indeed, one of data-driven instruction's greatest strengths is that it does not require faculty buy-in—it creates it. Buy-in is generated through tangible achievements. As long as faculty members are at least willing to try the methods outlined in this book, they will eventually come to believe in them. Focus on the fundamentals, achieve results, and faith in the program will follow.

Reliance on Poorly Implemented "Professional Learning Communities"

A second false driver is inappropriate faith in unstructured "professional learning communities," meetings designed to ensure that teachers collaborate and share experiences with one another. Obviously, it is critical that teachers share strategies and knowledge, but collaboration for collaboration's sake is not inherently valuable. In implementing data-driven instruction, what matters most is not how much time is used for faculty collaboration but rather how meaningfully such time is employed. Professional learning communities can offer significant benefits, but only if they are explicitly focused on analyzing student learning and identifying key action steps based on that analysis. The original definition of professional learning communities was intended to do just that; too many schools get off track.

Year-End Assessment Analysis

Many schools invest a great deal of time in creating elaborate analyses of the end-of-year assessment. Such reports are often exhaustively detailed, breaking down student results by every conceivable demographic or academic attribute.

Year-End Assessment Analysis—Performing an Autopsy

Many educators have referred to year-end assessment analysis as equivalent to performing an autopsy. If you had a sick child, what would you do? You would seek medical help. No one would recommend waiting until death to determine what made the child sick—they would hold you liable for that child's life! Yet schools do just that with student achievement. Rather than identifying what's making a child's learning "sick" during the school year and finding the right medicine to attack the disease (that is, make it possible to learn more effectively), schools wait to analyze year-end assessment results after some of the students have already died—that is, failed to learn. Rick DuFour stated it succinctly in 2004:

"The difference between a formative and summative assessment has also been described as the difference between a physical and an autopsy. I prefer physicals to autopsies."

Yet despite the huge amount of data it generates, analysis of these tests is of little use to the students who took them. Indeed, it may show what went wrong, but it comes too late to make a difference. Rather than pouring time into figuring out what students failed to learn at year's end, it is much more effective to focus on interim assessments and avoid failures altogether.

These false drivers are not, by themselves, undesirable. All schools want teacher buy-in, all want professional collaboration, all want year-end tests to be carefully examined, and all want detailed analyses. With scarce time and resources, however, schools cannot afford to invest in initiatives that will not lead directly to student excellence.

IDENTIFYING THE REAL DRIVERS: AN EFFECTIVE METHODOLOGY

It is easy to note the pitfalls and false drivers; the harder task is to identify the real drivers of data-driven instruction—the steps that reliably lead to outstanding student achievement. And with so many books about data, it can be difficult to know what is effective and what is not. This book does not purport to compete in that arena. *Driven by Data* bases its entire framework on the foundation of real schools, nationwide, that have set the standard for student achievement. These star schools work with students who have traditionally struggled in the U.S. educational systems. They have high free or reduced lunch populations and have used data to drive change in their results, becoming some of the highest-achieving schools in their respective districts, or at least placing themselves among the most improved. It is from this small subset of schools that the drivers were built.

What are the core action steps that these incredibly successful urban schools have taken to guarantee student achievement? Which action steps are consistent across multiple schools in different cities so as to suggest a universal applicability? The answers to these questions are the core drivers for data-driven instruction, presented in the first four chapters of this book. In fact, I am willing to stake the claim even more strongly: my colleagues and I have yet to meet a school that implements all of these drivers and does *not* make student achievement gains. In the following chapters I present the key drivers that will help schools reach their goals.

Core Concepts: Introduction

- Data-driven schools are those that use data to turn school focus from "what was taught" to "what was learned"
- Effective data-driven instruction is based on strong assessment, analysis, action, and culture.
- Schools that fail to implement data-driven instruction normally make one of eight critical mistakes:
  - Poor quality interim assessment
  - Secretive interim assessments
  - Infrequent assessments
  - Curriculum-assessment disconnect
  - Delayed results return
  - Separating teaching from analysis
  - Ineffective follow-up
  - Not making time for data
- Schools often waste resources on *false drivers*, which appear to cause success but do not. These include:
  - Attempts to create total faculty buy-in.
  - Investments in poorly defined "professional learning communities."
  - Focus on analyzing year-end results.
  - Any and all analysis that is not directly tied to concrete action.

Data-Driven Success Story

Williamsburg Collegiate Charter School: Perfecting the Model

The Results

New York State Assessments: Percentage at or Above Proficiency,
Fifth Through Seventh Grade

Cohort	Class of 2009		Class of 2010	
Subject	English and Language Arts	Math	English and Language Arts	Math
2005–06	56%	65%	—	—
2006–07	85%	100%	66%	92%
2007–08	**92%**	**100%**	**87%**	**100%**
Cohort gains	+36	+35	+21	+8

Source: #1 Public Middle School in New York City, NYCDOE Report Card 2007

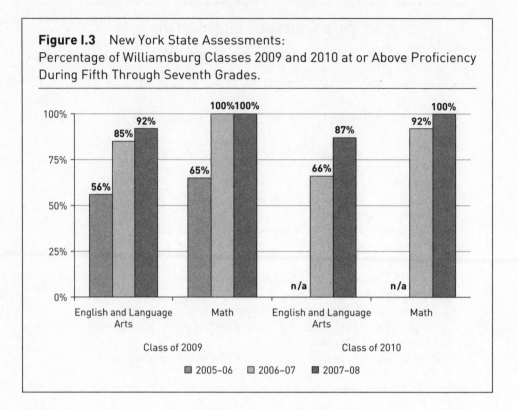

Figure I.3 New York State Assessments: Percentage of Williamsburg Classes 2009 and 2010 at or Above Proficiency During Fifth Through Seventh Grades.

The Story

Of all the case studies in this book, Williamsburg's comes the closest to showing a perfect implementation after struggling in the school's first year. When Julie Kennedy founded Williamsburg Collegiate Charter School in 2005, she had never implemented interim assessments before and had no framework through which to view assessment. In addition, Kennedy cites three other core mistakes in the first year:

- Teachers were poorly acculturated in data. Although they attended an introductory professional development using many of the materials found in the Data-Driven Instruction Teacher Workshop, they had little follow-up training and only minimal conversations about assessment results.
- Teachers and leaders did not devote the time necessary to create effective interim assessments: Kennedy found herself piecing together assessments the night before, with teachers having no chance to see them in advance.

- There was no yearlong vision and calendar: Williamsburg wasn't intentional about establishing the assessment calendar from the beginning, causing teachers to deprioritize the assessment cycle.

In 2006–07, Kennedy and school leaders started by building an intentional implementation calendar. She trained a teacher team to finish the assessment creation over the summer and scheduled all professional development days to be directly aligned to the interim assessment cycle. She improved her own ability to lead data analysis meetings by accessing a community of experts to help her increase her content knowledge to offer concrete guidance to teachers.

Kennedy's biggest contributions to the field, however, come in the laser-like focus she brought to teacher action plans and accountability. While doing observations, Kennedy would open up the analysis spreadsheet for that teacher and identify the standards that the teacher was addressing in that moment. Then she would see if the teacher was addressing questions to the students who most needed development on that standard, and she would analyze the quality of the questioning and student handouts to see it they matched the rigor of the interim assessment. Kennedy began leveraging the best practices of one of her star teachers, Stephanie Ely, to increase teacher action plans across the board: tracking student performance through Do Nows and exit tickets, building "review stations" with students placed strategically in classroom groups where they needed the most work, and aligning tutoring to student learning needs. They also created the novel "Student Assessment Reflection Template" (Appendix). In the words of Kennedy herself, "Assessment analysis became the fabric of how we planned our lessons every day. It kept the conversation alive at all times." It is no surprise, then, that Williamsburg Collegiate is now consistently one of the highest-achieving urban public middle schools in New York City.

Key Drivers from Implementation Rubric

- *Near-perfect implementation of every aspect of rubric:* Kennedy intentionally implemented every driver in the rubric. Each component was tightly woven into the daily fabric of the school.

Introduction Reflection and Planning

Take this opportunity to reflect upon data-driven instruction at your own school or district. Answer the following questions:

- What are the most common mistakes and false drivers that make people struggle at your school?

  _____

  _____

  _____

  _____

- What are the first action steps that you could take to address these pitfalls?

  _____

  _____

  _____

  _____

- Who are the key people in your school—the ones you need to share these steps with for data-driven instruction?

  _____

  _____

  _____

  _____

- How are you going to get the people on board?

  _____

  _____

  _____

  _____

Assessment Analysis Action Culture

PART ONE

The Framework

Assessment

Where's the Bar for Learning?

AN OPENING STORY

In one of the first years of implementation of data-driven instruction in our North Star middle school, we had a principal intern who was supervising one of our sixth-grade math teachers. One morning, he came to my office and put a sheet of paper in front of me: it was the Do Now worksheet that he had just seen used in the classroom.

"What do you notice?" he asked me. I reviewed the worksheet and saw ten problems on basic addition of fractions.

"This looks like a basic review of fractions," I answered.

"Exactly," the intern replied. "But the interim assessment we just reviewed asks students to solve word problems with fractions, and even the fractions themselves in those word problems are more complex than these ones. Yet the teacher is confident that she's preparing her students to master adding fractions."

These might seem like commonsense conclusions to many of you, but for us at North Star, the principal intern's insight was a watershed moment in identifying the common disconnect between what the teacher was teaching and what the interim assessment was measuring. What ensued was a deeper look at assessment at all levels of teaching.

Data-Driven Success Story

Morrell Park Elementary/Middle School: Data in the War Room

The Results

Maryland State Assessment: Percentage at or Above Proficiency, Third Through Eighth Grades

Math	3	4	5	6	7	8
2005–06	41%	37%	46%	24%	6%	2%
2008–09	100%	93%	89%	83%	74%	79%
3-year gains	+59	+56	+43	+59	+68	+77
Reading	3	4	5	6	7	8
2005–06	49%	49%	41%	38%	37%	32%
2008–09	89%	93%	86%	79%	77%	79%
3-year gains	+40	+44	+45	+41	+40	+47

Figure 1.1 Morrell Park Students on the Maryland State Assessment: Percent Proficient in Third Through Eighth Grades.

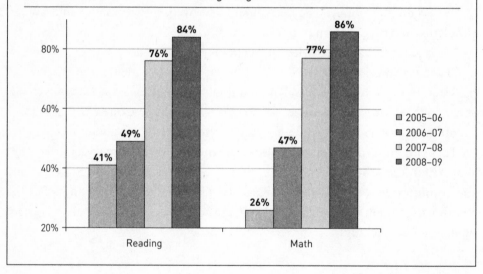

The Story

When Sean Conley began his principalship, Morrell Elementary/Middle School was a historically failing school: student achievement had remained consistently below 50 percent proficient, with scores often in the teens or twenties. The school was *zero-based*, which meant every teacher had to reapply and Conley was able to decide which teachers to hire. Conley quickly identified the best teacher in the school and asked her to let other teachers see what she was doing. By asking her to be an instructional coach, Conley sent a message that teachers needed to share their best practices with each other. The teachers started by creating common monthly math assessments, and they analyzed the results to determine which skills needed whole-class instruction, small-group re-teaching, or individual support. As they analyzed the results as a grade-level team, if one teacher had better results on one standard and another did better on a different standard, the team would regroup *all* the students from the grade into groups that were taught by the teacher most skilled at that particular standard. While they weren't able to launch a common assessment in literacy in 2006–07, they created a child-friendly writing rubric and had students analyzing writing responses and editing their own to meet the rubric.

In 2007–08, Conley focused his efforts particularly on literacy. He incorporated leveled texts and individual reading plans for students based on their reading assessment results. He increased instructional time and opportunities for teachers to pull out students who needed extra support. The main office was turned into a "war room" where all assessment information was posted so that teachers and parents could see it. Every faculty meeting started with celebrations and some sort of data about the students. The conversation among faculty members shifted from "The test is not fair" to "What do we have to do to move students?" Homework was differentiated to what students needed, and the district's Mathworks program continued to provide opportunities for teachers to plan the teaching of a standard aligned to the rigor of the state tests.

After moderate gains in 2006–07, results skyrocketed in 2007–08 and 2008–09. A school that had once had fewer than one in five students proficient had tripled its performance and achievement. Conley had transformed a failing building into a true school of learning.

Key Drivers from Implementation Rubric

- *Common interim assessments:* By creating common math assessments, grade-level teams were able to analyze results together and establish common goals and lesson plans.
- *Teacher action plans:* The strategic decision to re-teach difficult standards according to teachers' strengths was a creative approach to making teaching more effective.

TOWARD MEANINGFUL RIGOR: CREATING THE ROAD MAP

Assessment is the first core principle of data-driven instruction. Whether it is praised for emphasizing a "results orientation" or condemned for "teaching the test," the practices of data-driven instruction are inextricably bound up with the process of assessment.

Ask a teacher to define what the students should be learning, and chances are the teacher will talk about conforming to school, district, or state standards (or to the standards embedded in a mandated textbook or curriculum). Yet while meeting such standards is necessary, it is nearly impossible to measure a teacher's success simply based on a list of standards. To illustrate this, consider a basic standard taken from middle school math:

> *Understand and use ratios, proportions and percents in a variety of situations.*
>
> —New Jersey Core Curriculum Content Standards for Mathematics, Grade 7, 4.1.A.3

To understand why a standard like this one creates difficulties, consider the following premise. Six different teachers could each define one of the following six questions as a valid attempt to assess the standard of percent of a number. Each could argue that the chosen assessment question is aligned to the state standard and is an adequate measure of student mastery:

Six Assessment Questions "Aligned" to the Same Standard

1. Identify 50% of 20:
2. Identify 67% of 81:
3. Shawn got 7 correct answers out of 10 possible answers on his science test. What percent of questions did he get correct?
4. J.J. Redick was on pace to set an NCAA record in career free throw percentage. Leading into the NCAA tournament in 2004, he made 97 of 104 free throw attempts. What percentage of free throws did he make?

5. J.J. Redick was on pace to set an NCAA record in career free throw percentage. Leading into the NCAA tournament in 2004, he made 97 of 104 free throw attempts. In the first tournament game, Redick missed his first five free throws. How far did his percentage drop from before the tournament game to right after missing those free throws?
6. J.J. Redick and Chris Paul were competing for the best free-throw shooting percentage. Redick made 94% of his first 103 shots, while Paul made 47 out of 51 shots.
    a. Which one had a better shooting percentage?
    b. In the next game, Redick made only 2 of 10 shots while Paul made 7 of 10 shots. What are their new overall shooting percentages?
    c. Who is the better shooter?
    d. Jason argued that if Paul and J.J. each made the next ten shots, their shooting percentages would go up the same amount. Is this true? Why or why not?

Though these six questions differ tremendously in scope, difficulty, and design, all of them are aligned to the state standard. Indeed, even if the standard was made more specific and called for "higher-order problem-solving skill," choices four, five, and six would still all be plausible options. If teachers were given this standard without clarification and commentary, no one could fault them for teaching only the skills needed for a question like number four, even if the end-of-year state test demanded the skills needed to answer a question like number six.

From this, one can grasp an important truth: Standards are meaningless until you define how you will assess them.

CORE IDEA

- Standards are meaningless until you define how you will assess them.

The level of mastery that will be reached by a given class is determined entirely by what sort of questions students are expected to answer. This turns conventional wisdom on its head: instead of standards defining the sort of assessments used, the assessments used define the standard that will be reached.

Although this is initially counterintuitive, it's a principle that is constantly visible in the world around us. No one would start building a house without creating the blueprints, or training for the Olympics without identifying what

```
┌─────────────────────────────────────────────────────────────────┐
│                          CORE IDEA                                │
│                                                                   │
│  •  Assessments are not the end of the teaching and learning      │
│     process; they're the starting point.                          │
│                                                                   │
└─────────────────────────────────────────────────────────────────┘
```

benchmarks define success. Likewise, we should not first teach and then write an assessment to match; instead, we should create a rigorous and demanding test and then teach to meet its standards.

In effective data-driven instruction, the most important tests are *interim assessments:* formal written examinations taken at six- to eight-week intervals during the school year. Interim assessments give standards a clear definition of the level of rigor needed to succeed. Rather than have each teacher choose a level of rigor in response to vaguely written standards, the effective data-driven school leader or teacher works to create challenging interim assessments that set a high bar for student achievement.

As one of the better-known facets of data-driven instruction, interim assessments have been the focus of a great deal of academic research. Thus far, the evidence strongly suggests that, when properly applied, interim assessments are among the most powerful drivers of academic excellence.[1] Why?

Some Advantages of Interim Assessments

- *Road map for instruction:* This point cannot be made too emphatically— rigorous interim assessments define the standards and provide a road map to rigorous teaching and learning. When educators know precisely what skill level their students must reach on each standard, they will have a clear framework for creating a challenging and dynamic curriculum. Traditional curriculum scopes and sequences do not do this on their own.

- *Improvement in teaching:* Well-designed interim assessments serve to identify weaknesses during the course of the school year. Meticulous attention to results and a constant feedback loop allow teachers to improve their craft, changing strategies in response to changing needs.

- *Targeted Focus:* By creating concrete benchmarks, interim assessments allow for classroom strengths and weaknesses to be clearly identified and systematically targeted. In providing a baseline standard for comparison, interim assessments offer a comprehensive checkpoint of where a class needs to go and what it will take to get each of the students to that level.

- *Accountability:* The cumulative nature of interim assessments helps hold teachers and principals accountable for student learning results throughout the year. Rather than waiting for a year-end result, interim assessments make it possible to identify failed teaching strategies while there is still time to fix them.

- *Visibility:* Interim assessments allow for performance to be charted graphically so that school leaders and staff may see visual evidence of improvement.

- *Checking for understanding without teacher support:* Because of their formal written nature, interim assessments measure student understanding without what is often called "scaffolded" support (teacher hints and guidance in problem solving), which can often reveal great differences between student output when supported by the teacher and when not!

- *Preparing students for high-stakes assessment:* The written format can also be used to simulate the high-stakes tests by which states and many businesses measure academic achievement. Unlike other types of assessments, interim examinations can adopt the structure and content of end-goal tests to determine whether students have precisely the skills they need.

INTERIM ASSESSMENTS VERSUS IN-THE-MOMENT ASSESSMENTS

A body of research (primarily championed by Paul Black and Dylan Wiliam) asserts that *in-the-moment assessments*—checking for student understanding in the very moment something is learned—have even more power than interim assessments in building student achievement.[2] I agree that, done skillfully, real-time assessments do have a powerful effect on improving teaching—they give teachers immediate data on which students aren't learning and why.

What in-the-moment assessments lack is a sense of the larger year-end goal. By being the starting point, interim assessments have the ability to create what Kim Marshall terms the "ripple effect": they influence every component of

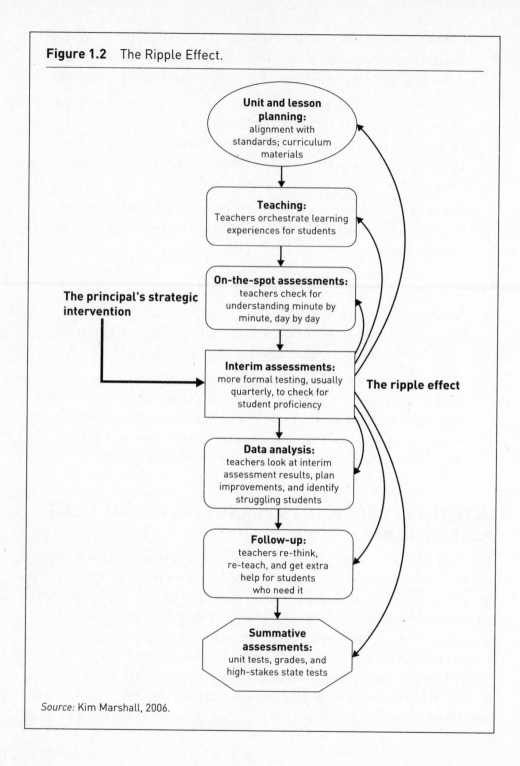

Figure 1.2 The Ripple Effect.

Unit and lesson planning:
alignment with standards; curriculum materials

Teaching:
Teachers orchestrate learning experiences for students

On-the-spot assessments:
teachers check for understanding minute by minute, day by day

The principal's strategic intervention

Interim assessments:
more formal testing, usually quarterly, to check for student proficiency

The ripple effect

Data analysis:
teachers look at interim assessment results, plan improvements, and identify struggling students

Follow-up:
teachers re-think, re-teach, and get extra help for students who need it

Summative assessments:
unit tests, grades, and high-stakes state tests

Source: Kim Marshall, 2006.

Planning a Road Trip: The Need for Interim Assessments

To use a simple analogy, imagine a road trip. When you check to make sure you have enough gasoline, your tires have enough air, and nothing is going wrong with the motor while you're driving, you're doing in-the-moment assessments. If you do not do these things, you'll never make it to your destination, so in-the-moment assessments are critical!

However, if you don't have a road map, it doesn't matter how well your car is running: you could be headed to the wrong destination! Interim assessments provide the road map. Within that context, in-the-moment assessment becomes a very powerful, necessary tool. I discuss these further as a follow-up strategy in Chapter Three, on action.

---

the teaching process. Figure 1.2 shows how interim assessments can drive unit planning, lesson planning, teaching, in-the-moment assessment and follow-up, and finally improved year-end results.

Quality interim assessments have the power to fundamentally improve every aspect of academic performance. To realize this potential, however, you need a sound framework for interim assessments.

THE BUILDING BLOCKS OF EFFECTIVE ASSESSMENT

All these principles contribute to the practice of writing a quality assessment. If standards are meaningless until you define how to assess them, and assessments are the starting point rather than the end, then a few basic building blocks emerge for writing quality assessments:

- Assessments must be the starting point.
- Assessments must be transparent.
- Assessments must be common.
- Assessments must be interim.

Assessments Must Be the Starting Point

The first step to creating interim assessments is knowing when to start writing them. Traditionally, assessments are written near the end of the semester or quarter they are reviewing. In this arrangement, the material taught in class determines the standards to which students will be held on the interim examination. In contrast, for data-driven instruction to be effective, this process must be reversed, meaning *interim assessments should be created before teaching ever begins.* In data-driven instruction, the rigor of the actual assessment items drives the rigor of the material taught in class. As explained earlier in this chapter, when assessments are written before teaching begins, teachers can adjust the curriculum and lessons to make sure all necessary skills are addressed. (This requires teacher accountability, also discussed in Chapter Three.)

Assessments Must Be Transparent

As part of this approach, assessments must be transparent and available to teachers and school leaders from the start of the school year. More broadly speaking, teachers, students, parents, and community members should all know exactly what skill level the students will reach and what steps they will take to get there. As demonstrated earlier, *standards are not sufficient to drive teaching to appropriate rigor.* Of course, this does not mean giving out copies of test answers to students on the first day of class, but it does mean publicly posting the exact sorts of skills needed so that every member of the school community knows what to expect. By making assessment expectations transparent and clear, schools can take control of their curriculum and guide learning based on their vision. *Since this is the area where districts fail more than any other, Chapter Five includes a whole section of coping mechanisms to employ when forced to use secretive district-mandated assessments.*

Assessments Must Be Common

It is essential to use the same examinations across all classes in a given grade-level and content area. If individual teachers develop and administer their own assessments, this generates problems similar to the six different levels of mastery demonstrated in the "Percent of a Number" questions. Assessments administered by individual teachers also make it nearly impossible to meaningfully track test-to-test progress or to coordinate fully shared standards across the entire student body. Furthermore, the process of creating and sharing a common assessment is itself a valuable opportunity for faculty to share ideas and collaborate to create the best curriculum possible for all students.

Assessments Must Be Interim

While schools and teachers assess in some form all the time, the key assessments—the ones driving change in schools making dramatic gains in achievement—are interim assessments. Interim assessments need to happen at least quarterly, and should ideally be given every six to eight weeks at the middle and high school levels.[3] If assessments are administered less frequently, then weaknesses will go unrecognized until it is too late to correct them. If assessments are administered far more frequently, then teachers cannot do the depth of analysis described in Chapter Two without burning out.

WRITING OR SELECTING THE RIGHT INTERIM ASSESSMENT

Once the fundamental logistics are in place, one can turn to the task of writing or selecting the test itself. The success stories I've included in this book show that effective results can emerge either from creating rigorous interim assessments at the school level or selecting already available assessments. Either choice can lead to success so long as one applies the core principles listed here.

Start from the End-Goal Exam

All public schools (and even most private schools) face the high stakes of end-goal tests by which student achievement is measured. At the primary school level, such assessment often includes statewide or districtwide exams; at the secondary level, it could include SAT/ACT scores or AP/ IB assessment results. In any case, when

---

CORE IDEAS: Interim Assessment

- Start from the end-goal exam.
- Align the interim assessments to the end-goal test.
- If acquiring assessments from a third party, be sure to see the test.
- Assess to college-ready standards.
- Design the test to reassess earlier material.
- Give teachers a stake in the assessment.

Data-Driven Success Story

Achievement First: A System That Makes the Grade

The Results

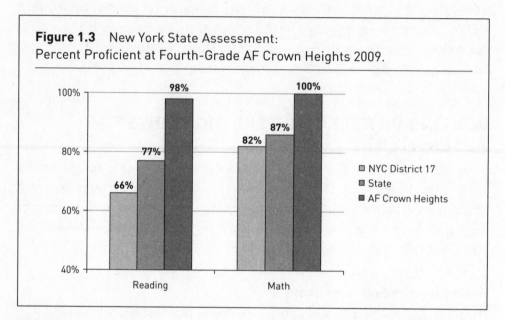

Figure 1.3 New York State Assessment:
Percent Proficient at Fourth-Grade AF Crown Heights 2009.

Legend:
- NYC District 17
- State
- AF Crown Heights

Reading: 66%, 77%, 98%
Math: 82%, 87%, 100%

The Story

Some schools are data-driven from the start and have built a model for other schools to follow. Achievement First schools, founded in 2005, built on the data-driven legacy of Doug McCurry and Amistad Academy in New Haven, Connecticut. In 1999, McCurry was a lead teacher at Amistad, and he began experimenting with assessments in math and grammar as a way to address his own struggle to know whether the students were learning or not. He looked at state standards, made a sequence, and started building prototype interim assessments. Right away he saw that assessments needed to move away from covering specific units and become cumulative for the year, to allow for retesting of standards. By 2000, McCurry had moved into a leadership role at Amistad and launched interim assessments in math across the whole school, but there were no systems to guarantee analysis or action. A number of teachers were resistant to using interim assessments, and this created more of a "he said, she said" defensiveness between teachers and leaders around the results on each assessment. Despite the resistance, however, certain teachers made remarkable gains from one cycle to the next, and that shifted the dynamic in the school. Since then, Amistad has consistently outperformed the statewide proficiency average in Connecticut.

McCurry founded Achievement First (AF) with Dacia Toll in 2002, and they created an infrastructure to wield across multiple schools. Over the next seven years, AF launched additional systems, creating a process of teacher review of the interim assessments to build in transparency. McCurry built more training around what good analysis looked like, and AF moved from paper-and-pencil analysis to Excel spreadsheets to Athena, an online interim assessment platform designed to save teacher time and customize analytics. It also increased the amount of time in the school calendar given to conversations around data. By 2008, it had also built Data Days—four annual full professional development days devoted to data analysis and discussion with sample agendas and outcomes for those days. In doing so, it moved from surface-level analysis ("I'm going to re-teach that") to super-clear outcomes and a data-driven plan.

Achievement First Bushwick Elementary School is one example of this success. Principal Lizette Suxo began each Data Day with a schoolwide reflection: what were the common challenges across all grades? Are there things we should address schoolwide? Do we need intervention groups? If so, what students should be in each group, and what standards will each group be taught to master? This conversation led directly into grade-level planning. Teachers planned out the standards to be taught for the next six weeks (both new and re-teach standards) and then planned the specific lessons for the next nine days. Teachers and leaders alike used daily exit tickets and three-week targeted assessments to make in-course adjustments. The results tell the story: achievement is truly first at Bushwick and all its sister schools.

Key Drivers from Implementation Rubric

- *Ongoing professional development:* Four full Data Days set the tone for a laser-like focus on data.
- *Effective data reports:* One of the key drivers was the use of Athena, McCurry's automated results analysis system. Commercial interim assessments and analysis services are often problematic because they do not facilitate teacher-level planning, so AF built its platform with the end goal of data analysis meetings in mind, and that analysis is explicitly linked to the creation of a teacher action plan.
- *Implement action plans:* Action plans were explicitly connected to teaching, and everyone in the building monitored student learning to assess the quality of the action.

designing or selecting interim assessments, it is critical that decisions be made in reference to the specific demands of the end goal and not to vague, ill-defined academic standards, as discussed earlier in this chapter.

Align Interim Assessments to End-Goal Test

Once the specific sorts of questions that are employed by the end-goal test are noted, schools should work to create or select interim assessments that are aligned to the specific demands of the end-goal examination. This alignment should not be limited to content but should also follow the format, length, and any other replicable characteristic of the end-goal test.

Be Sure to See Any Third-Party Test

Test sales representatives have a very simple goal: to sell more tests. Because of this, they will do anything in their power to convince schools that their exam is aligned and will meet their needs. Don't take their word for it. Instead, school leaders and teachers should personally inspect actual copies of the product to see how well it lines up with the end goals in question—remembering that no third-party test is perfect. Find something that seems close, then push to modify the examination to exactly align with your school's academic goal. *This is one of most overlooked steps in schools and districts that do not have well-aligned interim assessments.*

Assess to College-Ready Standards

At every level, it's important to realize that the skills needed to pass state tests are often insufficient to ensure success in college or other postsecondary environments. As such, a final goal of well-written interim assessments is that they prepare students not only for a state test but also for college and beyond. High schools have a clearer path to do this, as they can look to align with the SAT/ACT, AP/IB, or the demands of a college research paper. Elementary and middle schools require more creative thinking. Here are some examples of college-ready rigor for those grade spans:

Elementary School Reading   Set higher reading-level expectations: At the elementary level, an easy way to push for greater rigor is to evaluate students' progress at meeting above-grade reading levels. For example, rather than expect kindergartners to meet the equivalent of Fountas-Pinnell Level B, push for Level C or D by the end of the year. (See Myth 3 in the upcoming section for additional ideas on early elementary reading rigor.)

Elementary School Math   Set higher grade-level expectations—for example, prompt each grade level to accomplish a certain percentage of the standards for the subsequent grade level. For example, second graders can accomplish all the operations standards associated with third grade. North Star Elementary School (see Success Story) has done this aggressively from Kindergarten. Using the TerraNova as a guide, they have established interim assessments for Kindergarten that measure all the K standards and half the first-grade standards. First grade then measures all first- and second-grade math standards, and second graders prepare to master all standards on the third-grade state test. Imagine how pleased third- and fourth-grade teachers will be receiving all their students already grade-level proficient at the start of the year!

Middle School Math   Embed algebra in every strand. Most eighth-grade state tests have a rudimentary inclusion of basic linear equations or expressions, but few measure all of the rigor of a high school Algebra I curriculum. Middle schools can quickly increase the college-ready rigor in their classrooms by exploring algebraic applications for each mathematical strand that they teach. For example, a fifth-grade teacher presenting addition of fractions could add a question like the College-Ready Example into the class Do Nows or in-class activities:

College-Ready Example — Algebra in Fifth-Grade Math

Write an expression for the following:
   Mr. Smith has b books in his classroom. He gives three of them to students. Then he splits the rest of them evenly on his two bookshelves. How many books are on each shelf? Justify your answer.

Middle School Reading   Push for deeper reading of the text: Adding college-ready rigor to reading can be challenging. Giving students harder texts to read is laudable, but it does not accomplish this task in itself: if the book is well above the students' reading level, vocabulary knowledge might limit their ability to comprehend the text. Still, an overlooked strategy is choosing text with grade-level vocabulary but complex meaning. This allows the teacher to assess for more critical reading than is often possible with middle school novels. The box gives an example of a poem that has very accessible language but requires deep, critical thinking:

College-Ready Example — Rigor in Middle School Reading

Chicago Poet
by Carl Sandburg

I saluted a nobody.
I saw him in a looking-glass.
He smiled—so did I.
He crumpled the skin on his forehead, frowning—so did I.
Everything I did he did.
I said, "Hello, I know you."
And I was a liar to say so.
Ah, this looking-glass man!
Liar, fool, dreamer, play-actor,
Soldier, dusty drinker of dust—
Ah! He will go with me
Down the dark stairway
When nobody else is looking,
When everybody else is gone.

1. In stanza 1, Sandburg looks into the mirror and says, "Hello, I know you," but then calls himself a liar to say so. How is this possible when he is looking at himself? (Inference)
   A. He is still figuring out his identity.
   B. He is insulting himself because he is angry.
   C. He does not recognize his physical self.
   D. He is being playful and joking.

2. Which of the following questions might Sandburg want to ask of this "looking-glass man"? (Asking questions)
   A. Where are your friends?
   B. Where are you right now?
   C. How are you feeling?
   D. Who do you want to be?

Design the Test to Reassess Earlier Material

Additionally, effective assessments revisit material from earlier in the year. In many fields, such as math, this review is vital to retaining information and learning new concepts. It also ensures that teachers have the opportunity to see if their re-teaching efforts were effective. One such method of review is to make tests longer as the year progresses; a second is to test all material from day one and then track improvement as the students actually learn the concepts being tested. No matter which method is chosen, however, it is important that review of past material is made a central part of interim assessments. *This is a common, critical mistake of schools and districts where assessments fail: they convert interim assessments into unit tests (just covering material in that time period) rather than cumulative assessments.*

Give Teachers a Stake in the Assessment

Finally, when assessments are created or selected, teachers should have meaningful input. This is critical, because it ensures accountability; teachers who are included in the assessment writing or selection process become invested in the assessments' effectiveness. Give teachers a stake in the assessment, and you'll give them a stake in the results.

ASSESSMENT MYTHS DISPELLED

Before discussing the key steps to writing effective interim assessments, it's important to address some of the common misperceptions surrounding testing. Given the widely conflicting attitudes and understandings of assessment, it is unsurprising that many myths and half-truths surround the assessment process. Before going any further, it is useful to dispel some of the more prominent and problematic of these myths:

- Multiple-choice questions just aren't rigorous.
- Tests such as the SAT don't really measure student learning.
- Doing well in early elementary reading assessments will guarantee proficiency in the upper elementary grades and beyond.

MYTH 1: Multiple-Choice Questions Just Aren't Rigorous

Reality: In the eyes of many teachers and school leaders, multiple-choice questions are vapid and low-rigor exercises in test taking, useful only because they are easy to score. From this viewpoint, assessments that employ such questions cannot test more sophisticated concepts and do not require rigorous critical thought. Yet while this observation seems intuitively obvious, it is incorrect. Consider the three questions in the box, each of which pertains to the main idea or theme of the story "Little Red Riding Hood."

Three "Little Red Riding Hood" Assessment Questions

1. What is the main idea of this story? (open-ended response)
2. This story is mostly about:
   a. Two boys fighting
   b. A girl playing in the woods
   c. Little Red Riding Hood's adventures with a wolf
   d. A wolf in the forest
3. This story is mostly about:
   a. Little Red Riding Hood's journey through the woods
   b. The pain of losing your grandmother
   c. Everything is not always what it seems
   d. Fear of wolves

In comparing the last two questions, it is easy to see that question 3 is far more demanding. Clearly, some multiple-choice questions are more rigorous than others. But is question 3 less rigorous than the open-ended question 1? The answer: it depends on the rubric used for question 1. If it merely requires that the student identify a wolf and a girl, then it will be the easiest of the three; if it demands a nuanced, five-paragraph explanation of the symbolism and word choice of the story, then it is the most difficult. Implicit in these questions are two important truths: first, for multiple-choice questions, the options define the rigor.

If the choices present are very similar to one another, as in question 3, then the test will require a far higher degree of knowledge. A high degree of comprehension is also required when the options include complex vocabulary and prior knowledge. Thus, depending on their answer options, multiple-choice questions can offer as much rigor as any open-ended response prompt (simply look at Advanced Placement exams for an example of this). For open-ended questions, by contrast, the rubric defines the rigor. Sometimes these rubrics are explicit and transparent for the students, including anchor papers detailing exactly what "proficient" looks like. In other cases, these rubrics are internal metrics in a teacher's mind that the students have not been explicitly taught. Either way, the rubric drives the rigor.

CORE IDEAS: Multiple Choice

- In a multiple-choice question, the *options* define the rigor.
- In an open-ended question, the *rubric* defines the rigor.
- Any good assessment will combine multiple forms to achieve the best measure of mastery.

Even with the greatest rubric or the best wrong answer choices, multiple-choice questions and open-ended questions still measure different aspects of rigor of the same standard. One requires putting thoughts together in your own words; the other involves distinguishing critically between various plausible actions. These two angles simulate real life and also every testing situation students will face in the future. Thus, a truly rigorous test should be created from open-ended responses with challenging rubrics and multiple-choice questions (or other formats) with challenging options. Both test critical skills, and when it comes to creating effective and rigorous assessments, both are necessary, complementary sides of the same coin.

MYTH 2: Tests Such as the SAT Don't Really Measure Student Learning

Reality: A second common misconception holds that standardized assessments like the SAT are simply tricky tests that don't really show student mastery.

While this is sometimes true, it is not categorically correct. Consider the two questions below:

Two Questions on Quadratic Equations

1. Solve the following quadratic equation:

$$x^2 - x - 6 = 0$$

2. Given the following rectangle with the lengths shown below, find the value of x:

x | Area = 6

$x - 1$

If you solve question 2 algebraically, you arrive at the same quadratic question that is listed for question 1. However, you needed mastery of many additional mathematical concepts to set up the equation: properties of a rectangle, area, distributive property, and more. Question 1 also has two possible answers: -2 and 3. In question 2, however, the student must eliminate -2 as a possible answer, because a rectangle would not have a negative side!

Question 1 is taken straight from an algebra textbook; question 2 is from the SAT. The issue with the SAT question is not that it's trying to trick the student; it's that it requires a deeper, more conceptual understanding of quadratic equations, as well as the ability to apply it in the context of geometric properties. So when a student struggles with the SAT but does well in algebra, the first thing a teacher or leader must consider is whether the rigor of class instruction matched the rigor of the SAT. Defining the rigor of the questions on assessments to the highest bars that students are expected to reach makes sure that students will master any sort of test put in front of them.

SAT Rigor: The Experience of a High School Math Teacher

In the first round of implementation of data-driven instruction at North Star Academy Charter High School, our school leaders designed interim assessments that were aligned both to the New Jersey state test and the SAT. After we implemented the first round of interim assessments, one of the math teachers complained that there were too many SAT prep questions that weren't really connected to teaching high school math. As a school leader, I had a choice to make about how to respond. I could explain to the teacher why I thought the assessment was a valuable tool with rigorous SAT questions embedded, or I could try to get her to reach the conclusion herself. I opted for the latter. I said that I appreciated her concern and invited her to look at the assessment with me to identify the questions that were problematic. We then identified the questions that were aligned to the rigor of the SAT, and with each one I asked her, "Are these skills that your students should know in your class?" After each question, she acknowledged that the question did indeed measure standards she was teaching. We repeated this exercise throughout the entire test, and the teacher slowly realized that her concern was not about SAT prep but the high level of rigor of the questions. Without challenging her directly, our whole conversation had shifted from test prep critique to how much additional work it would take students to reach a higher level of standards mastery. The rest of our time was focused on new strategies and schoolwide systems to support student learning.

Too often our critiques of tests are done from the 20,000-foot aerial view. However, when you get up close and examine actual test items, you start to discover the real issues of rigor (or the lack thereof).

MYTH 3: Doing Well on Early Elementary School Reading Assessments Will Guarantee Proficiency in the Upper Elementary Grades and Beyond

Reality: Although it might seem counterintuitive, schools assess more in early elementary school than at any other grade level: there are individual reading assessments, observation checklists, sight word checks, and so on and on. This is justifiable because the ability to read is one of the critical foundations of

Data-Driven Success Story

North Star Elementary: Exploding Expectations

The Results

2008–09 TerraNova Exam: Kindergartners' Median National Percentile

Reading			Language			Math		
Pre-test	Post-test	Change	Pre-test	Post-test	Change	Pre-test	Post-test	Change
27.5	95.3	+67.8	42.6	96.7	+54.1	29.3	97.4	+68.1

Figure 1.4 North Star 2008–09 TerraNova Exam: Kindergarten — Median National Percentile.

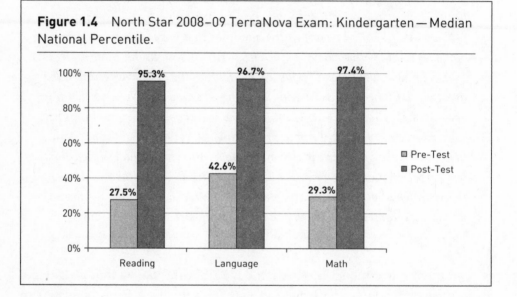

The Story

When founding principal Julie Jackson began planning the launch of North Star Elementary School, almost everyone she talked to argued that data-driven instruction did not really apply to K–2 education. "Save testing for the older grades." "Child development in Kindergarten is so irregular that it's too difficult to measure." "Children need to develop at their own pace." Because of her experience as a high school principal who witnessed firsthand the challenges of first-generation college students in their initial years as undergraduates, Jackson was determined to break the stereotypes of what elementary school students could do. First, she selected a leveled reading assessment that targeted critical reading comprehension in addition to fluency, accuracy, and decoding—the STEP assessment out of the University of Chicago. By doing so, teachers avoided the trap of only teaching reading for fluency and accuracy and also focused on Kindergartners' ability to make inferences and understand the purposes of stories. Teachers targeted lessons directly toward the areas in reading where the students were struggling, whether it was the vowel sounds, the ability to draw meaning from a picture, or making a connection between the beginning and end of a story.

Jackson's colleague, Christian Sparling, designed interim math assessments that not only covered Kindergarten material, but also half the standards from first grade as well. Unsatisfied with the lack of rigor of most Kindergarten math curricula, they supplemented their math program with story problems and more time to apply the mathematical principles in exercises. They built a comprehensive assessment calendar, trained all teachers in the principles of data-driven instruction, and posted class results in the teachers' room after each round of interim assessments. The Kindergarten teachers collaboratively planned lessons and consistently targeted deficient standards and struggling students throughout the year.

By the end of the first year of the school, Jackson and her team of teachers had accomplished extraordinary results. At the beginning of the year, only three of the seventy-eight Kindergartners were reading. By the end of the year, all but three were reading on the first-grade level. The median national percentile scores on the TerraNova placed North Star students in the upper 10 percent of all students nationwide. For 2008–09, Jackson and the elementary school set the goal to accomplish all second-grade math standards by the end of first grade, and preliminary results strongly suggest that they will meet that goal. By exploding expectations for what is possible in K–2 education, North Star Elementary School is redefining elementary education.

Key Drivers from Implementation Rubric

- *College-ready interim assessments:* Jackson set the interim assessment rigor to match first grade, not just Kindergarten, causing teachers to shoot higher with their students and keep in mind the larger goal.
- *Collaborative lesson planning:* The Kindergarten teachers identified lead planners for each subject, and the planners led the creation of lesson plans that everyone agreed to implement. After teaching, they discussed the strengths and weaknesses of the lesson, and they developed even more effective lessons based on that feedback.
- *Accountability:* Jackson reviews all lesson plans as well as observing classes to look for alignment with the key standards from assessment analysis.
- *Deep analysis:* By creating an innovative analysis spreadsheet for the leveled reading assessment results, teachers were able to identify the precise letters, sounds, and reading strategies that needed attention.

elementary education. The issue at hand, however, is whether schools are using the right assessments to prepare critical readers.

Consider four different early literacy assessments, all testing students at Level C on the Fountas-Pinnell scale (a K–1 reading passage).

Four Early Literacy Assessments

Story text (assume that every line is a separate page and accompanied by a picture):

> When I grow up, I want to put out fires.
> I want to play ball.
> I want to go to the moon.
> I want to teach school.
> I want to fix cars.
> But now, I am happy to be a kid.

Here are the comprehension questions required by four major early childhood assessments:

DRA (Diagnostic Reading Assessment)
Students need to

- Re-tell the story.
- Make a personal connection.

DIBELS (Dynamic Indicators of Basic Early Literacy Skills)

- No test for comprehension given: fluency in reading combined with proper decoding via nonsense words is considered an adequate predictor of comprehension.

Running Record (this is a sample; there are many different versions)

- Students need to: Tell what happened in the story.
- Answer "right there" basic comprehension questions.

STEP (Strategic Teaching and Evaluation of Progress) Assessment
Students need to answer the following questions

- What is the first job the girl thinks about doing?
- What job would make her leave earth?
- What does she think she will do as a teacher?
- Why does the girl say that for now she is happy being a kid?

Each test claims to be an accurate, adequate predictor of future reading performance. They all monitor how quickly a student reads, with how many mistakes (and each has unique additional components focused on decoding, spelling, and other areas). However, they vary significantly in how they assess for comprehension.

Considering that most elementary educators consider the assessments discussed in this section to be interchangeable, it is striking how each one requires a radically different level of mastery of reading comprehension. As is true in later grades, the assessment selected goes a long way in determining just what will be learned—and therefore what will be taught. While every elementary teacher that I know strives for deep understanding with each year's students, seeing students pass an assessment that doesn't require critical comprehension can lull any teacher into a false sense of security about the student's progress. Particularly in urban schools, ignoring the importance of selecting rigorous assessments for the early years of education will leave students at a tremendous disadvantage as they move toward later grades. Countless schools have shared their experience of having students with excellent mastery on DRA or DIBELS turn out to struggle with state assessments. It is not that the state assessments are unfair measures of student learning at the early grades; it is that the state assessments ask for critical reading comprehension that the other assessments did not. Choosing an effective early assessment that measures not only fluency, decoding, and basic comprehension but also inferential thinking will push schools and teachers to introduce more rigor and better prepare young students for the challenges ahead.

BOILING DOWN TO THE ESSENCE: THE FIVE CORE DRIVERS OF ASSESSMENT

If a single theme unifies the ideas outlined in this chapter, it is that effective assessments are those written with tremendous attention to detail. Schools must take the time to properly and specifically align their tests, to consider in detail the standards they need to approach, and to review the rigor of questions not based on myths and common knowledge but on their own observations. Though often neglected or overlooked, these fundamental principles of assessment creation invariably define the rigor of a school and, in doing so, determine what students will achieve.

In sum, what follows is a rubric that consolidates this information into five key drivers for the principle of assessments.

Assessment: Five Core Drivers

- *Transparent starting point:* Assessments need to be written before the teaching starts, and teachers and schools need to see them in advance: they define the road map.
- *Common and interim:* Assessments should apply to all students in a grade level and should occur every six to eight weeks.
- *Aligned to state tests and college readiness:* Assessments should be aligned to state tests in format, content, and length, and also aligned to the higher bar of college readiness via SAT/AP/IB exams, research papers, and so on.
- *Aligned to instructional sequence:* Assessments should be aligned to the teachers' sequence of clearly defined grade-level and content expectations, so teachers are teaching what will be assessed.
- *Reassessed:* Interim assessments should continuously reassess previously taught standards.

APPLICATION: FIRST STEPS FOR TEACHERS AND LEADERS

So what is the most effective way to implement these principles of assessment as a classroom teacher, school leader, or multicampus or district office leader? What follows are the first steps that could be taken to put this into action.

Level 1—Teachers

In some schools, teachers will have a fundamental role in the creation of interim assessments. If that is the case, please view the steps discussed at the district and multicampus level. If, however, you work in a school where you do not have input into the interim assessment, the following steps can help you develop in-class assessment tools that will raise the bar for driving change in your classroom:

- Analyze the interim assessment or end-goal test.
- Build your in-class assessments prior to teaching the unit.
- Plan lessons to meet the rigor of that assessment.
- Where applicable, set your college-ready goal.

Analyze the Interim Assessment or End-Goal Test   Acquire the closest version that you can find of your state test, interim assessment, or other year-end assessment by which your students' learning will be measured. (This will vary from state to state: some states have actual prior-year state tests available, others have one practice test, some just have sample questions. You can also try to acquire the interim assessments from a high-achieving school in your state—assessments that have been proven to work and be aligned to the state test.) Jon Saphier, author of *The Skillful Teacher,* offered me the following precise question to use when analyzing the end-goal assessment: "What are the skills and knowledge needed to master each assessment question?" In the case of a multistep word problem or analytical essay, this list could be quite extensive. This serves as the starting point for determining what to teach your students. Ask yourself, which of these skills and knowledge elements do the students already know, and which ones will I need to teach them?

Build Your In-Class Assessments Prior to Teaching the Unit   Before teaching your next unit, design your unit-ending assessment. As you work on it, create questions that mirror the format of the end-goal test that you acquired in the first step. Make sure you have questions that match the rigor, format, and question type. At the same time, include *building-block questions:* questions that are below the rigor of the end assessment but are necessary steps toward proficiency. In math, this could include basic computation skills even as you are pushing for word problem application. In literacy, this could include using a lower-leveled text at first even as you push for students to eventually demonstrate comprehension on grade-level passages.

Plan Lessons to Meet the Rigor of That Assessment   Once you've designed your in-class assessment, start planning your lessons. With the end assessment clearly defined, you have a road map for all the skills and knowledge elements—and to what degree of rigor—that you will need to teach to ensure that your students are proficient on the unit-ending assessment. Keep referring back to the actual assessment questions while you plan to make sure that every activity sets up the students to succeed at that level of rigor.

Where Applicable, Set Your College-Ready Goal   As stated earlier, proficiency on state assessments is a necessary but insufficient bar for preparing our students for success in college and life beyond. If your students are currently well below grade level, state test proficiency goals could be an appropriate step for the moment. Once you start to achieve that, higher goals can continue to drive needed student college readiness.

Data-Driven Success Story

South Bronx Classical: Excellence in Real Time

The Results

TerraNova: Percent at or Above Grade Level

Grade	Kindergarten			First Grade		
Year	Reading	Language	Math	Reading	Language	Math
2006–07	50%	53%	79%	70%	65%	67%
2007–08	92%	85%	93%	82%	94%	95%
2008–09	**98%**	**97%**	**97%**	**93%**	**100%**	**98%**
Gains	+48	+44	+19	+23	+35	+31

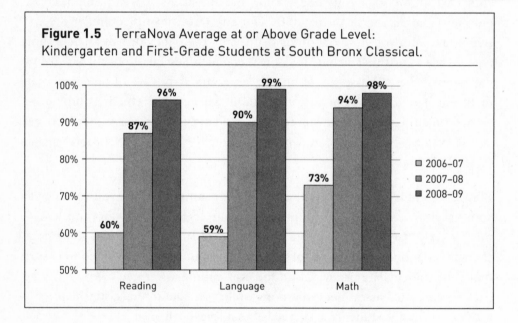

Figure 1.5 TerraNova Average at or Above Grade Level: Kindergarten and First-Grade Students at South Bronx Classical.

The Story

Located in a gritty New York neighborhood, South Bronx Classical was founded in 2006 to serve a student body where 100 percent are minority students and 90 percent qualify for free or reduced lunch. When Scott Hudnor took over as principal in 2007–08, he was determined to put data-driven instruction in place. Having attended the Data-Driven

Instruction Comprehensive Leadership Workshop (see Chapter Twelve), Hudnor first focused on creating effective interim assessments.

In the summer of 2007, Hudnor assembled a team of teachers who worked to identify precisely what level of rigor the New York State exam and the national TerraNova exam required, and what specific skills were needed for students to reach them. Once they knew exactly what their end goal required, Hudnor and his team set about creating a series of interim assessments in math and in English and language arts. Rather than simply implement regular interim assessments, however, South Bronx Classical created an aggressive follow-up system in which students took daily math assessments and daily English assessments to track their performance in real time. This up-to-the-minute awareness of student strengths and weaknesses was coupled with formal tests every two weeks that served as miniature interim assessments within the larger structure of quarterly tests. Critically, Hudnor made sure that each layer of this assessment structure was built into the academic calendar before the year began.

Once South Bronx Classical's multilayered, real-time assessment structure was in place, the school was able to implement effective and rigorous follow-up to aggressively target standards that posed problems for students. Every teacher at the school spent at least two of the ten weekly "specials" periods (such as gym class) tutoring small groups of students on key re-teaching standards. In 2008, the school added daily twenty-minute re-teach blocks devoted to these standards. Daily assessments were constantly updated to reflect student achievement, with areas of weaknesses reinforced and spiraled back into teaching as soon as they were identified. And as the facts have shown, this single-minded focus on knowing exactly what students have learned has paid off in a tremendous way!

Key Drivers from Implementation Rubric

- *Aligned assessments:* In creating interim assessments, South Bronx Classical staff made sure that they worked backwards from the original text of their end-goal exam to ensure aligned rigor.
- *Ongoing assessment:* By tracking student understanding through interim assessments, bi-weekly tests, and short daily quizzes, South Bronx Classical staff knew exactly what students were learning and what standards needed work, and they knew it in real time as teaching was occurring.
- *Teacher action plans:* Hudnor and his staff were willing to think outside the box to find time for critical re-teaching. By making targeted re-teaching a key priority and adapting the nonacademic schedule to fit it in, South Bronx Classical was able to greatly increase the amount of effective teaching time in the school day.
- *Deep analysis:* South Bronx Classical looked closely at student answer choices to determine precisely where the learning gap was occurring.

Level 2—School-Based Leaders

Coaches, assistant principals, principals, and other school-based leaders all have different levels of authority and interaction with teachers. The degree to which each of the following steps is implemented will depend on your role. Here are the critical first steps you can do in the area of assessment.

Make Sure Your Interim Assessments Are Aligned and Rigorous   The first thing to do is analyze the quality of the interim assessment vis-à-vis your state test. Acquire the closest version that you can find of your state test. (Some creative means of doing so are listed in the Level 1 Teacher section.) Line up actual test items from both assessments that are assessing the same standard, and determine if the interim assessment is meeting or exceeding the rigor of the state assessment. Exhibit 1.1 models a guiding worksheet that could help with doing that analysis. If interim assessments are not aligned or rigorous, see Chapter Five for creative workaround solutions.

Manage and Support Teachers to Use Effective Assessments   Look at teacher materials and in-class assessments when observing. For example, observe the quality and the rigor of the actual activities and assignments going on in the classroom. Do the in-class assessments meet or exceed the rigor of the interim assessments and year-end assessments? (See the criteria established in the Level 1 section.) Do the teacher's activities and plans match the rigor of these assessments? Where are there gaps?

Facilitate teachers' creating high-quality, in-class assessments and planning backwards from them. Teachers can always use more planning time to focus on doing the activities listed in Level 1. Use individual meetings with teachers, grade-level meetings, and professional development time to give teachers the opportunities to do this sort of planning. Once the unit assessment has been properly aligned to the interim assessment, the planning process can mirror the work of Understanding by Design or Kim Marshall's curriculum units highlighted in *Re-Thinking Teacher Supervision and Evaluation*.[4] What makes the process so valuable is that the interim assessment has already clearly defined the bar for rigor, so the planning is double the value!

Level 3—District-Level or Multicampus Leaders

The biggest impact that district-level leadership can have is in the creation or selection of rigorous, high-quality interim assessments. One of the single most

Exhibit 1.1   Interim Assessment Evaluation Worksheet.

INTERIM ASSESSMENT ITEM	STATE TEST ITEM	THE RIGHT CONTENT Addresses the same standards, and addresses the standards as rigorously as the state test.	THE RIGHT FORMAT Reflects format and type of questions from state exam; (If applicable) reflects format of and types of questions from exam. Rubrics are used, if applicable. Wrong answers illuminate misunderstanding.	THE RIGHT COLLEGE-READY EXPECTATIONS Rigor and content seem appropriate for developing college-bound students. Content is "State test plus" in areas where state test is not college-preparatory. More complex than state tests (require additional critical thinking and application). More standards covered within the test and within the same question.	COMMENTS Comments and suggestions to improve question.
1		Yes/no	Yes/no	Yes/no	
2		Yes/no	Yes/no	Yes/no	
3		Yes/no	Yes/no	Yes/no	
4		Yes/no	Yes/no	Yes/no	
5		Yes/no	Yes/no	Yes/no	
6		Yes/no	Yes/no	Yes/no	
7		Yes/no	Yes/no	Yes/no	
8		Yes/no	Yes/no	Yes/no	
9		Yes/no	Yes/no	Yes/no	

limiting factors in schools' achievement growth are poor interim assessments mandated by their districts. The five core drivers of assessment are listed here. Using this checklist, does your district or network have quality interim assessments?

If your district's interim assessments don't meet all the criteria listed here for each subject, then your critical task is to redesign them. Here are some key points that are worth reiterating.

Interim Assessments are instructional tools first, validity tools second: Many companies that sell interim assessments do not allow schools to see their product—either before or after administration—because they want to keep the results "valid." It cannot be said more strongly: if standards are meaningless until you define how to assess them, then curriculum scope and sequences lack a road map for rigor without a transparent assessment. Transparent assessments allow teachers to plan more effectively and increase rigor across schools. The goal is not to compare schools (that's the purpose of summative state tests!)—it is to guide instruction at the classroom level. This is not possible without transparent assessments.

Don't take anyone's word for it—check out the test itself: Since assessments define standards, then it is insufficient to align an interim assessment to a scope and sequence alone. You must compare it with the end assessment to make sure it assesses standards at a similar or higher bar of rigor (see the Level 2 section for more details). Ask the assessment creator to prove alignment by showing actual tests in comparison to your state tests.

Involve teachers and leaders in the interim assessment selection or creation process: Don't underestimate the talent of your highest-achieving teachers and leaders: they can be an invaluable resource in building a quality interim assessment program.

Chapter One: Reflection and Planning

Take this opportunity to reflect upon assessment at your own school or district. Answer the following questions:

*   After reading this chapter, what are the key action steps around assessment that you are going to implement in your school (and that you can realistically do)?

    _____

    _____

    _____

    _____

*   Who are the key people in your school with whom you need to communicate this plan and have on board?

    _____

    _____

    _____

    _____

*   How are you going to get them on board? What are you going to do when someone says no? (What's Plan B?)

    _____

    _____

    _____

    _____

*   Set the key dates for each action step, write them here, and then put them in your personal agenda or calendar to hold yourself accountable for implementing these steps.

    _____

    _____

    _____

    _____

Analysis

Diving Deep—What Happened and Why?

AN OPENING STORY

What follows is the actual conversation (based on a video transcript) between the principal of North Star Academy Downtown Middle School, James Verrilli, and teacher Rachel Josephs around the results of an interim assessment. Josephs taught fifth-grade literacy, and her results on inference questions were not as good as those of some other teachers:

> "So what's the data telling you?" Verrilli asked to begin the meeting. Josephs had done significant analysis in preparation for the meeting, so she launched into what she had discovered. She pulled out her action plan, in which she had written all the core analysis of why students didn't answer certain questions correctly. After fifteen minutes of analysis, Josephs switched her focus to the performance of her lowest-skilled reading group.
>
> "The Orange group was pretty similar to the other group with the exception of inference with the nonfiction passage . . . many of them got #18 wrong." Josephs proceeded to pull out the test and open it up to question #18. "Let me look at that question again."
>
> Verrilli scanned through her action plan to see what steps she had listed to address this skill. "So here you've got in your action plan that you're going to use some nonfiction sources like *Sports Illustrated, Body Baggage*. How are you going to use them to do inference?"

"I guess I will rewrite test questions with multiple-choice responses and ask the students to prove why they chose the answer they did—always continuing to talk about the skill of inference and why it's important as a reader. So I guess the best strategy would just to be looking at each question and assuming they're all possible and which is the most likely answer and why."

Verrilli had been mostly listening and asking questions up until this point, but here he decided to suggest an action step generated by another teacher, a woman named Gennival. "Yeah," he said. "One thing that Gennival and I talked a little bit about that helps in developing this skill is in learning to find more pieces of evidence that go with it. What we found in the sixth grade is that the students were thinking that the inference is a guessing game—that you just want to guess right. But what they didn't realize was that inference is clearer if you gather evidence from the story. That there should be clues in the story that let you know what it was. So Gennival was talking about doing exercises like, 'On the street corner the men are undoing the fire hydrant. What's happening?' So most students think there's a fire. Then she adds, 'It's late July and it's ninety-five degrees.' So now they think it's a hot day and people are untapping the hydrant to play in the water. So the students can see that more information can actually get you closer to what might be inferred."

Josephs wrote these ideas down in her action plan. "Got it," she said. "Because when I give them sample answers, they always have to provide proof, but when they were looking at inference they weren't looking for evidence, so I think you're right."

In some ways, there is nothing noteworthy about the conversation between Verrilli and Josephs. In other ways, considering the results Josephs got—she consistently made forty-point gains in student achievement—and all the precursors that led up to this meeting and what resulted from it, this conversation is at the heart of what makes effective analysis so powerful.

Data-Driven Success Story

North Star Academy Downtown Middle School: Setting the Standard

The Results

- Highest Achieving Urban Middle School in New Jersey
- Education Trust National Dispelling the Myth Award, 2007
- USDOE Title 1 Distinguished School Award, 2006

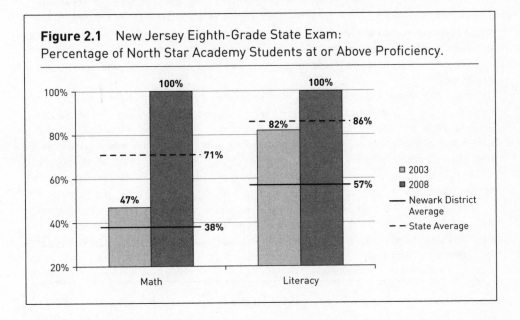

Figure 2.1 New Jersey Eighth-Grade State Exam: Percentage of North Star Academy Students at or Above Proficiency.

The Story

When James Verrilli co-founded North Star Academy in 1997 with Norman Atkins, he was driven to fulfill the mission of the school's name: to create student stars who would shine brightly—just as Frederick Douglass did with his abolitionist newspaper, *The North Star*. The school started by building a strong student culture, working on character development, and developing dedicated teachers, and the first few years of state test results were promising. North Star Academy served 90 percent free or reduced lunch, 90 percent African American students in the heart of Newark's Central Ward, and it was outperforming the Newark District and neighborhood schools from which the students came. However, its students were still lagging behind their statewide peers, especially affluent and white students.

In an effort to increase student achievement, in 2003 Verrilli and his colleagues visited Amistad Academy in New Haven, Connecticut. After observing data analysis meetings around Amistad's use of interim assessments aligned with Connecticut standards, Verrilli gathered a team of lead teachers and spent the summer of 2003 designing and writing interim assessments for fifth through eighth grades in literacy and math. That fall, they launched a fully developed interim assessment calendar with time for assessment, analysis, and re-teaching. Before the first round of assessments, the teachers were fairly skeptical of the value of the assessments. After seeing results fall below what they expected and doing deep analysis of assessment results, however, teachers began to pay more attention to student learning. The end of 2004 saw the first significant gains in achievement.

From 2004 through 2006, Verrilli implemented the interim assessment cycle even more systematically. He increased the rigor on the interim assessments, launched formal data-driven instruction training for new teachers, and sharpened the re-teaching focus with a series of professional development workshops around checking for understanding. From that point forward, teachers were in a continuous self-improvement cycle, always trying to improve their teaching to increase student achievement on each interim assessment. North Star began to formally train instructional leaders in leading assessment analysis meetings, and student achievement results consistently outperformed the statewide average, even surpassing the performance of white and affluent students in New Jersey. By 2008, North Star's results were among the highest of all schools in New Jersey, regardless of income level.

Key Driver

- *Execution of all aspects of implementation rubric:* The Data-Driven Implementation Rubric in the Appendix came out of North Star's experience in implementing these systems. In each subsequent year, North Star sharpened its focus and identified the key drivers in assessment, analysis, action, and culture that laid the foundation for the rubric that exists today.

FOUNDATIONS OF EFFECTIVE ANALYSIS

Imagine a swimmer and her coach. The swimmer is a hard worker in practice, but when she goes to her first competition she finishes in third place. If the coach skips the meet and only reads the results in the newspaper, his advice will probably be that his student should focus on swimming faster. Had the coach actually gone to the pool, however, he would have seen that his swimmer was actually the fastest in the pool, and that her slow time was the result of her being the last racer off the starting blocks. This simple story, taken from the 2004 film *Man on Fire,* reflects a powerful truth: schools that take a superficial approach and "read the newspaper" will not draw the right conclusions about how to lead their students' success. Only with a "view from the pool" can anyone begin to see what must be done. This is the insight from which we all must draw guidance when we start to put data-driven instruction into practice. Of course, we cannot watch our students take the SATs or state exams (without facing serious legal consequences), but we can do the next best thing by employing effective, rigorous analysis on the results of interim assessments.

If assessments define the ultimate goals, analysis identifies the strategy and tactics needed to get there. By examining raw interim assessment data effectively, teachers and school leaders can systematically identify their students' strengths and weaknesses and determine what specific steps they must take to achieve their goals.

DATA REPORTS: CHARTING A COURSE TO SUCCESS

Good assessments provide a tremendous amount of raw data, but great analysis is impossible unless that data is recorded in a readily useful form. Effective data report charts are those that organize student results in a way that allows for analysis at many important levels:

- Question level (the most overlooked level of analysis)
- Standard level (all questions measuring the same standard)
- Individual student level
- Whole class level

It is essential that those creating the data report template keep the ultimate users—teachers and school leaders—in mind. To that end, report templates must have a teacher-friendly learning curve. Templates need not be overly simplistic, but they must be designed so that most teachers can, with reasonable effort, master their complexities. Templates that are too difficult to be useful will lead to frustration, not to results.

What might some effective templates look like? One good example is the data template from North Star Academy in Newark, New Jersey. This particular template is reprinted in blank form in the Appendix, but Table 2.1 presents a small section of it.

In this chart, each of the core principles is highlighted. Every blank space represents a question that the student answered correctly. Every letter represents the wrong answer the student chose on a multiple-choice question. A number presents the number of points awarded on an open-ended response. In the school, the results are color-coded: above 75 percent is green, between 60 percent and 75 percent is yellow, and less than 60 percent correct is red. That makes it easy to look at the class performance by question, by standard, and overall. As added value, the scores are sorted from strongest to weakest, allowing you to look for questions that separate proficient from nonproficient students (for example, question 11 in the table). The color schemes also make it easier on the eye, and even if printed on a black-and-white printer (the reality at most schools), shades of gray clearly distinguish between the green, red, and yellow of the original.

This sample spreadsheet embodies one more core principle that is important to highlight:

Table 2.1 North Star Interim Assessment Results Analysis Template

Question standards:
1. (1) Computation: add and subtract decimals and money
2. (NSA) Fractions in Context: +/-
3. (2) Computation: 3 x 2 multiplication
4. (3) Computation: division by 1–2 digits
5. (4) Fractions: add and subtract mixed numbers
6. (5) Computation in Context: multiplication
7. (6) Computation with money: subtraction
8. (5) Computation in Context: division
9. (5) Computation in Context: division
10. (7) Estimation and rounding: division
11. (8) Estimation and rounding: addition of decimals

Student:	MULT. CHOICE: % CORRECT	OPEN-ENDED: % CORRECT	COMBINED PROFICIENCY SCORE	1	2	3	4	5	6	7	8	9	10	11
Moet	82%	81%	81%											
Jateel	82%	62%	76%									C		
Terrell	79%	42%	69%					C						
Aniya	79%	38%	68%					C					B	
Juwan	68%	58%	66%					A						B
Aziz	74%	42%	65%					A				D	B	D
Juan	63%	58%	62%					D		E		D		B
Shannon	71%	31%	60%											B
Maniyah	71%	31%	60%		C									D
Kabrina	63%	38%	56%		C			A		C			B	B
Keshawn	55%	54%	55%		B		B	A				D		B
PERCENTAGE CORRECT:	95%	85%	100%	95%	40%	90%	90%	90%	80%	60%	45%			

TOTAL: 85%

Repeated 6–1 Standards:

Comp: +/- decimals/money (1):	95%
Comp: 2 x 2 multiplication (3):	100%
Comp: divide by 1–2 digits (4):	95%
Multiply/divide in context (6,8,9):	87%

Estimation/Rounding (10,11):	53%
Charts: missing element (2,3):	75%
Add/subtract with money (7):	90%

TEAM NAME	Multiple-Choice	Open-Ended	COMBINED
	69%	47%	63%

To illustrate how these core principles can be applied effectively in different styles of data reports, a few templates have been included in the CD-ROM. Pick one that meets your technical needs—anything will do as long as it meets the requirements stated here!

Beware the False Driver of Overreporting

If test-in-hand analysis between principals and teachers is the real driver of student achievement, then schools don't need lots of fancy data reports to drive change. This is especially important in the current landscape, where companies and districts are marketing the fact that they have forty or more data reports, as if volume were more important than quality. Incredible amounts of time are wasted looking at reports that analyze the same data in multiple ways or are a few steps removed from the classroom-level analysis. Moreover, *the more pages an assessment report has, the less likely the teacher will use it.* Keep it simple: a one-page data report (or at most two pages) per classroom is plenty—you don't need more!

A Note on Commercial Products

Finally, many commercial companies now offer analysis sheets of their own. As was true for commercial versions of interim assessments, it is essential that school leaders *personally examine these sheets* to make sure that they contain all relevant information. Beware: if you cannot have the test in hand when using these analysis reports, they will be of little value no matter what information they contain (see next section for more details on this point).

RESULTS ANALYSIS: GOING TO THE POOL

Just as the coach in *Man on Fire* needed to carefully examine the race in order to help his swimmer, educators must carefully parse assessment data to best help their students. With effective templates in hand, one must dig in to test results and see what the data holds. Although there are many ways to approach this critical task, some methods are more effective than others. The following sections describe a few of the best.

Test-in-Hand Analysis: The Scoreboard Analogy

Imagine a basketball game where the scoreboard was covered. Imagine the game was competitive, but at no time did you know what the score was or who was leading. As a coach, how could you possibly guide your players in the final minutes of the game? Should you be fouling the other team to stop the clock (as if they were losing), or should you work to hold on to the ball and "milk the clock"?

Using interim assessments is equivalent to taking the cover off the scoreboard so you can see how you're doing as a team. Without assessment, your teaching is blindly moving forward without thought of what is most needed in each situation. (Darlene Merry, former vice president of New Leaders for New Schools, can be credited with this analogy!)

Work with the Test in Hand

First off, it is absolutely essential that assessment analysis be done *test-in-hand*, with teachers constantly comparing results posted on the template with the assessment questions themselves. Results provide almost no meaningful information unless they can be seen in the context of the assessment itself, a fact illustrated in nearly every example in this section.

Do Question-Level Analysis and Standard-Level Analysis Side by Side

With the test in hand, the most basic strategy for results analysis is to look over the template and identify the questions and standards on which students generally performed poorly. When combined with clear and easy-to-read data report templates, this strategy allows educators to quickly identify weaknesses and act on them. Teachers should constantly ask *why* students bombed given questions. Did students all choose the same wrong answer? Why or why not? By comparing similar standards to one another or by examining trends within given standards, teachers can find the trends in student errors. Do results in fractions influence division of mixed numbers? Do systemic failures in sequence have any relation to the ability to summarize? By understanding the linkages between disparate standards, educators can better understand *why* a given question posed problems. At the level of the individual standard, consider if students performed similarly on all questions or if they found some harder than others. If so, why? Here's an example:

Standard-level Analysis of Student Performance: Sixth-Grade Math Sample

Ratio-Proportion Results Overall:	70%
Ratio-Proportion — General (Questions 12, 21):	82%
Ratio-Proportion — Rates (Questions 22, 30):	58%

If one looked only at performance on all Ratio-Proportion questions, the teacher would assume that most students are doing well and a third of the students need overall remediation. Looking at the first breakdown of the standard, however, it would appear that this teacher should re-teach rates. Upon looking at the individual question results, however, one finds the following information:

Question-level Analysis of Student Performance: Sixth-Grade Math Sample

Student Performance on Rates Questions:

Question 22:	35%
Question 30:	80%

At this point, the only way for the teacher to determine what occurred is to look at the actual test items themselves. Here are the two questions and the most commonly chosen wrong answer for question 22:

22. Jennifer drove 36 miles in an hour. At this rate, how far would she travel in $2\frac{1}{4}$ hours?

   A) 72 miles (most commonly chosen wrong answer)

   B) 80 miles

   C) 81 miles

   D) 90 miles

30. If a machine can fill 4 bottles in 6 seconds, how many bottles can it fill in 18 seconds?

A) 24

B) 12

C) 8

D) 7

It appears that students knew how to calculate a rate in question 22, but they were unfamiliar with multiplying by a mixed number (and so most decided to simply multiply 36 by 2). Could operations with mixed numbers be the problem? A look back to the test and performance on related standards reveals that, sure enough, students performed dismally on mixed-number operations:

Related Standards Analysis: Sixth-Grade Math Sample

Multiply and divide mixed numbers (Question 5):   40%

In one simple question analysis, the power of "being at the pool" comes alive. Without test-in-hand analysis, the teacher either would have re-taught ratio and proportion generally or, just as ineffectively, would have re-taught rates. Both of these efforts would have led to little change in student achievement. Imagine the implications of this type of analysis on all of the standards on given interim assessments: proper test-in-hand analysis saves countless hours of valuable re-teaching time and energy.

Core Idea

- Test-in-hand analysis is not one possible way to analyze student error—it is the *only* means by which to do effective analysis.

Search for Separators

Another important technique is to seek out questions on which the generally stronger academic students outperform their weaker peers. Such questions are relevant because they reveal areas where smaller group focus or pullout groups would be highly effective at targeted instruction. Looking closely at the North Star Academy Results Analysis Template in Table 2.1, the three lowest-achieving

A Doctor's Diagnosis: Deep Analysis to Find the Cause

Try to remember the last time you visited the doctor when you were sick with something unfamiliar. You told the doctor what your symptoms were (fever, chest pain, or whatever). The doctor then did a physical exam—probing by hand, listening to your breathing with a stethoscope, and so on. The doctor then formed a hypothesis of what was causing the sickness, and depending on both observation and your description, might have ordered one or another series of tests from the lab. When those results came back, you got a final diagnosis and a plan for surgery, recovery, or medication.

A doctor's approach to treating a patient is essentially what we're asking teachers to do with their students' learning. It would be unacceptable in the medical profession to administer medication or perform surgery without having a sound hypothesis about the cause of the problem. As a doctor, you start with the basic level of analysis (the patient's description), then you dig deeper with the physical examination, and even further with tests or X-rays that give you analysis that your hands cannot provide. By analyzing assessment data at the standards level and item level, and finally looking at the assessment questions themselves, you perform the same level of diagnosis. By re-teaching the standard based on your analysis, you are administering medication. If your analysis was deep and thorough, you will most often get it right the very first time of re-teaching. If not (as in a difficult medical case), it might take multiple approaches.

If you diagnose like a doctor, your teaching will be more targeted—and more effective.

students answered question 2 incorrectly. Those results clearly indicate that targeted re-teaching and support for those three students on that particular standard could help them catch up to their peers. On the other end of the spectrum, the top third of the class answered question 11 correctly, suggesting that they could be given a stretch assignment while the teacher focuses on re-teaching that standard to the rest of the class—either learning a more challenging application or standard or serving as tutors to their peers during that re-teaching session.

Scan by Student

Additionally, it's important to review performance not just between questions but also for individual students. Consider the case of Kenyatta:

Student-by-Student Analysis Sample

Question	1	2	3	4	5	6	7	8	9	10	11	12	13	14	15	16	17	18	19	20	21	22	23
Kenyatta					A				D					C	D	A	B	D	D	D	C	D	A

Following the guidelines listed with Table 2.1 (every blank space is a correct answer, and every letter represents the wrong choice on a multiple-choice question), the teacher can quickly conclude that something happened starting on question 14 that completely changed Kenyatta's achievement up to this point. When this analysis is done in comparison to her peers (as can be accomplished in a spreadsheet like the one demonstrated in Table 2.1), Kenyatta outperformed her peers in the first half of the assessment, yet she finished with the lowest score in the class due to her performance on the second half.

If one only "read the newspaper" and looked at the girl's overall score, it would be easy to conclude that Kenyatta was one of the weakest students in the class. The fact that she performed as she did after this question could mean many things: perhaps she fell asleep, perhaps she's a slow test taker who rushed and filled in answers at random at the end; or perhaps she got bored. What these results do *not* indicate, however, is a lack of academic ability. As this example demonstrates, it is critically important to carefully examine anomalies in individual student performance before reaching any conclusion. Without it, Kenyatta could have been placed in endless re-teaching sessions, while she might have needed only a good night's sleep and a strong breakfast before an assessment.

In short, without a student-level analysis like this, it's easy to reach significantly wrong conclusions as to why a student is struggling. Student-by-student analysis like this helps teachers identify the right approach for each student.

The following guide lists questions that teachers can ask themselves about their assessment results. These are the questions that were modeled in the preceding discussion.

Core Idea — Questions to Ask During Interim Assessment Analysis

Global Questions ("reading the newspaper")

- How well did the class do as a whole?
- What are the strengths and weaknesses in the standards: where do we need to work the most?
- How did the class do on old versus new standards? Are they forgetting or improving on old material?
- How were the results in the different question types (multiple choice versus open-ended, reading versus writing)?
- Who are the strong and weak students?

"Dig in" Questions

- Bombed questions — Did students all choose same wrong answer? Why or why not?
- Break down each standard: Did students do similarly on every question within the standard or were some questions harder? Why?
- Compare similar standards: Do results in one influence the other?
- Sort data by students' scores: Are there questions that separate proficient and nonproficient students?
- Look horizontally by student: Are there any anomalies occurring with certain students?

FAST TURNAROUND — LAYING THE FOUNDATION FOR EFFECTIVE ACTION

Finally, for analysis to be useful it must be timely. Assessment results that are not returned and analyzed in a timely manner are wasted. Because of this, it's important to put systems into place to ensure that the insights of data-driven instruction are quickly put to use. Ideally, schools should design their calendar to ensure that interim assessments are analyzed within forty-eight hours of being scored. One example of this can be seen at Greater Newark Academy, where the calendar includes several half-days following each round of interim assessment to allow for analysis, resulting in a three-day turnaround from results to action plans. By keeping the analysis process under a week, schools can ensure that information gained from data-driven analysis is quickly applied to the classroom and that re-teaching targets weaknesses while material is still fresh in students' minds.

Data-Driven Success Story

Greater Newark Charter School: Achievement by Alignment

The Results

New Jersey NJASK Eighth-Grade State Exam: Percentage at or Above Proficiency

Year	2004	2005	2006	2007	GAINS	District Average	State Average
Math	7%	26%	73%	82%	+75	38%	71%
Literacy	46%	63%	73%	80%	+34	57%	82%

Source: NJDOE School Report Card

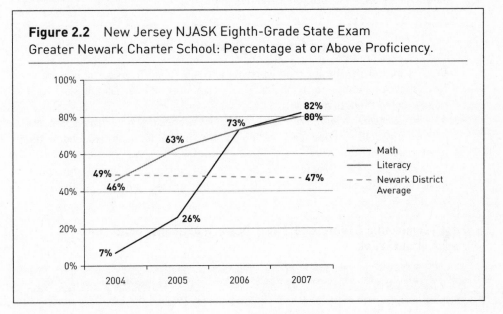

Figure 2.2   New Jersey NJASK Eighth-Grade State Exam
Greater Newark Charter School: Percentage at or Above Proficiency.

The Story

In the summer of 2004, Greater Newark Academy was a study in contrast. Despite a solid school culture with few discipline issues, math scores placed it as one of the lowest-achieving schools in the state. Principal Pete Turnamian decided to visit his neighbor down the street, James Verrilli of North Star Academy (whose story appears earlier in this chapter). Verrilli shared North Star's assessment model and gave Turnamian all his fifth- through eighth-grade interim assessments, analysis spreadsheets, and assessment calendar.

Turnamian's priority was to implement the interim assessments in a low-stakes environment: The assessments were a starting point to understand what students were learning and what they weren't. The biggest initial reaction was that teachers felt they were teaching to the test; it would take a year and a half for teachers to turn the corner and buy in to the assessments. As part of the school transformation, Turnamian built a voluntary team of teachers dedicated to moving from "good to great." They used the interim assessments to align teaching to New Jersey standards with far more consistency.

By 2006–07, Greater Newark had solidified a streamlined forty-eight-hour analysis process. Teachers were more and more precise in their analyses, doing more line-item analysis and developing a targeted monthly cycle of meetings to address re-teaching of difficult standards. The shift of focus to what was learned from what was taught seeped into every area of the school: principal observations, weekly assessment designs by the teachers, and even grading systems. Re-teaching evolved from occurring during a one-week re-teach to being embedded in all six weeks subsequent to an interim assessment. The commitment to the system bore great fruit: Greater Newark Academy had one of the strongest three-year achievement gains in the state, and the school eliminated the achievement gap between its students and the state.

Key Drivers from Implementation Rubric

- *Build by borrowing:* Rather than worrying about building from scratch, Greater Newark took neighboring North Star's assessments and analysis templates and implemented them to great effect.
- *Aligned assessments and curriculum:* The school aligned the interim assessments with its curriculum sequence, creating a cohesion that focused teaching on the most important standards.
- *Immediate analysis:* Greater Newark could be used as a model for quick turnaround: assessments were administered, graded, and analyzed within one week.

Fast Turnaround Example: Greater Newark Academy's Interim Assessment Week

	MONDAY	TUESDAY	WEDNESDAY	THURSDAY	FRIDAY
Morning	Literacy Interim Assessments (during class)	Math and Science Interim Assessments (during class)	Regular Classes	Regular Classes	Regular Classes
Afternoon	Grade Assessments (during free periods)	Grade Assessments (during free periods)	Grade Assessments (during free periods)	Faculty Meeting: Create Action Plans based on Assessment Results	During Free Periods: 1-to-1 Analysis Meetings with Instructional Leader

After each interim assessment week, the following week was devoted to re-teaching difficult standards.

THE ANALYSIS MEETING: TEACHER AND LEADER SIDE BY SIDE

Many schools have seen the value of creating effective tools for assessment data analysis. However, an often overlooked and equally critical component is the leadership training needed to lead effective analysis meetings with teachers. Too often schools assume that simply sitting down with the data is sufficient to ensure quality analysis. That assumption is fundamentally flawed. Proper leadership and teacher training is a crucial component to guarantee quality analysis. Such meetings need a clearly understood rationale and a set of tools, and school leaders should learn this material in the course of preparing to lead such meetings.

Rationale

As their name suggests, *interim assessment analysis meetings* are conferences between teachers and instructional leaders in which results gathered from the last interim assessment are analyzed and discussed. Unlike traditional post-observation conferences, which are based on a relatively small portion of teaching, interim assessment data span the entire test period. As a result, analysis meetings offer insight into months of student learning. Additionally, analysis meetings allow for more specific and nuanced advice than traditional observations since yearlong trends can be systematically assessed and analyzed. Analysis meetings also work to increase accountability by providing school leaders with a concrete record of class achievement.

Finally, and most important, such meetings are integral to changing from a culture focused on what students were taught to a culture focused on what students actually learned, which is the crux of data-driven instruction. Of course, this is not to say that traditional observations do not play an important role; they do. But interim assessment analysis meetings greatly enhance the effectiveness of observations to make them a more powerful tool to target and improve student achievement.

Who Should Conduct the Meeting   Ideally, the school principal should conduct data analysis meetings, since this makes it possible to directly supervise the implementation of data-driven instruction. That said, most schools are simply too large for the principal to hold regular face-to-face meetings with all teachers. In these situations, meetings should be distributed among the principal and other school instructional leaders who have a formal supervisory role: assistant principals, coaches, team leaders, head teachers, and so on.

One-on-One Meetings or Group Meetings?   Both one-to-one conferences and group meetings can be effective means of analysis, each with advantages and disadvantages. Small and large schools each have used these approaches, so the decision is not always just one of school size. Large schools have trained all coaches, department chairs, and team leaders to lead one-to-one analysis meetings with every teacher, while small schools have led group meetings. Generally speaking, one-to-one meetings focus on individual accountability and allow teachers to focus entirely on their own students and their unique learning needs. Alternatively, group meetings allow teachers to share best practices and resources that have worked and to plan new lessons together. At the risk of oversimplifying, one-to-one meetings can sharpen the focus on analysis, and group meetings can amplify the repertoire of teaching strategies in the action phase. To that end, this chapter addresses one-to-one meetings, while the next discusses group protocols. But the following discussion is still relevant to group settings and does not require significant adjustment to implement in that setting.

Before the Meeting   To quote Muhammad Ali, "The championship is decided before you enter the ring." Most errors in analysis meetings come from a lack of effective precursors. Consider the following errors:

Poor Preparation = Ineffective Analysis Meetings
Sample Failures and Their Root Causes

NOTE: Teacher responses based on rates questions (question 22 and question 30) presented earlier in this chapter.

FAILURE #1

> TEACHER: "I have to teach rates better, so I have selected some new approaches to teaching rates more effectively ... "

LEADER: "OK. What new approaches are you going to use?"

ROOT CAUSE: Analysis of questions 22 and 30 revealed that students were struggling not with rates but with multiplying mixed numbers! This teacher is about to embark on a misdirected action plan. The only way for leaders to identify this problem is if they have done the assessment analysis themselves in advance of the meeting.

FAILURE #2

TEACHER: "I'm frustrated by this test because it has a number of standards that I didn't even know I had to cover!"

ROOT CAUSE: The lack of transparency of the assessment—not letting teachers see the tests in advance—sets a teacher up to fail: A teacher cannot clearly lead a class to mastery without knowing the end goal!

FAILURE #3

TEACHER: "The test is completely what I expected. It didn't teach me anything, because I already knew exactly how they were going to do."

ROOT CAUSE: Interim assessments are so powerful because that they expose our limitations in predicting student performance perfectly. Most teachers think they know their students' performance far better than they actually do. A simple exercise done in advance of the meeting could have solved this problem: asking teachers to predict the performance of their students on each question of the assessment. The areas of disconnect between prediction and performance give us great insight into how well we know our students!

FAILURE #4

LEADER OR TEACHER: "So what we need to do is plan some effective lessons around multiplying mixed numbers." But after effective analysis, nothing is written down or recorded at the meeting.

ROOT CAUSE: Few people are adept at following through on a plan without writing something down. In the context of an analysis meeting, the "writing" needs to occur on something that the teachers will reference when designing their lesson plans. If you allow a great analysis conversation to end without nailing down what will be done and when, it is highly unlikely that all actions will be implemented as effectively as they could.

The following precursors can make sure that all of these failures are avoided and thus doubles the impact of the meeting:

Core Idea: Precursors for Effective Analysis Meetings

Before Giving Interim Assessment

- *Six weeks prior:* Teachers review assessment and plan toward the rigor of those assessments.
- *A few weeks prior:* Teachers predict student performance on each assessment question, choosing one of three options:
  a. Confident they'll get it right
  b. Not sure
  c. No way they'll get it right
- *Professional development (timing flexible):* Teachers receive model of how to do assessment analysis and complete action plan, and they see model of effective and ineffective analysis meetings.

Immediately Following Interim Assessment Administration

- *Teacher analysis:* Teachers do analysis of results prior to meeting, trying to answer the fundamental question: *why* did the students not learn it?
- *Teacher action plan:* Teachers complete action plan explicitly linked to analysis.
- *Leader analysis:* Leader analyzes teacher results personally in preparation for the meeting.
- *Review of teacher plan:* Instructional leader collects each teacher's action plan and analysis in advance and makes sure it meets preestablished expectations.
- *Content expertise:* If the subject in the assessment is beyond the expertise of the instructional leader, the leader identifies an expert within or outside of school to call on for extra support.

In addition to averting the failures just discussed, these precursors have some additional benefits. The single most effective way to ensure a quality analysis meeting is to model both effective and ineffective meetings with the faculty and school leaders in a nonjudgmental way. The leadership training modules presented in the second half of this book provide excellent resources that motivate teachers to see the benefits of these meetings while also implicitly setting the expectation for what is effective and ineffective analysis. Moreover, by asking teachers to fill out an action plan prior to the analysis meeting, a leader makes it possible to see in advance if the teacher has done a thorough analysis.

Before moving to details of the meeting itself, it is important to note the final precursor. Analysis meetings work most effectively when the instructional leader can make specific, well-informed suggestions about the data being examined. In many schools, instructional leaders are charged with leading analysis meetings in areas in which they do not have complete content mastery. For example, a K–12 math coach whose experience is really in K–8 math winds up having to lead a meeting for the advanced placement calculus teacher. Or a high school principal must lead a meeting for a Spanish teacher without knowing the language. Ideally, leaders are identified within the school who can lead these teachers. Given that this option will not always be available, leaders should make plans to access someone with greater content expertise for whenever that will be necessary.

Getting Started

Often the most challenging aspect of an analysis meeting is knowing how to begin. Fortunately, there are a few tried-and-true ways to start analysis meetings:

- So . . . what's the data telling you?
  This line accomplishes several critical goals; not only does it firmly ground the meeting in the data but it also allows the teacher to take control and begin to reach independent conclusions and feel more invested in the process of analysis.

- Congratulations on your improvement in _____; you must be very proud!
  Beginning on a positive note can be a good way to show familiarity with the data and at the same time acknowledge the accomplishments of the teacher.

- So the [paraphrase the teacher's main frustration—for example, geometry scores did not improve]. I'm sorry to hear that. So where should we begin our action plan?
  If the teacher had expressed frustration over a certain area, this is a good way to directly address it and move on from problem to solution. Of course, one must be sensitive to the context, and it may not be helpful to begin unless the issue in question is one that has already been discussed.

Data-Driven Success Story

Explore Charter School: Face-to-Face

The Results

New York State Exam: Percentage of Students At or Above Proficiency

Year	English and Language Arts	Mathematics
2005–06	51%	68%
2006–07	55%	68%
2007–08	**75%**	**92%**
2008–09	**84%**	**98%**
Gains	**+33**	**+30**

The Story

In 2004, after attending the Data-Driven Instruction Comprehensive Leadership Workshop (see Chapter Twelve) and follow-up workshops as part of New Leaders for New Schools' principal training program, Kinnari Patel came to Explore Charter School of Brooklyn, New York, with the goal of implementing data-driven instruction. Eighty percent of the students at Explore qualify for a free or reduced lunch, 90 percent are African American, and performance was not where it should be. During her first year, Patel worked with a team of teachers to create an initial set of interim assessments. Although the first tests focused only on second grade, by the end of the year every class in the school had at least some interim assessments.

The next year (2005–06), Patel focused on creating a robust assessment calendar that included time for analysis and assessment. She and her staff also continued to refine the interim assessments, working backward from sample questions from the state exam to ensure alignment with the end-goal test. During this ongoing assessment creation process, Patel made a point of allowing teachers to look at the tests and to voice their opinions. Additionally, the leadership at Explore made sure to keep data in simple templates with teacher-friendly learning curves and to implement entire weeks for re-teaching to focus on standards that students found difficult.

In the third year (2006–07), even more assessments were rolled out and turnaround time improved tremendously. Yet despite these improvements and despite the buzz surrounding data-driven instruction, student achievement still was not significantly improving. Rather than give up on data, however, Patel realized that there was still a piece missing: effective face-to-face assessment analysis meetings. During her fourth year at Explore (2007–08), Patel put tremendous emphasis on improving instruction through face-to-face meetings. While in the past Patel had conducted data meetings at

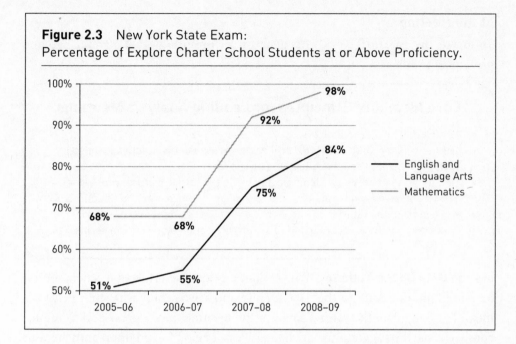

Figure 2.3 New York State Exam:
Percentage of Explore Charter School Students at or Above Proficiency.

the whole grade level, that year she put special emphasis on individual meetings that focused both on the nitty-gritty mechanics of individual standards and on the big picture of student performance. Although such conferences were never evaluative or hostile, they were intense and focused on the exact steps needed to boost student achievement. Patel never looked back.

Key Drivers from Implementation Rubric

- *Aligned interim assessments:* Explore looked directly to the text of the New York state test and then worked backward, which ensured that rigor was aligned.
- *Face-to-face meetings:* Although everything else was in place, no progress could be made until emphasis was placed on meeting with teachers to determine what the data meant and what strategies would be adopted. The dramatic success of Patel's fourth year highlights the critical importance of the principal-teacher data conference in achieving results.
- *Teacher-owned analysis:* The biggest product of the analysis meetings was teachers assuming full ownership for their results, looking closely at what they could do to improve.

At the Meeting

To make the meeting work effectively, it is important that several baseline principles be adhered to:

> ## Core Idea: Key Principles for Leading Analysis Meetings
>
> - Let the data do the talking.
> - Let the teacher do the talking. (Or if necessary, push the teacher to do so!)
> - Always go back to specific questions on the test.
> - Don't fight the battles on ideological lines (in the larger picture, you'll lose).
> - You've got to know the data yourself to lead an analysis meeting effectively.
> - Keep in mind the difference between the first assessment and the third.
> - Make sure analysis is connected to a concrete action plan you can verify.

Let the Data Do the Talking   Rather than explicitly assert what teachers should or should not do, point to the data at hand and ask teachers what they believe it means. Making data the central focus of the meeting does a great deal to reduce conflict, since the suggestions for change are not being forced upon a teacher but instead are presented as the logical results of objective facts.

Let the Teacher Do the Talking   It is extremely important that teachers own the process of assessment and analysis, and to that end it is critical that they be allowed to reach their own conclusions. School leaders should prompt their faculty to explain their interpretation of the data and should guide them to the changes that the results suggest they should make. Adults learn best when they find answers on their own.

Always Go Back to the Test and Back to Specific Answers   During this process, it's critical that both teacher and school leader have copies of the assessment in front of them. This allows for more detailed and productive recommendations and analysis.

Know the Data Yourself to Have an Effective Meeting   Armed with nuanced knowledge about classroom data, school leaders can ensure insightful and productive meetings.

Don't Fight Battles on Ideological Lines (Nobody Wins)   Rather than becoming bogged down in debates on pedagogical philosophies, focus on the narrowly defined task at hand. Indeed, one of the greatest strengths of the analysis meeting is that it shifts the discussion from irresolvable ideological dilemmas to a series of practical, pragmatic questions that can be targeted and addressed.

Keep in Mind the Difference Between the First Assessment and the Third
Though analysis meetings should always be teacher led, school leaders must be willing to change their tone if improvement has not occurred. When weaknesses persist after several analysis meetings, this must be acknowledged, and other solutions (such as outside help) should be presented.

Make Sure Analysis Is Connected to a Concrete, Verifiable Plan   Finally, it's absolutely vital that any solutions reached at the analysis meeting be written down and put into action as part of a concrete, verifiable plan. Even the best insights will be meaningless if they aren't in a form that can readily be put into practice.

Dealing with Resistance

Initially, it is likely that at least some teachers will be resistant to the very idea of the analysis meeting, especially when data-driven instruction is first introduced. Telltale signs of resistance might include phrases like these:

- "This is just test prep."
- "The students just make silly mistakes."
- "I taught it, and they knew it in class but just didn't perform on the test. I don't know why."

Such responses are unproductive and can quickly derail the analysis meeting. How then should you respond? The sidebar lists the most common errors that school leaders make when dealing with such assertions.

Dealing with Resistance

Three Common Errors and an Effective Response

Ineffective Approach #1: The Accepter

TEACHER: "The students just made silly mistakes."

LEADER: "Why do you think they made those silly mistakes?"

ERROR: This sort of response is dangerous because it legitimizes the belief that the reason students failed to learn had nothing to do with teaching and everything to do with students' failure to learn. In effective data-driven education, the emphasis must shift from what was taught to what was actually learned, a process that will not happen if responses like these are accepted.

Ineffective Approach #2: The Fighter

TEACHER: "The students just make silly mistakes."

LEADER: "That's an unacceptable answer; we believe in accountability, and your attitude needs to change."

ERROR: If the instructional leader is too strident and overbearing, then the teacher will likely shut down, become defensive, and ignore the data. The benefit of using data-driven analysis is that it need not be personally charged; by making an aggressive gesture the leader has forfeited this advantage.

Ineffective Approach #3: The Pedant

TEACHER: "The students just make silly mistakes."

LEADER: "If you look to question 18, you'll see that based on the results in the lower column this error stemmed entirely from misunderstanding mixed numbers."

ERROR: Spoonfeeding one's own complete interpretation of the data takes ownership of the analysis, causing teachers to feel disconnected from the actual process of analysis and making it less likely that they will own making the change. Additionally, because teachers observe their students on a daily basis, it is likely that the conclusion they would reach on their own would be as useful as the one the school leader has made—if not more so.

Effective Approach: The Guide

TEACHER: "The students just make silly mistakes."

LEADER: "Let's look at question 6; why do you think so many students got this question wrong?"

RIGHT: Responses like this one redirect the conversation immediately back to the essential question: What errors did the students make when answering a certain question? The response is not judgmental, nor does it allow teachers to drift into superficial analysis. Considered in the abstract, this may seem like an obvious response—but in practice it can require intentional training to make sure not to fall into one of the ineffective approaches.

A handful of key phrases can greatly add to the preparation of a school leader. In addition to the response listed for the "the guide," here are a number of conversation starters and redirectors that enhance assessment analysis meetings.

Core Ideas: Conversation Starters and Redirectors During Analysis Meetings

Starters

- "Congratulations on the improvement on _____ from last time!"
- "So . . . what's the data telling you?"

Redirectors for Resistant Comments

- "Let's look at question _____. Why did the students get it wrong?"
- "What did the students need to be able to do to get that question right? How was this more than what they are able to do with you in class?"
- "What's so interesting is that they did really well on question _____ but struggled on question _____ on the same standard. Why do you think that is?"

Synthesizers for Quality Analysis

- "So what you're saying is . . . [paraphrase and improve good responses]"

Making It Work

- "So let's review your action plan and make sure we have incorporated all these ideas."
- [When new analysis or action is proposed during the meeting] "Let's go back to your action plan and add these new actions."

Analysis meetings will not be easy at first, but in time they will become a critical part of any leader's arsenal in improving performance and building a better school. Combined with the other analytical techniques presented so far, such meetings represent a powerful tool for moving from examining data to taking action.

Analysis: Five Core Drivers

- *Data reports:* User-friendly, succinct reports that include item-level analysis, standards-level analysis, and bottom-line results.
- *Immediate turnaround* of assessment results, ideally within forty-eight hours.
- *Teacher-owned* analysis, facilitated by effective leadership preparation for analysis meetings.
- *Test-in-hand* analysis between teachers and instructional leader: the only means by which to do effective analysis.
- *Deep* analysis: Moving beyond *what* students got wrong to answer *why* they got it wrong.

APPLICATION: FIRST STEPS FOR TEACHERS AND LEADERS

So what is the most effective way to implement this type of analysis as a classroom teacher, school leader, or multicampus or district office leader? What follows are the first steps that could be taken to put this into action.

Level 1—Teachers

If your school has effective analysis templates, your work is perfectly focused: analyze the results as demonstrated in this chapter. (That detail does not need repeating here!) You can turn to your instructional leader and colleagues for support in this analysis.

If your school lacks adequate analysis templates, take one of the Excel templates provided in the CD-ROM that accompanies this book and adapt it to meet the needs of your class and your assessment. It is a worthy substitute if you don't have access to a tailored analysis template.

Level 2—School-Based Leaders

You play a critical role in ensuring that all teachers in your school analyze their assessments results effectively. Here are the three fundamental steps to this quality analysis:

- *Lead assessment analysis meetings:* Follow the guidelines set out here and work side by side with your teachers.

- *Train all instructional leaders in your school to lead effective analysis meetings:* Part Two of this book provides high-quality professional development activities to develop leaders in this area. This training allows you to distribute instructional leadership more effectively and guarantee that analysis is done consistently across the school.

- *(If possible) Select, change, or adjust analysis templates to meet criteria listed in this chapter:* Some principals have the authority to design or select their own assessment analysis tools. See Level 3 for details on proper criteria for making or selecting an effective template.

Level 3—District-Level or Multicampus Leaders

District-level leadership has a significant impact on school performance in two critical areas: the selection or creation of effective analysis templates and the process for quick turnaround of assessment results. These components are often connected to the choice of whether to have a districtwide analysis tool or let schools design their own. Districts have been successful with both approaches. If a district or organization decides to select a company to provide these services, here are the core criteria for selection:

- *Analysis sheets should be one page per classroom:* One well-packed page with item-level, standards-level, and student-level analysis is all a teacher needs. Do not sacrifice item-level analysis for all the other analysis that can be done—all power of change in teaching practice will be lost without item-level analysis!

- *Turnaround should be forty-eight hours to one week maximum:* See the discussion of fast turnaround in Greater Newark Academy, earlier in this chapter.

- *Teachers need the test in hand to do the analysis:* Make sure schools have access to the interim assessment when doing analysis of the results.

Chapter Two: Reflection and Planning

Take this opportunity to reflect upon the analysis process at your own school or district. Answer the following questions:

- After reading this chapter, what are the key steps around analysis that you are going to implement in your school (and that you can realistically do)?

  _____

  _____

  _____

  _____

- Who are the key people in your school with whom you need to communicate this plan and have on board?

  _____

  _____

  _____

  _____

- How are you going to get them on board? What are you going to do when someone says no? (What's Plan B?)

  _____

  _____

  _____

  _____

- Set the key dates for each action step, write them here, and then put them in your personal agenda or calendar to hold yourself accountable for implementing these steps.

  _____

  _____

  _____

  _____

Action

Changing Teaching to Enhance Learning

CHOOSING—TO ACT

After implementing effective assessments and engaging in deep, nuanced analysis, school leaders face the most daunting task of all: putting their plans into practice. Although it is based on gathering information, data-driven instruction is worthless unless that information is actually employed in the classroom. Unfortunately, data-driven instruction often gets misrepresented (and incorrectly implemented) as a numbers game akin to accounting. What is completely missing from this representation is the impact this approach has on the students themselves. When action is implemented effectively, students can perceive how their learning has improved. What follows are actual quotes from students about their experiences with data-driven instruction implemented well:

"The teachers use the assessments to become better teachers. They see what they didn't teach very well and re-teach so we can learn it better. So we end up learning more."

"I like the assessments because they help me know what I need to work on. Every time I have something new to learn, and my teacher pushes me to keep learning those new things."

Quotes from middle schools student at North Star Academy Downtown Middle School (see Success Story at the start of Chapter Two).

"My teacher would do anything to help us understand. He knows that science can be a hard subject so he will teach and re-teach the lesson until everyone gets it."

"Mr. G always accepts nothing less than each student's personal perfection. He is constantly telling us that we owe ourselves only our best work. If you do not understand something from class, he will make sure you get it before the day is over. He makes sure to stay after school so that we are able to go to him with anything we need."

"Ms. J is a special teacher because she wakes up the power that we all have in ourselves. She has taught us writing skills that are miles ahead from where we started because she cares about our future."

Developing effective action, therefore, is about changing student learning at its core. How, then, does one ensure that good plans become good practice?

Data-Driven Success Story

Thurgood Marshall Academy Charter High School: Teachers and Leaders Together

The Results

District of Columbia Comprehensive Assessment System (DCCAS) Exam: Percentage at or Above Proficiency, Tenth Grade

Year	English/Language Arts	Mathematics
2005–06	38%	33%
2006–07	43%	50%
2007–08	70%	61%
2008–09	67%	72%
3-year gains	+29	+39

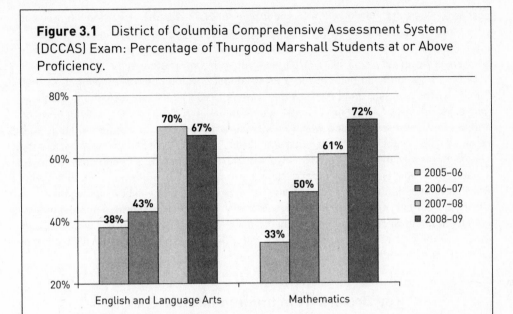

Figure 3.1 District of Columbia Comprehensive Assessment System (DCCAS) Exam: Percentage of Thurgood Marshall Students at or Above Proficiency.

- Highest-achieving open enrollment high school in Washington, D.C., in reading, 2008
- Second highest achieving open enrollment high school in Washington, D.C., in math, 2008

The Story

When Alexandra Pardo assumed the role of academic director (equivalent to principal) at Thurgood Marshall Academy, she confronted a culture that was very resistant to data-driven instruction. The student body was 100 percent African American and 70 percent free or reduced lunch, and only a third were proficient on the city's assessments (DCCAS).

In 2006–07, Pardo launched a data-driven instruction model connected to standards-based teaching. The administrative team made in-house benchmark assessments that were administered every six weeks, which clashed with the instructional culture that had been predominant up to that point. Teachers were unaccustomed to assessing the progress of their students on interim assessments, and they were often overwhelmed by the data reports that were created by the administrative team. Despite the challenges, math scores jumped moderately that year; reading scores also rose, but not so far. Upon closer examination of student performance, teachers and administrators noticed that while students had done relatively better on multiple-choice questions, they had really struggled (sometimes not even answering) on open responses. The students also weren't receiving instruction in all the math content prior to the assessment: students needed additional instructional time to take geometry earlier in their high school year.

In the summer of 2007, Pardo attended the Data-Driven Instruction Comprehensive Leadership Workshop (see Chapter Twelve). Armed with those tools and with the latest assessment results, Pardo built a stronger plan for 2007–08. She discarded the previous year's interim assessments and established a process where teachers and administrators built more rigorous interim assessments together, increasing teacher buy-in while also ensuring quality control. The administrative team created more teacher-friendly data reports, and Pardo established a professional development calendar that allowed a half-day for assessment analysis within a week of each interim assessment. On those half-days, teachers formed grade-level teams that analyzed the results, looking at which standards were mastered and which needed re-teaching. They made action plans with targeted focus on the most challenging standards. Teachers consistently went back to the action plan and analyzed how students were doing. For struggling students they launched a Saturday Academy, and both teachers and administrators tutored students daily who were struggling. Students themselves were engaged in the process by graphing their test scores all year long and tracking their development. The school celebrated improvements, both for students and for teachers. All the hard work paid off: Thurgood Marshall Academy made dramatic gains in achievement, becoming the highest-achieving open enrollment high school in Washington, D.C.

Key Drivers from Implementation Rubric

- *Common assessments:* Creating a common interim assessment with teachers was a critical first step in the data-driven process.
- *Teacher action plans:* Teachers consistently reviewed their progress on the action plans and adjusted the plan when needed to meet student learning needs.
- *Engaged students:* Involving high school students in tracking their progress and celebrating achievement was essential for their commitment to self-improvement.

THE ACTION PLAN

Immediately following analysis (done individually, in groups, or in a leader-teacher analysis meeting) teachers should draw up *action plans* that describe how they will apply the insights they have gained. Although they vary greatly, effective action plans all share a fundamental principle: they are explicitly tied to conclusions from analysis and are designed to put such conclusions into practice. Beyond this general principle, successful action plans share several key characteristics:

- *Correct analysis:* If analysis is not sound, then plans won't improve student results (see Chapter Two for more on analysis).

- *New strategies:* Action plans are only worth creating when a school believes it has room for improvement. If an action plan calls for a continuation of the status quo, then it is a waste of time and resources since more of the same will not yield different results. Plan with purpose, not for the sake of planning in itself.

- *Specific time of implementation:* Any and all suggested changes should be clearly marked with a date and a time for implementation; if a plan is made without a specific and well-defined time for action then it will probably be neglected due to the perpetual demands competing for a teacher's time.

Exhibit 3.1 presents one example of an action plan that conforms to each of these principles. The format was initiated by Amistad Academy and Achievement First and has been imitated in varying degrees by schools across the country.

Exhibit 3.1 Action Plan Template.

Pages 2–3 of Action Plan Results Analysis

RE-TEACH STANDARDS: What standards need to be re-taught to the whole class?	ANALYSIS: Why didn't the students learn it?	INSTRUCTIONAL PLAN: What techniques will you use to address these standards?

6-Week Instructional Plan

WEEK 1 DATES _____	WEEK 2 DATES _____	WEEK 3 DATES _____
Standards for Review and Re-Teach	Standards for Review and Re-Teach	Standards for Review and Re-Teach
New Standards	New Standards	New Standards
WEEK 4 DATES _____	WEEK 5 DATES _____	WEEK 6 DATES _____
Standards for Review and Re-Teach	Standards for Review and Re-Teach	Standards for Review and Re-Teach
New Standards	New Standards	New Standards

Exhibit 3.2 Sample Action Plan: Fifth-Grade Math.

Date: 10/27–31	Date: 11/3 — 11/7	Date: 11/10 — 11/14	Date: 11/17 — 11/21
Standards Spiraled in Do Now	**Standards Spiraled in Do Now**	**Standards Spiraled in Do Now**	**Standards Spiraled in Do Now**
10/27 — Multiplication	11/3 — Algebraic Subtraction	11/11 — Comparison	11/18 — Place Value: Value Identity
10/30 — OE (Exponents)	11/4 — Place Value: Value Identity	11/12 — OE (Eggs)	11/21 — WP with MC
10/31 — Add/Subtract WP, Comparison	11/5 — OE (Locker)	11/14 — WP with MC	
	11/7 — WP with MC		
Mini-Lesson?	**Mini-Lesson?**	**Mini-Lesson?**	**Mini-Lesson?**
	11/3 — Algebraic Subtraction/finding total		
Re-Teach Standard Heart of Lesson?	**Re-Teach Standard for Heart of Lesson?**	**Re-Teach Standard for Heart of Lesson?**	**Re-Teach Standard for Heart of Lesson?**
10/30: Open-Ended Explanations. Sample student responses from the NSA will be distributed and discussed.	11/6: Factors/Primes/Multiples: Identify (rectangular arrays). Discuss divisibility. Review array terminology and connect to multiply concepts.		
Checking for Understanding	**Checking for Understanding**	**Checking for Understanding**	**Checking for Understanding**
	Grade 11/3 homework (Expressions)	Grade DN 11/11 (Expressions)	
	Grade 11/4 homework (PV)	Grade OE 11/12 (Factors: Identify)	
	Grade 11/7 DN (WP)		
Standards Spiraled into Assessment	**Standards Spiraled into Assessment**	**Standards Spiraled into Assessment**	**Standards Spiraled into Assessment:**
10/28: Multiplication Quiz — whole numbers		11/11: Division Quiz	11/19: November Skills Check
Multistep WP		Whole Number Ops: multistep WP	Spiraled standards from NSA 5.1
Multiplication		Open-ended explanations	
Standards Spiraled into Homework	**Standards Spiraled into Homework**	**Standards Spiraled into Homework**	**Standards Spiraled into Homework**
10/30: Learning from Mistakes (all)	11/3: Expressions (Algebraic Subtraction)		
10/31: NSA Review homework (all)	11/4: PV: Value Identity (Switch digit)		

For schools that are new to making action plans, a simple piece of advice: *keep action plans simple.* A large stumbling block can be developing overly complex, lengthy action plans that get teachers tied up in analysis and too far away from implementing the action plan itself. By being very simple at the beginning, action plans give momentum to the whole process. Later you can add more thorough analysis piece by piece. Exhibit 3.2 is an example of a completed action plan for the four weeks following the interim assessment.

PUTTING IT INTO PRACTICE: ACTION IN THE CLASSROOM

After drawing up an action plan, data-driven schools must finally take the leap and change their actual classroom practices. In the end, implementing new approaches to difficult standards will lead to better teaching and thus better learning. This cycle of planning new lessons also develops the content knowledge of the teachers and expands the repertoire of potential teaching methods to use with future students as well. This leads to a somewhat obvious but often overlooked point:

Core Idea

- Lesson plans must be done with action plan in hand.

Often, an action plan is created in school (either individually or with a grade-level team) and then stored in some sort of assessment binder. If teachers do their lesson planning at home (which is often the case), those action plans can often be vague memories at the time of planning. If your school has a mandated lesson plan template, one effective way to resolve this problem is to add a reflection section to the very beginning of the weekly lesson plan template. On a weekly basis, teachers can highlight any particular skills they are re-teaching based on their action plan, and this keeps that action plan present for both the teacher and the school leader.

Data-Driven Success Story

Capitol Heights Elementary School: Data in the "Blue Book"

The Results

Capitol Heights Elementary School Students: Percentage at or Above Proficiency

Year	English and Language Arts	Mathematics
2004–05	25%	16%
2005–06	26%	34%
2006–07	41%	54%
2007–08	44%	57%
Three-year gains	+19	+41

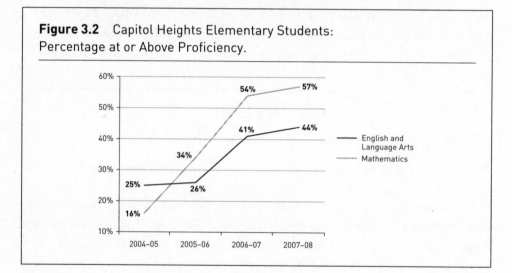

Figure 3.2   Capitol Heights Elementary Students: Percentage at or Above Proficiency.

- Most Improved Elementary School in Sacramento Public Schools District
- USDOE Title 1 Distinguished School Award, 2007

The Story
Robert Spencer arrived at Capital Heights Academy in January 2005 during a difficult transition. Housed in an old building, the school served 70 percent free and reduced lunch students, mostly African American or Latino. Spencer immediately presented a vision that at the time seemed completely unrealistic: that Capitol Heights would be the best school in Sacramento. He "wore his vision on the collar" and tackled discipline and instruction at the same time. After initiating regular observations and evaluations,

Spencer launched the 2005–06 school year with a first wave of data-driven instruction. The "Blue Book" came to define Capitol Heights' approach to data. The blue binder had four tabs: student profiles, pacing guide, lesson reviews, and interim assessment data. At any point, Spencer would walk into a classroom, pick up the Blue Book, and have a rich conversation about data connected to lesson plans, pacing guides, and student needs. For example, Spencer would sit down with a teacher to look at the performance of students in a leveled reading group. They looked student by student to design in-class strategies and extra-class support for particularly struggling students. By using the Blue Book, Spencer's evaluation of instruction became less subjective and more targeted. Spencer also implemented procedures that created a positive culture around the results from interim assessments. Capital Heights Academy tracked student achievement with EduSoft, celebrating successes in morning assemblies. Spencer also tried to make sure that teachers didn't feel defeated with initial poor results, writing notes of encouragement to teachers. At the end of that year, student achievement went up 48 points on California's Academic Performance Index (API).

In 2006–07, Spencer worked with key personnel to bring everything up another notch. As a part of the Aspire schools, he launched the "Cycle of Inquiry" that was built around identifying a challenging standard to tackle. Teachers gave a pre-test, created and delivered lessons based on pre-test results, and administered a post-test to monitor progress. Spencer worked with his after-school director to establish an often-overlooked component of high-achieving schools: they took a standard after-school program and built it to be completely data-driven. The after-school director led tutors to use data to decide what to teach the students and where to focus. The ensuing eighty-five-point gains in API represented the highest achievement growth in the district and earned the USDOE Title 1 Distinguished School Award. In the 2007–08 school year, Capitol Heights fine-tuned the cycles of inquiry and coaching support. The API continued to climb as the teachers built even stronger collaboration.

Key Drivers from Implementation Rubric

- *Accountability:* The Blue Book allowed Spencer and any instructional leader to check instantaneously for alignment between lesson planning, student learning needs, and assessment results.
- *Ongoing professional development:* Spencer developed two professional development tracks: one for new teachers and one for returning teachers. He aligned all professional development time with the data: he was adamant that no time or money be spent on any professional development that wasn't connected to the core learning goals identified in the data.
- *Transparent starting point:* By creating pre- and post-tests themselves, teachers were able to understand the end goal for each unit and teach more explicitly to mastery of those standards.

The box below shows a sample from a ninth-grade literacy class.

Sample Lesson Plan Reflection Box
Ninth-Grade Literacy Lesson Plan

Reflection
Students continue to struggle with characterization. I think there's a twofold problem there; one issue is that the level of vocabulary used in the answer choices is pretty high. We're continually trying to close vocabulary deficits with direct vocabulary instruction, word parts, and vocabulary-in-context questions. The other problem is that we haven't addressed the skill as purposefully as necessary in the class novels. We're going to start with a focus on characterization and draw on some inferencing skills when we begin *The Color Purple*. It seems authentic because Walker's work is so character-driven.

While every standard requires unique, content-based instruction, some powerful tools are not content-specific, and they can greatly enhance most lessons:

- *Ongoing assessment:* Constantly checking for understanding tightens the feedback loop between interim assessments. (See research on formative, in-the-moment assessments presented in Chapter Two.) To make sure the goals of the action plan are being met with every lesson, teachers should employ oral review, dipsticking, dry erase boards, cold calling, and other questioning techniques to gauge student comprehension as new material is taught. Such "in-the-moment assessment" is critical for ensuring that the action plan is actually achieving results, and can also provide real-time insights into *why* a given lesson is succeeding or failing.

- *Re-write and tighten objectives with assessment in mind:* From the outset, teachers should be encouraged to write more specific objectives that target the learning needs identified in the assessment analysis. This action can move teachers away from big objectives ("Students will make inferences") to the aspects of that objective that need the most attention ("Given three pieces of evidence, students will make inferences about a character's purpose"). To follow through with the example from *The Color Purple*, the next box presents the assignment that reflects that tightened objective.

The Color Purple

Reading Response Journal

For the *last* letter in this section, answer four comprehension questions:

1. Whom is the letter from and to?
2. What happens in the letter?
3. What is the writer feeling?
4. What happened since the last letter?

Event	Inference About Character	Explanation

Complete the characterization grid for any character in this section *except Celie.*

- *Do more with Do Nows:* Do Nows—a common practice of a five- to ten-minute individual work assignment to start the class—and other quick-check activities should be used to assess in-the-moment comprehension of new material. Special attention should be paid to focus Do Nows on the rigor of the standards targeted for review by the action plan; to this end, one helpful exercise is for teachers to collect targeted quick-check activities throughout the week and then let students correct their errors on the fifth day of each week.

- *Use differentiated instruction:* Teachers should generate strategies to work with select student groups while other students are working independently.

This is especially important if the action plan calls for the targeting of specific segments of the class or if there is a wide range of student ability levels on a given standard.

- *Use exit tickets to enter student learning:* A properly executed exit ticket—a brief class-ending activity to check for understanding of that day's lesson—that is aligned to the rigor of the interim assessments can give teachers immediate feedback about how well the students learned the standards of that given day.

- *Build peer-to-peer support strategies:* Given proper materials, students can be among the most effective teachers of their peers. To highlight how this principle can work even with the youngest students, I recently watched a first grader at North Star Elementary School peer tutor a new first grader for thirty minutes while the rest of the students were in reading groups. He used a set of flash cards prepared by the teacher to build sight word vocabulary that this student particularly needed, and then he listened to his peer read to him, correcting him in the same way the teacher does. If a first grader can provide effective support, then a student of any age can do so!

- *Make homework meaningful:* Re-design homework with the assessment end goals in mind: target the assignment to the areas that are most beneficial for the students to review.

One of the most effective ways to put all these possibilities into action can be to have a general faculty professional development meeting where everyone generates ideas for each aspect of the lesson plan that can increase the rigor and re-teaching possibilities.

North Star Academy gathered together the highest-achieving teachers—people who regularly made achievement gains of thirty points or more in their classrooms—and asked them to identify all the non-content-specific strategies that they use to re-teach standards and drive rigor in their classrooms. The resulting list is also a handout in the Appendix: "Increasing Rigor Throughout the Lesson: Data-Driven Classroom Best Practices." These activities confirm the research done on effective data-driven instructional strategies.[1] This list can serve as an excellent resource for principals and teachers alike to find ways to add high-leverage activities to daily lessons.

Increasing Rigor Throughout the Lesson

Data-Driven Classroom Best Practices

1. Objectives: Rewrite and tighten with assessments in mind.
   - Connect objective to how the students will be assessed.
   - Write "know and do" objectives: Students will know _____ by doing _____ .
   - Look at test questions beforehand to be sure the skills assessed on the test were worked into the daily lesson.
   - Write an assessment of the skills immediately after the objective, at the top of the lesson plan.
   - First write assessment questions that align to the objective; then break the objective into smaller chunks that will ensure mastery of all the skills needed to answer the question correctly.
   - Use verbs from Bloom's taxonomy to ensure that the objective is rigorous.
2. Do Now (five- or ten-minute individual exercise to start class).
   - Use Do Now as a re-teach tool: write questions that students struggled to master on the last interim assessment.
   - Use mixed-format questions for a skill: multiple choice, short answer, open-ended, and so on.
   - Organize questions sequentially according to difficulty.
   - Spiral objectives, skills, and questions from everything previously learned to keep student learning sharp.
   - Develop Do Now tracking sheet for teachers and students that shows student performance on the skills in each Do Now.
   - Make Do Nows that look like a test question and make sure they are reviewed in class.
   - Observe students' answers during Do Now and note kids with wrong answers to follow up with them during oral review.
   - Add multiple-choice questions to Do Now to allow real-time assessment.
   - Add why and how questions (for example, Why did you choose this answer? How do you know your answer is correct?) for different levels of learners and to push thinking.
   - Revisit yesterday's objectives in the Do Now.
   - Collect and grade four straight Do Nows, and for the fifth day let students correct their previous four Do Nows for extra points toward their Do Now grades.
3. Question to check for understanding and increase engagement.
   - Develop whole-class responses to student answer (for example, snap your fingers if you agree, stomp if you don't) to engage 100 percent participation.

Increasing Rigor Throughout the Lesson (*continued*)

- Use cold call: avoid just calling on students with hands raised.
- Move from ping-pong to volleyball: instead of responding to every student answer yourself, get students to respond to each other: "Do you agree with Sam?" "Why is that answer correct or incorrect?" "What would you add?"
- Script questions in advance of the lesson to make sure they scaffold appropriately and address rigor at varied levels.
- Have an observer record teacher questions: highlight where students are succeeding and where they can grow.

Student Error: Techniques for Helping Students Encounter the Right Answer

- Have student who struggled initially repeat correct answer eventually produced by the class.
- Use whiteboards to have every student write down response to question: whole class shows answers simultaneously so teacher can immediately check to see how many students answered correctly.
- Write questions in plan to specific students who are struggling with a standard; jot down their responses in the plans during class.
- Note in your book or lesson plan what questions students answer incorrectly; call on them again when you revisit that sort of question later in the week.
- Choose "No opt out": do not let student off the hook when struggling with an answer.

"Think" Ratio: Techniques to Reduce Teacher Talk and Push Student Thinking

- Require students to support answers with evidence from the text.
- Feign ignorance (for example, write a wrong answer that student gives on the board, let students find the error rather than correcting it yourself; pretend you don't even know that the answer is wrong).
- Ask students: "put it in your own words" about a classroom definition, concept, and so on.
- Reword question to force students to think on their feet about the same skill.
- Use Wait Time to give more students the chance to think through the answer.
- Model "Right is right": press to get the 100 percent correct answer.
- Check for student use of specific strategies and not just correct answers.
- Ask "what if" questions: "What if" I took away this information from the problem, how would you approach it?
4. Differentiate instruction—teach students at different levels.
    - Create leveled questions for assessments.
    - Include a bonus section of challenging questions.

- Prepare different Do Nows, worksheets, and so on for students at different levels.
- Use data (tracking sheets, interim assessments, exit tickets) to determine the degree of scaffolding and extra support each student needs.
- Group students according to the skills they need to develop.
- Communicate and collaborate with skills room and special education teachers to develop appropriate scaffolding for special needs students.
- Implement station work.
- Create individual "work contracts"—so students have a clear path of what they are working on.
- Use Do Now, exit tickets, and assessment data to drive small-group re-teach sessions.
- Create assignments with menu options by level (easy, medium, hard)—students can choose or teacher can assign.
- Have observers sit by lower-achieving students during an observation to provide extra support.

5. Peer-to-peer support strategies.
- Observe student work carefully during independent work—enlist strong students to help weaker students determine right answer during review of assignment.
- Have students teach parts of the lesson to small groups of their peers.
- Have students run stations.
- Train peer tutors—teach student tutors how to ask questions instead of giving answers and how to get tutee to do most of the talking.
- Think, pair, share: have students think of answer, talk with partner, and then share as a large group.
- Turn and talk: students turn toward a partner and explain answers to a question.
- Peer to group: student models think-aloud.
- Implement peer editing and revision.
- Develop study groups that jigsaw activities and content.
- Create mentoring relationships: twelfth to tenth grade, eleventh to ninth grade, and so on.

6. Student self-evaluation.
- Create weekly skills check with a tracking chart: students track their own progress on each skill.
- Go over tests after grading them—"Why is choice A wrong?" and similar questions.
- Have students grade own papers based on rubric.
- Give students independent practice worksheets with answers on the back so that students can check their own work once completed.

Increasing Rigor Throughout the Lesson (*continued*)

- Create a cumulative rubric (adding skills as taught): have students do periodic self-evaluations with the rubric.

7. Exit tickets (brief class-ending activity to check for understanding of that day's lesson):
   - Create a tracking sheet to match the exit ticket.
   - Assess the same skills through varied methods.
   - Align format to interim assessment.
   - Grade immediately.
   - Immediately follow up (breakfast, lunch, home-room).
   - Answer essential questions on exit ticket.
   - Follow up data from exit ticket with following day's Do Now.
   - Use exit ticket to determine small-group re-teach.
   - Engage instructional leaders to design effective exit tickets for newer teachers.
   - Monitor whether exit tickets reflect scope and sequence.

8. Homework:
   - Develop homework center targeting specific skills identified by interim assessments.
   - Review problem areas within homework assignment in class soon after assignment.
   - Have students fix homework errors and teach them how to scrutinize errors.
   - Make tracking sheet by skill.
   - Incorporate spiraled review in homework assignments: include questions and tasks from previously learned standards.
   - Create leveled homework (student-specific).
   - Design homework that is aligned with interim assessments, state test, SAT.
   - Use homework for open-book quizzes.
   - Encourage homework completion with classwide or schoolwide competition.
   - Include above-grade-level challenge problems.

The Audible: Immediate Action in the Classroom

Too often schools undervalue the importance of acting quickly on assessment analysis. No matter how well you plan your lesson and teach the standard, moments will come when students do not learn effectively. Football coaches know this well.

When a less experienced quarterback is at the helm of a football team, generally the coach plans a series of plays in advance of the game and calls all the plays himself. Even if the quarterback notices something about the defense (for example, they are planning on blitzing) that will cause the play to fail, the team won't be able to make an adjustment on that play and will wait until the next down—or even halftime—to consider a more effective strategy. Great quarterbacks, however—Peyton Manning on the Indianapolis Colts is a modern-day example—are empowered to make "audibles": on-the-spot changes to the play based on what they read in the defense. This adds incredible versatility to a football team and makes its maneuvers much more difficult to defend against.

Using the strategies discussed here for immediate action quickens the feedback loop and allows you to check for understanding consistently between interim assessments. Teachers are essentially making more "audibles," which if applied effectively will lead to student learning in their classrooms.

ACTION OUTSIDE THE CLASSROOM

Beyond the classroom, there are steps school leaders can take to improve follow-up throughout the school:

- *Align after-school tutoring:* Most schools have some sort of after-school tutoring program, but the tutors often lack guidance on how to support the students other than helping them with their homework. The simple act of sharing assessment results with tutors and showing them the goals for each of the students can immediately double the impact of tutoring efforts.

Data-Driven Success Story

Monarch Academy: Vision and Practice

The Results

California State Tests: Percentage at and or Above Proficiency, School Aggregate

Year	English and Language Arts	Mathematics	API
2005	21%	43%	625
2008	37%	75%	776
Gains	+16	+32	+151

USDOE Title 1 Distinguished School Award

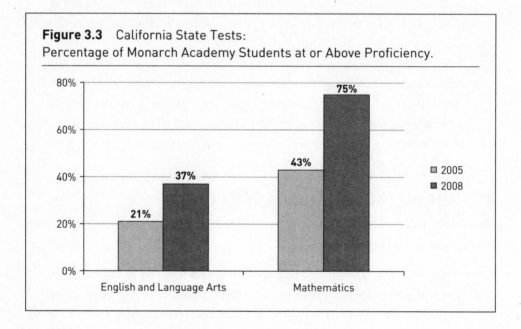

Figure 3.3 California State Tests: Percentage of Monarch Academy Students at or Above Proficiency.

The Story
When Tatiana Epanchin became principal of Monarch Academy charter school in California, her top priority was to create a compelling vision of what data could do for her students.

As a school in which 95 percent of students received free or reduced lunches and 80 percent of students were English language learners, Epanchin faced a daunting challenge. Inspired by the Data-Driven Instruction Comprehensive Leadership Workshop (see Chapter Twelve) she took while training to become a principal, she recognized the critical importance that data-driven instruction could play in greatly improving student achievement. During her first year on the job (2005–06), Epanchin constantly worked to create a sense of efficacy among the faculty, a belief that every student could learn and every student could achieve. During the first year, she constantly gave the Monarch faculty articles about other successful urban schools using this model and told them that they too could make data work.

Rather than rely on "talking the talk," however, Epanchin and her team also "walked the walk" of data-driven practices. During the 2005–06 school year, Monarch Academy set a goal of being public about data, a goal it met by posting data in common areas and in classrooms and ensuring that data reports drove all faculty meetings. Additionally, special effort was made to recognize the legitimate importance of teaching test-taking skills and to show students the important role such tests will play in the rest of their education and lives.

In the next year (2006–07), Monarch made a special effort to create an after-school tutoring program for students and to hold data meetings every week with administrators. By this point, the fundamental structure of the school had been altered. Even when Epanchin went on maternity leave for half of the 2007–08 school year, student test scores remained strong. Monarch has continued to achieve remarkable results, and has done so through a mix of compelling vision and effective practices.

Key Drivers from Implementation Rubric

- *Introductory professional development:* Rather than dismiss test-taking skills as "silly," Monarch rightly realized that for better or worse standardized tests would have a role in their students' future, and that they had better be prepared. Data-driven schools work best when they prepare students for the world as it is, not someone's idea of how the world ought to be.
- *Ongoing professional development:* A large part of creating a data-driven culture is instilling the belief that teachers can actually make this happen. By constantly reinforcing her vision that all students can learn and that data-driven instruction would be effective, Epanchin helped create a more involved and effective faculty.
- *Action outside the classroom:* Epanchin made sure to align after-school tutoring to the action plans in each classroom to increase the quality and quantity of targeted support that students received.

- *Make every second in school count:* When designing the academic calendar, school leaders should take into account time needed for the re-teaching that action plans might require. All efforts should be made to use every minute of school time for learning and growth. Indeed, creative data-driven schools have not shied from using breakfast, lunch, and even hallway time as opportunities to teach and review. Here is a sample comment from a teacher action plan for fifth-grade math (North Star Academy Clinton Hill Campus, October 2009) that shows how each minute is aligned and used effectively:

> In terms of student progress, there are a number of students (6–8 per team) who continue to struggle with the mechanics of division. This week we will continue to spend class time solidifying this skill, as well as time in the small group and Breakfast Club sessions. Breakfast Club is beginning this week for the six students who are having the most difficulty with basic operations, to provide additional time devoted to these concrete skills twice per week in a more individualized setting. In addition, the small-group schedule for the coming month has been adjusted based on interim assessment results, with additional students attending specific meetings based on needed subject areas.

- *Bring all hands on deck:* To make these efforts possible, consider how staff members in the school beyond just the teachers can support the process. With the proper coordination and training, secretaries, parent volunteers, teacher aides, and other adults can provide many of these in-school supports.

ACCOUNTABILITY: ROLE OF THE SCHOOL LEADER

School leaders clearly play a critical role in ensuring implementation and building accountability. Here are some of the most effective ways to make sure that action is happening:

- *Observe more smartly:* Classroom observations can be used to target key moments of re-teaching and rigor. Julie Kennedy, principal of Williamsburg Collegiate Charter School, has mastered this strategy. When she prepared to observe a classroom, she would bring the interim assessment results spreadsheet with her and open it up in the classroom.

As she observed the class, she looked at the spreadsheet to determine which students were struggling with particular standards. Then she would observe teacher questioning to see if those students were being given opportunities to practice that difficult standard. For example, in a fifth-grade reading class, she noticed that during Read-Aloud the teacher predominantly asked prediction questions, even though that was a reading strategy the students had already mastered! Moreover, when she asked inference questions, she called on the students who had mastered that standard rather than on those who needed the extra help. When Kennedy brought this information to the teacher's attention, the teacher was grateful to have another set of eyes looking for these issues, and she became more intentional in shaping and directing her questions.

Having the assessment analysis and action plans at hand is like putting on 3-D glasses! Leaders can observe both for implementation of those plans and for indications that the rigor of the classroom activities meets the rigor of the upcoming assessment. Such analysis for rigor is extremely difficult without a well-defined assessment as the guide.

- *Review lesson and unit plans with the action plan in mind:* This same mentality can be brought to the review of curriculum unit plans and lesson plans. Do the in-class assessments (writing products, projects, tests, and so on) meet or exceed the rigor or the interim assessments? If you have a mandated lesson plan format for all teachers, you can add a "Reflection" box that can help you see how the teacher has integrated the action plan (see a sample of this at the beginning of the "Putting It into Practice" section earlier in this chapter). Additionally, do the lesson plans use every effective strategy to re-teach a difficult standard? "Increasing Rigor Throughout the Lesson: Data-Driven Classroom Best Practices" (see pages 81 through 84) provides an excellent tool that coaches, department chairs, and mentor teachers can use as a resource to insert more rigor into a lesson on any content.

- *Lead assessment analysis meetings:* Chapter Two highlights the clear connection between analysis and action, and the critical role of school leaders in this process. Facilitating assessment analysis meetings shifts the focus from what was taught to what students learned, and it allows you to work with teachers to make targeted action plans addressing student needs.

Exhibit 3.3 Observation Tracker: Global Summary Page.

Teacher Name	Observations	Yearly Improvement Goals	Latest Core Changes (from DDI Analysis Meeting, Lesson Plan Review or Observation)
Smith	7	Teach to the objective. Make sure 100% of students are on task. Use more wait time in questioning.	Close the loop on all student misunderstandings. Do not settle for "Do you agree?" Push further by asking "Why?"
Doe	9	Make sure 100% of students are on task. Final check for understanding. (Check back with all students who struggle.)	Use "Agree" and "Disagree" questions to poll for understanding, rather than re-explain.
Johnson	10	Think ratio. (Make sure that students do the heavy lifting.) Integrate NJASK skills and algebra skills effectively. Final check for understanding with struggling students (no opt out).	Review Positive Framing to change tone in class. Call on every student at least twice in the class. Use combination of cold-call and hands to do this.
Brown	7	Stretch it. Students need to be asked to consider each others' thoughts in the course of each class. Questioning technique — avoid asking questions that imply that the answer is wrong. Expand key concepts section on the lesson plan.	Put directions for all group activities on a worksheet or on the overhead. Determine what structure for activities is best — partnered, individual, or group? Script questions in lesson plans in hierarchy. Too much scaffolding lowers cognitive demand. Probe by asking students to explain why after big assertions.
Total Observations:	70		
Average per Teacher:	7.7		

- *Change the focus of existing teacher-principal meetings:* Pre-observation and post-observation conferences can be transformed into pre- and post-assessment conferences. Leaders and teachers can preview upcoming lesson plans with the action plan as guidance, or they can look at exit tickets to see how students learned during that lesson.

- *Track observations and recommendations:* One of the biggest challenges as a principal is to keep track of the different plans and recommendations that each teacher is trying to implement. For an effective tool to manage teachers in this area, try something like the Observation Tracker that I created for this purpose (Exhibit 3.3).

GROUP WORK THAT WORKS: THE RESULTS MEETING PROTOCOL

Chapter One warned of the false driver of professional learning communities with a focus on collaboration for collaboration's sake. Teacher team meetings can be ineffective for many reasons: agendas are not tied directly to student learning goals as measured by interim assessments; conversations drift off target even with a proper objective; or time seems too short to accomplish anything productive.

In schools across the country, results-focused meetings have been among the most important levers in leading to student achievement. They are what Richard DuFour originally intended when he coined the term "professional learning community."[2] To highlight that focus, principals at North Star Academy refer to the following meeting style as the Results Meeting Protocol. This protocol closely follows the protocol originally set up by the Brazosport (Texas) School District (the dramatic gains in achievement accomplished there were highlighted by Mike Schmoker in *The Results Fieldbook*).[3] The protocol presented in Exhibit 3.4 is a simple variation of this district's highly effective approach. Designed to be implemented in a fifty-five-minute block (though it can easily be reduced or extended for teams that have shorter or longer meeting times simply by reducing or expanding the time in each section), the meeting is a versatile and effective framework for approaching any number of problems. Specifically, it is used to address how to re-teach a standard that proved particularly difficult on the last interim assessment.

When it is implemented properly, teachers note the advantages of the results meeting format immediately. Following the agenda keeps the meeting on task and keeps the group from straying to other topics. The group is also forced to

Exhibit 3.4   Results Meeting Protocol.

Results Meeting Protocol

Agenda for Teacher Teams When Looking at Interim Assessment Data

- *Identify roles:* Timer, facilitator, recorder (2 minutes)
- *Identify objective* to focus on (3 minutes unless objective is given)
- *What worked so far* (5 minutes) [Or: What teaching strategies did you try so far?]
- *Chief challenges* (5 minutes)
- *Brainstorm* proposed solutions (10 minutes)
- *Reflection:* Feasibility of each idea (5 minutes)
- *Consensus* around best actions (15 minutes)
- *Put in calendar:* When will the tasks happen? When will the teaching happen? (10 minutes)

(TOTAL TIME: 55 minutes; can be adjusted for more or less time)

Brainstorming Protocol	Reflection Protocol
Go in order around the circle: Each person has 30 seconds to share a proposal.	1 minute—silent personal/individual reflection on the list: What is doable and what isn't for each person.
If you don't have an idea, say "Pass."	
No judgments should be made; if you like the idea, when it's your turn simply say, "I would like to add to that idea by . . . "	Go in order around the circle once: Depending on size of group each person has 30-60 seconds to share their reflections.
Even if 4-5 people pass in a row, keep going for the full brainstorming time.	If a person doesn't have a thought to share, say "Pass" and come back to him/her later.

Consensus and Calendar Guidelines

- Identify key actions from brainstorming that everyone will agree to implement:
  - Make actions as specific as possible within the limited time.
- Identify key student-teacher guides or tasks needed to be done to be ready to teach:
  - Identify *who* will do each task.
  - Identify *when* each task will be done.
- Put date for re-teaching on *calendar*.
- Spend remaining time developing concrete elements of lesson plan:
  - Do Nows
  - Teacher guides (for example, what questions to ask the students or how to structure the activity)
  - Student guides, homework, and so on

come up with action steps—even when people feel they haven't had enough time to do so. (This is a key teachable moment, showing teachers that they'll never have enough time to design a perfect action plan, but that an imperfect action plan is better than no plan at all.) Finally, focusing on a standard and the particular assessment questions that students struggled to answer provides for a pinpointed, precise attack on the learning problem.

Focus on one standard, not ten: What makes this protocol work is that it dives deeply into one standard rather than trying to cover ten on the surface. One standard done deeply has far greater impact than the same time spent on superficial analysis. Unfortunately, schools regularly mistake breadth for quality.

Making Sure the Protocol Works

Even the best protocol requires strong school leadership to maximize effectiveness. The following steps can drive the quality of these meetings.

- *Model a results meeting for the teachers:* Modeling the results meeting for the faculty allows everyone to see it in action before implementing it in their teams.

- *Run the first sets of results meetings in one common space:* For the first rounds of implementation, use all-faculty professional development time so that all your teacher teams can implement the results meeting in the same common space. This allows you to float from team to team, giving feedback about the implementation of the protocol and identifying strong leaders on each team who are driving implementation. Such observations can help you identify which teacher teams are ready to work independently (for example, during department meeting time) and which teacher teams might require additional support.

- *Be specific about the objective and the solution:* Make sure that all proposed solutions are specific to the level of the individual assessment question. If they're not, teams run the risk of global, ambiguous action steps that will not lead to real change.

- *Firmly facilitate:* Whoever is chosen as facilitator must be active at keeping the team focused on the task; for this reason, the facilitator should ideally be a teacher who is respected by the whole staff and who will be serious and focused.

Data-Driven Success Story

Dodge Academy: Turnaround Through Transparency

The Results

Illinois ISAT Exam: Percentage and of Students at or Above Proficiency

Reading			Math			Science		
2005	2008	Four-Year Gains	2005	2008	Four-Year Gains	2005	2008	Four-Year Gains
32.5	69.7	**+37.2**	21.6	79.4	**+57.8**	20.5	58.1	**+38.6**

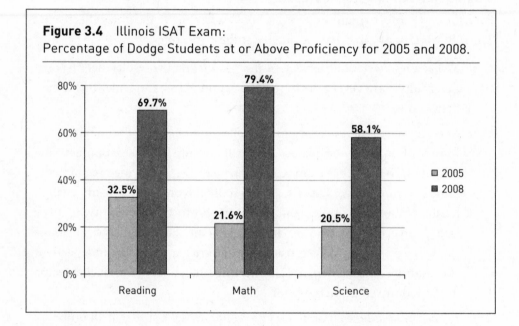

Figure 3.4 Illinois ISAT Exam:
Percentage of Dodge Students at or Above Proficiency for 2005 and 2008.

Highest Gaining K–8 School in Chicago, 2006

The Story

When Jarvis Sanford became principal of Illinois's Dodge Academy in 2004 (85 percent free or reduced lunch, 97 percent African American), he inherited a struggling school that had been closed just one year earlier for poor performance. In his first year, Sanford's goal was to show teachers what good instruction looked like and how data-driven instruction would get them there. To this end, Sanford made all teachers take the statewide ISAT test for themselves so they knew their end goal. Because Dodge implemented effective data analysis templates, teachers were able to quickly identify student weaknesses and discuss what steps were needed to boost student achievement. Data began to change the way teachers taught. Yet although many positive steps were taken in the first year, teacher resistance remained strong, and at the end of year one the gains were minimal.

The next year (2004–05), Sanford brought in key faculty leaders to increase teacher involvement and participation. Members of his leadership team also attended the Data-Driven Instruction Comprehensive Leadership Workshop and follow-up workshops (see Chapter Twelve). Along these lines, Dodge Academy committed fully to the idea of transparency in data-driven analysis, acknowledging that it might not achieve "perfect practice," but it would achieve "public practice." This translated into posting of interim assessment results outside every classroom and informing all parents exactly how students were doing. Teachers also knew exactly what would be on each interim assessment and prepared for it accordingly.

But Sanford wasn't finished. By the third year (2005–06), teachers had a clear idea about exactly what had to be taught at each grade level, which meant they could focus entirely on boosting achievement. Additionally, Dodge aggressively engaged students in the process of data-driven instruction. In every class at Dodge, the students each met individually with teachers to discuss where they were, where they needed to be, and precisely what they had to do to improve along objective, measurable benchmarks. This proved so effective that soon students were approaching teachers on their own.

In 2005–06, Dodge Academy saw unprecedented gains in all subjects on the ISAT, with over thirty-point gains in both math and science. Reading results showed similar growth a year later, as Dodge began a period of four consecutive years with achievement gains, making it consistently one of the highest-achieving public schools in Chicago.

Key Drivers from Implementation Rubric

- *Effective data reports:* Because the data templates used at Dodge clearly identified student strengths and weaknesses, teachers could quickly identify areas to improve and rapidly address them.
- *Transparency:* By putting special effort on making the process of data-driven instruction transparent to all stakeholders at the school, Sanford was able to overcome initial teacher and community resistance and achieve remarkable results.
- *Student engagement:* Students are critical partners in making data a reality. When students knew the precise goals they needed to reach and how they could reach them, they became far more motivated and as a result learned far more.

- *Avoid broad ideological debates:* Though nuanced discussions on pedagogical theory are often engrossing, they have no place at the action meeting. Action-results meetings should focus almost entirely on the specific, concrete challenge of the moment, since it is here that data-driven instruction can make its greatest impact.

- *Split larger groups:* If a group has more than eight or nine people, then (after the initial presentation of the problem) split it into smaller groups, each with its own timer, facilitator, and recorder. At the end of the meeting, all groups can reconvene and share results, which allows everyone to benefit from the insight of the subgroups.

- *Mark all dates:* After the meeting ends, be sure to clearly record exactly when the tasks agreed upon will be carried out and when re-teaching will occur. Doing so ensures that the actions agreed upon at the meeting are actually carried out.

- *Consider repeating the cycle:* If a task is especially important or the students are still struggling to master the standard, do not hesitate to redo the results meeting after the first round of implementation. This second meeting allows the group to evaluate the effectiveness of the first action plan and to develop even more precise action steps for a second round of re-teach implementation.

STUDENT ENGAGEMENT: TAKING ACTION INTO THEIR OWN HANDS

The strategies mentioned up to this point guide leaders and teachers in making action effective. But I would be remiss if I did not discuss the actions that should be taken by the most integral members of the data-driven process: the students

---

Core Idea

- Data-driven student engagement occurs when students know the end goal, how they did, and what actions they can take to improve.

---

themselves. In a truly effective data-driven school, students will be co-participants in improving their own learning.[4]

Simply put, students need to know where they're headed and what it will take to get there.

Williamsburg Collegiate School in New York City has one of the most effective student engagement templates that I have seen. Consider the first and last page of the school's template, shown in Exhibit 3.5:

Exhibit 3.5 Student Reflection Template: Williamsburg Collegiate Charter School.

Questions	Standard/Skill: What skill was being tested?	Did you get the question right or wrong?		Why did you get the question wrong? Be honest.	
		Right	Wrong	Careless mistake	Didn't know how to solve
1	Algebra substitution: add				
2	Algebra substitution: add 3 numbers				
3	Algebra substitution: subtract				
4	Translate word problems				
5	Solve equations				
6	Elapsed time — find end time				
7	Elapsed time — find elapsed time				
8	Elapsed time — word problem				
9	Elapsed time — word problem				
10	Elapsed time — word problem				

Using your test reflections, please fill out the following table:

Type of Error	Careless Errors	Did Not Know How to Solve
Number of Errors		

Williamsburg Collegiate Student Assessment Reflection Template copyright © 2010 by Uncommon Schools.

Exhibit 3.5 *(continued)*

If you have …	You are a …	In class you …	During class you should …	During assessments you should …
More careless errors than "don't know's" …	RUSHING ROGER	Are one of the first students to finish the independent practice Want to say your answer before you write it Often don't show work Get assessments back and are frustrated	SLOW DOWN! Ask the teacher to check your work or check with a partner Push yourself for perfection, don't just tell yourself "I get it." Take time to slow down and explain your thinking to your classmates Keep track of your mistakes, look to see if you keep making the same ones over and over	SLOW DOWN. You know you tend to rush, so make yourself slow down. REALLY double-check your work (since you know you tend to make careless errors) Use inverse operations when you have extra time
More "don't know's" than careless errors	BACK-SEAT BETTY	Not always sure that you understand how to do independent work Are sometimes surprised by your quiz scores	Ask questions about the previous night's homework if you're not sure it's perfect Do all of the problems with the class at the start of class Use every opportunity to check in with classmates and teachers to see if you're doing problems correctly	Do the problems you're SURE about first Take your time on the others and use everything you know Ask questions right after the assessment while things are still fresh in your mind

***Are you a Rushing Roger?* Then answer question 1:**

1. In your classwork and homework, if you notice you keep making similar careless errors, what should you do?

***Are you a Back-Seat Betty?* Then answer question 2.**

2. When you get a low score on a quiz, what should you do?

Clearly, this exercise allows students to share ownership in their improvement process. As a related activity, students can be asked to chart their performance throughout the year and to offer explanations as to why their results showed the trends they did. Doing this is not only a challenging and relevant exercise, it also allows schools to reinforce the central principle that academic achievement is everyone's responsibility. As a result, no effective action strategy is complete without including students in the mechanics of data-driven instruction.

In the context of school management, a great many things are easier said than done. Action will never be easy, but by employing the strategies necessary for effective student, teacher, and school leader action, data-driven schools can ensure that their plans become reality.

Action: Five Core Drivers

- *Planning:* Teachers plan new lessons collaboratively to develop new strategies based on effective analysis.
- *Implementation:* Explicit teacher action plans are implemented in whole-class instruction, small groups, tutorials, and before- and after-school supports.
- *Ongoing assessment:* Teachers use in-the-moment checks for understanding (Do Nows, questioning, exit tickets) and in-class assessment to ensure student progress between interim assessments.
- *Accountability:* Instructional leaders review lesson and unit plans and give observation feedback driven by the action plans and student learning needs.
- *Engaged students:* Students know the end goal, how they did, and what actions they are taking to improve.

APPLICATION: FIRST STEPS FOR TEACHERS AND LEADERS

So what is the most effective way to put data-driven instruction into action as a classroom teacher, school leader, or multicampus or district office leader? What follows are the first steps that could be taken in this process.

Level 1—Teachers

Four of the resources discussed in this chapter are of the highest leverage for teachers:

- Action Planning Worksheet
- Increasing Rigor Throughout the Lesson: Data-Driven Classroom Best Practices
- Student Assessment Reflection Template
- Results Meeting Protocol

Each of these is available on the CD-ROM for your use. It works best to have these documents present while you plan each lesson. Make sure you're addressing the standards in need of re-teaching, and adjust each component of your lessons with the instructional practices listed in the "increasing rigor" document.

Level 2—School-Based Leaders

Here is where the "rubber meets the road." Assessments, analysis, and action plans are meaningless if they are not implemented. These are the most effective ways to ensure that teaching practice is changing to meet students needs:

- *Launch results meetings to give teachers time to plan jointly:* Allocate professional development time to build action plans and problem solve using the results meeting protocol. It can take time to become comfortable with the protocol. To that end, we recommend that for your initial launch you have all results meetings run simultaneously with all faculty gathered in the same large space. That way you can identify best practices and nudge groups that need more guidance. Over time, the results meeting protocol can become a part of the fabric of team meetings looking at data.

- *Observe for action plan implementation:* See the "Accountability: Role of the School Leader" section of this chapter for details. The use of an observation tracker can be particularly useful. Look for re-teaching in lesson plans, student notebooks, class materials, and the teaching itself. When you find best practices in one classroom, pass them on to other teachers.

- *Tighten re-teaching and support systems outside the classroom:* Are all staff members connected to the re-teaching process? Are there nontraditional staff members who could support individual students or small groups?

Are special education teachers and ELL teachers following the same protocols as regular education teachers? Often schools overlook the natural connection between the work of these support staff members and the work around interim assessments.

Data-Driven Success Story

True North Rochester Prep: Data-Driven Immersion

The Results

New York State Assessment: Percentage of True North Rochester Prep Students and at or Above Proficiency, Fifth and Sixth Grade

Year	2007	2008	2009
Fifth-grade math	87%	89%	92%
Fifth-grade literacy	61%	78%	88%
Sixth-grade math	—	98%	100%
Sixth-grade literacy	—	84%	94%
Seventh-grade math	—	—	100%
Seventh-grade literacy	—	—	100%

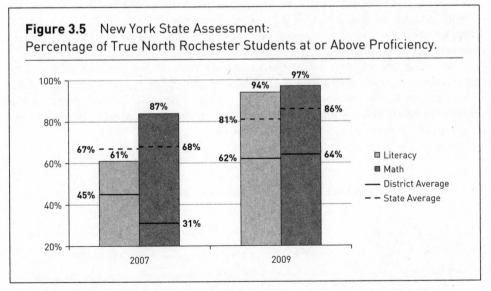

Figure 3.5 New York State Assessment: Percentage of True North Rochester Students at or Above Proficiency.

Highest Achieving Middle School in Rochester

The Story

When parents arrived at the first orientation meeting at True North Rochester Prep (80 percent free or reduced lunch, 98 percent students of color), they were immediately made aware of the importance of data for founding principal Stacey Shells: their children were led to a classroom to take a baseline assessment to determine how to serve their learning needs most effectively. Teachers had a similar experience in the first days of professional development before the school year started: emphasis on data-driven instruction and protocols for analyzing and acting on data were fundamental components of teacher training. In this way, Shells launched the data-driven cycle from the opening day: teachers analyzed results, made work plans according to students' needs, and selected books for students based on their individual reading levels.

The data-driven culture continued in every aspect of the school. Teachers were trained in creating effective assessment questions and how to analyze student data to drive planning and teaching. They looked closely at individual test items and incorrect answer choices to form hypotheses about student learning errors. Interim assessments were the focal point: teachers analyzed the test data and made explicit action plans for whole-class instruction and targeted tutoring groups. The scope of the re-teaching was based on the depth of the knowledge gap: some standards required just a day of instruction and others required five. Teachers were particularly effective in using ongoing assessment to track student progress after each round of interim assessments: daily exit tickets, Do Nows, homework assignments, and quizzes gave indicators of student understanding in each moment. Shells also focused teacher energy on their questioning strategies, analyzing student responses — and which students raised their hands to answer a question — to check for basic understanding.

With such strong implementation from the first few days of the school's founding, True North Rochester Prep set itself up for notable achievement. In the first year, the school already established itself as one of the highest-performing schools in Rochester. As the years progress, Shells has developed a stronger leadership team and shared data-driven leadership with her staff, and has expanded her efforts to include data-driven emphasis in history and science. She has also maintained a regular dialogue with principals at other Uncommon Schools to drive best practices continually in her school. The data-driven culture has become so embedded in the daily life of the school that it seems commonplace. What is anything but commonplace, however, are the extraordinary results that True North Rochester Prep attains each year.

> ## Key Drivers from Implementation Rubric
>
> - *Leadership team:* True North Rochester Prep's Leadership Team shared responsibility for proper implementation of interim assessments and keeping all eyes focused on student achievement.
> - *Ongoing assessment:* Shells created a data-hungry environment where teachers used every form of ongoing assessment to continuously check for student understanding.

Level 3—District-Level or Multicampus Leaders

If your districts have established effective interim assessments and analysis structures, you have done the most important things to set up principals to lead the core elements of action effectively. Your core work here is to block and tackle: keep everything else away from school leaders so they can focus on these elements. Here are some of the most important ways to do that:

- *Minimize requests to principals during interim assessment weeks:* Free up reporting requirements and off-site meetings during each interim assessment cycle so that principals can focus on their teachers during that time.

- *Join principals in doing building walk-throughs—post–interim assessments—to look for action plan implementation:* Join principals to analyze assessment data, observe analysis meetings, and walk around to see action plans being implemented in the classrooms.

- *Identify areas of strength to leverage best practices:* Often data-driven instruction focuses on areas of struggle. It is also important to build on your strengths. Look at the various schools and see which teachers and schools are performing most effectively. Ask those teachers and leaders to share their best practices and even lead professional development for others. Your role is to disseminate the practices that are working to reach a larger audience.

Chapter Three: Reflection and Planning

Take this opportunity to reflect upon action at your own school or district. Answer the following questions:

• After reading this chapter, what are the key steps around action that you are going to implement in your school (and that you can realistically do)?

_____

_____

_____

_____

• Who are the key people in your school with whom you need to communicate this plan and have on board?

_____

_____

_____

_____

• How are you going to get them on board? What are you going to do when someone says no? (What's Plan B?)

_____

_____

_____

_____

• Set the key dates for each action step, write them here, and then put them in your personal agenda and calendar to hold yourself accountable for implementing these steps.

_____

_____

_____

_____

Culture

Creating Conditions for Success

AN OPENING STORY

In our first year of implementation of data-driven instruction, we knew that one teacher in particular was going to be very resistant. As one of the most veteran teachers on the staff and well respected by her peers, she also wielded great influence on others. Although we had invited her to join a leadership team to launch the initiative, she was still unprepared for the poor results her students received on their first interim assessment. As we followed the protocols established in Chapter Two and Chapter Three, her students' performance notably improved, but she remained very unhappy and completely unconvinced that data-driven practices had anything to do with these improvements. She regularly sent us signals of her displeasure with this initiative and felt it was stifling her teaching. At the end of the year, students gained thirty points in proficiency from the previous year's cohort, despite the fact that this cohort had been even lower-skilled when they started the year! Despite all the signs of her accomplishments, the teacher was still unwilling to acknowledge any impact of data-driven practices and continued to advocate for removing these systems.

Two years later, however, we had a faculty meeting and were discussing whether we should shorten our analysis protocol and action plan to make it easier for teachers to complete. In the middle of the meeting, this same teacher raised her hand and said, "This is a critical reason why our students learn so effectively; we shouldn't shorten it at all."

It took two full years for the teacher to buy in to data-driven instruction, but in the meantime, her students still made dramatic gains in achievement. When implemented well, data-driven instruction drives achievement from the beginning—a critical factor that distinguishes it from many other initiatives that require teacher buy-in before they have any chance of success.

DEVELOPING CULTURE

If you feed "culture of high expectations" to an Internet search engine, you will find hundreds of articles devoted to the topic. More concretely, studies of high-achieving schools often talk about the influence of "culture" or "shared vision" in their success.[1] The question to ask, however, is not whether high-achieving schools have a strong culture of high expectations—they universally do—but what were the drivers that created such a culture in each school?

In traveling around the country, I have yet to meet any teachers or school leaders who did not believe they had high expectations for student learning. The difference, then, is not in what is said but what is practiced. How can a school demystify the process of improving expectations and operationalize it with concrete actions that have proven to yield results? Just as standards are meaningless until you define how to assess them, working to build a data-driven culture is fruitless until you define the concrete drivers that guarantee it.

Building Buy-In

Initial faculty buy-in is not a prerequisite for starting to implement data-driven instruction. (Which is just as well; it's easy to argue that any initiative that requires complete buy-in prior to implementation is likely to fail.) The best initiatives in schools—and elsewhere—do not require buy-in, they create it. In fact, the Camden County, Georgia, School District published a very persuasive article about the phases of data-driven instruction. It illustrated how teachers in their district moved from Phase 1 to Phase 5:

- Phase 1: Confusion and overload—"This is too much!"
- Phase 2: Feeling inadequate and distrustful—"How can two questions on a test possibly establish mastery of an objective? These questions are terrible!"
- Phase 3: Challenging the test—"That is a poor question. Answer 'b' is a trick answer."
- Phase 4: Examining the results objectively and looking for causes—"Which students need extra help and in what topic? Which topics do I need to re-teach in different ways?"
- Phase 5: Accepting data as useful information, seeking solutions, and modifying instruction—"Their inability to subtract negative integers affected their ability to solve the algebraic equation. I need to re-visit the concept of negative numbers and how to use them."[2]

Rather than hope that teachers enjoy the process from the very beginning, school leaders should anticipate that it will take various phases for everyone to see the value of data-driven instruction.

The article from Camden County, Georgia, is one of the few publications to discuss the hurdles and challenges that occur early on in the implementation of data-driven instruction. If you would like to look at an even more concrete example, read the case study included in the CD-ROM about Douglass Street School. While the names were changed to allow for a candid sharing of the details, the case study is a true story and can give more insight into how schools make dramatic gains in achievement despite initial resistance.

Data-Driven Success Story

Chicago International Charter School: Winning Converts

The Results

Illinois ISAT Exam: Percentage of Chicago International Charter School Students at or Above Proficiency

Year	English and Language Arts	Mathematics
2005–06	58.8%	61.5%
2006–07	72.1%	83.1%
2007–08	83.1%	85.5%
Two-year gains	+24.3	+24.0

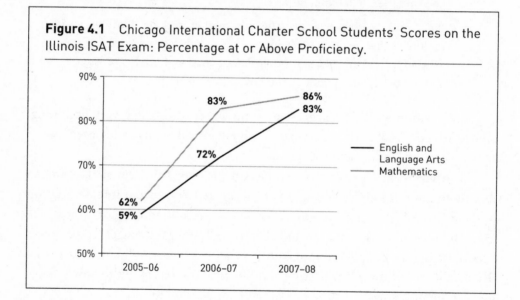

Figure 4.1 Chicago International Charter School Students' Scores on the Illinois ISAT Exam: Percentage at or Above Proficiency.

The Story

In 2005, the Chicago International Charter School (C.I.C.S.) Bucktown Campus was stagnating. With ineffective leadership and an unmotivated faculty, the school had seen almost no change in test scores since 2000. Turon Ivy set out to change this upon becoming principal at C.I.C.S.-Bucktown. Taking what he learned from the Data-Driven Instruction Comprehensive Leadership Workshop (see Chapter Twelve), Ivy introduced interim assessments to the school.

Yet although the new principal was enthusiastic about data-driven instruction, his teachers were considerably more wary. During the 2005–06 school year, resistance from the faculty was strong, a problem greatly compounded by the lack of communication and transparency that had been practiced by Ivy's predecessor. Rather than abandon the project of data-driven instruction, the leadership at C.I.C.S.-Bucktown put systems in place to win staff over and secure faculty participation. One of the most important parts of this process was running detailed professional development sessions to introduce faculty members to data-driven instruction and to show them its value in improving education. More important, during a time where many faculty members were apprehensive about testing, Ivy presented data-driven analysis not as a way for the administration to catch poor teachers but as an opportunity for the school to succeed as a whole.

In the next year, 2006–07, Ivy continued to win staff over, making professional development more systematic than it had been in the past and creating a transparent school calendar to allow for faculty participation and input. As more and more staff bought in, the few holdout teachers eventually left on their own accord to work elsewhere. Ivy continued to visit other high-achieving schools and attend data-driven workshops to bring additional best practices to the school. Additionally, C.I.C.S.-Bucktown began having teachers from different grade levels meet with each other so that teachers of younger students could coordinate their curricula to the demands of later academic years. As a result of this strong emphasis on effective professional development and staff involvement, Ivy was able to bring a formerly dysfunctional school from stagnation to success!

Key Drivers from Implementation Rubric

- *Introductory professional development:* If great care is not taken when setting up the professional development session that introduces data-driven instruction, the result can be a seemingly insurmountable level of faculty distrust and resistance. Framing assessments as opportunities for the entire school to improve its teaching as a whole is a great strategy for persuading wary staff to give them a try.
- *Build by borrowing:* Ivy looked for best practices in other high-achieving schools that he could bring to C.I.C.S.-Bucktown, and he also built systems for teachers to learn from each other within the school.
- *Implementation calendar:* By developing a transparent implementation calendar, Ivy removed the mystery of data-driven instruction and allowed teachers to understand clearly what was occurring each step of the way. Even teachers who were resistant knew what was expected of them and achieved stronger results.

> ## Core Idea
>
> - Data-driven instruction properly implemented does not require teacher buy-in — it creates it.

Much of what builds an effective data-driven culture is embedded within the drivers of assessment, analysis, and action. This chapter focuses on the remaining explicit structures that build buy-in and guarantee an effective data-driven culture. In my experience, following the drivers identified in this book will lead directly to increased student achievement.

IDENTIFYING AND DEVELOPING THE RIGHT LEADERSHIP TEAM

At the heart of this work is the identification of the school leadership team. School leaders should identify and cultivate relationships with key faculty leaders, ties that can be thought of as bridges to buy-in. As long as structures exist to ensure the participation of key school leaders, improved results will win over the rest of the faculty in time.

In the *Harvard Business Review* article "Informal Networks: The Company Behind the Chart," David Krackhardt and Jeffrey Hanson argue about the importance of making sure that the leadership team includes members of two important networks in an organization: the *expert network* and the *trust network*.[3] The expert network consists of those members with the greatest expertise: in the case of a school, your strongest teachers. These are the people teachers admire for the quality of their teaching. The trust network in a school, by contrast, consists of teachers to whom others turn for personal support or guidance. While not necessarily the strongest teachers, they are the ones with the greatest influence on their peers in the day-to-day working of the school.

Most school leadership teams already consist of leaders of the expert network. Securing the input and involvement of leaders of the trust network as well will go a long way toward creating a solid culture of data-driven instruction.

Involvement now, buy-in later: Once these staff members are identified, every effort should be made to include them in the process of implementing data-driven instruction. Of course, not every school leader will instantly embrace data-driven instruction, and some will initially dislike it. By keeping such faculty leaders involved in the process, however, the principal will be able to minimize resistance and at least ensure participation on the part of the most influential teachers. This is extremely significant, because as long as leaders are involved and willing to stay with the plan, then buy-in will inevitably follow.

THE CALENDAR

A story that sticks (author unknown): during one lecture, a time management expert set out a large glass container and a box of fist-sized rocks. After carefully placing rocks in the glass container, he came to a point where no more would fit. He then turned to the audience and asked: "Is it full?"

"Yes," came the reply.

He then produced a box of smaller pebbles and managed to fit a few into the container. "Is it full?" he asked again.

"Yes, it is now," was the answer.

From a small bucket he began to pour gravel into the spaces between the rocks and pebbles, every now and then shaking the container until no more would go in. "Is it full?"

"Probably not!" the audience replied.

Out came some fine sand, and he began to pour. With just a few gentle shakes, he was able to bring the contents of the container to the very brim. "Is it full?"

"No!"

Next came a pitcher of water and this he allowed to drip slowly into the container until, in time, the pitcher was empty.

"So," he asked, "what have you learned today?"

"Well," someone responded, "the lesson is that there is always room for more."

"Nope. The lesson is that if you don't put the big rocks in first, they won't fit."

The lesson of the story is clear: if certain key fundamentals are not secured first, then nothing else will be possible. Although this principle applies to many facets of life, it is especially apparent in data-driven instruction when it comes to creating a culture in which assessment, analysis, and action can thrive. The "jar" in this arena is the school calendar. The "big rocks" are interim assessments, analysis, and action. Without the "big rocks" firmly in place within this calendar, it is almost impossible to create a truly excellent data-driven school.

Schools live and die by their calendars: whatever makes it onto the schoolwide calendar trumps other activities that come later. Given that data-driven instruction is based upon timely and regular analysis, assessment, and action, placing these events on the school calendar first is essential for student achievement. Without being embedded in the structure of the calendar and school schedule, analysis and action are likely to be ignored, overlooked, or delayed, causing the project to fail. There are too many moving pieces in a school year to expect effective data-driven instruction to "just happen"; schools must consciously craft a calendar that lays the foundation for genuine progress.

> ### Core Idea
>
> - School calendars drive priorities: Make sure to schedule assessments, scoring, analysis, and professional development *before* placing any other events on the school calendar.

Here are the keys for developing an effective data-driven school calendar:

- *Make time for data:* The first critical feature of the calendar is that it blocks off time for interim assessments to be administered, scored, and analyzed. All too often, schools will make time to test but leave no time to grade exams, a situation that gives teachers and school leaders an excuse to postpone analysis until it is useless.

- *Note end-goal tests when placing interim assessments:* Beyond fixing the time for interim assessments, the schoolwide calendar must also take into account the state and national tests taken by students during the year. Given that interim assessments are most effective in six- to eight-week periods, plan the timing of the interim assessments working backward from the summative state and national tests, and then working forward for the rest of the school year after these assessments. (For example, if your state test is in February, plan for an interim assessment cycle the leads up to the February state test, and then after February you can start working toward the standards of the following year, allowing you to have a full calendar year of interim assessments).

- *Mark professional development:* As a further important feature, plan for professional development days before and after each round of interim assessments to allow for implementing each step of the data-driven process. This will also allow the school to provide content-focused professional development in response to the learning needs identified on the assessment.

- *Leave room for re-teaching:* Finally, and perhaps most important, an effective calendar is one that builds in time for the re-teaching necessitated by the assessment analysis. North Star Academy, for example, formally allots a week following assessments to re-teaching and reviewing earlier standards. Of course, this is not to say that this entire week is spent in review; in most cases, teachers integrate and spiral re-teaching while presenting new material. Nevertheless, the very existence of this re-teach week sends a powerful signal that assessment results will guide curriculum and that data results are to be taken seriously.

Exhibit 4.1 is an example of a yearlong assessment calendar. As can be seen from Exhibit 4.1, an effective calendar need not be overly complex or difficult to create, but it must include the basic elements outlined here if it is to be successful.

A second question often asked is how to structure the week itself when assessments occur and then analysis meetings and re-teaching. Chapter Two (Analysis) highlighted a one-week schedule used by Greater Newark Academy, and that can serve as a model.

Build by Borrowing

In building a data-driven culture, few skills are as vital as the ability to identify and adapt best practices from other successful schools. All the highest-achieving

Exhibit 4.1 Assessment Calendar.

Time Frame	Unit or Assessment	Notes
8 Weeks (8/25–10/10)	Unit 1	
10/13–10/17	Interim assessment 1	Approximately 1 hour per assessment. Aligned State Test objectives for 8 weeks
1 Week (10/20–10/24)	RE-TEACH Objectives from interim assessment 1	Re-teach based on test results analysis
7 Weeks (10/24–12/8)	Unit 2	
December 11 (7.5 weeks after first assessment)	Interim Assessment 2	Cumulative: All objectives Units 1–2 (@ 1:20 hours/exam)
1 Week (12/15–12/19)	RE-TEACH Objectives from interim assessments 1 and 2	Re-teach based on test results analysis
6 Weeks (1/2–2/9)	Unit 3	
4 days (2/9–2/13)	Interim Assessment 3	Cumulative: All objectives from units 1–3 (@ 1:40 hours/exam)
3 Weeks (2/26–3/16)	Unit 4, Re-teach of Units 1–3, and test preparation	Re-teach based on test results analysis
STATE TEST 3/19–3/23	STATE TESTING	
7 Weeks (3/26–5/18)	Unit 5	
7 weeks (5/21–5/25)	Interim Assessment 4	Cumulative: All objectives Units 1–5 (@ 2 hours/exam)
4 Weeks (5/28–6/22)	Unit 6 and Final Performance Task Preparation	
YEAR-END (6/25–6/29)	Final Performance Tasks	Oral presentations and large math projects

schools highlighted in this book are masters of "building by borrowing." They visited schools that were achieving better results than their own and borrowed any and every tool that could increase their own results. Leaders should strive to create an ethos in which teachers and school leaders perpetually seek out the best ideas beyond their building. During their initial roll-out of data-driven instruction, leaders should make an effort to visit effective schools and see data in action. Such visits will surely provide important insights into the mechanics of data-driven instruction, but they also provide something more important: hope. By seeing data-driven instruction succeed with their own eyes, school leaders and teachers will gain the confidence to articulate a compelling and coherent vision of what data-driven excellence looks like and what it will take to truly succeed.

One individual has taken this concept to another level. Doug Lemov, a fellow managing director at Uncommon Schools and manager of True North Rochester Prep (see success story), has devoted the past few years to finding the most accomplished urban school teachers in the country—"Master Teachers." He has videotaped them in action and identified the shared strategies that they all use to be so successful. He compiled these experiences into *Teach Like a Champion*, which includes a framework, actual video clips, and resources to be used in training teachers. Lemov is proving that teachers don't have to be born great; they can also be developed into high-achieving teachers. It is also much easier to believe in success when you can see examples of success with students like your own. This happens naturally in the assessment cycle when teachers see their own students improve on subsequent assessments. In these video clips, Lemov makes it possible for school leaders and teachers to "build by borrowing" without ever leaving their own schools!

Getting to Why

As you lead your school to build a culture of data-driven instruction, the most frequent and important question you will face is also among the simplest: why? Very often, people will ask why such dramatic changes are being made and, more fundamentally, why data-driven instruction matters at all. Implementing the core principles of effective professional development and building by borrowing will answer these questions effectively for most school staff members. However, other staff members will have lingering questions, and they will need a brief, personal "sales pitch." Indeed, if you cannot coherently defend data-driven instruction in a minute or less, then faculty, students, and community members will be much less likely to accept it.

Data-Driven Success Story

Samuel J. Green Middle School: New Orleans Rebirth

The Results

Louisiana Eighth-Grade State Exam: Percentage and of Students at or Above Proficiency

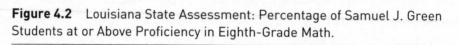

Year	2005	2006	2007	2008	2009:	GAINS
Math	8%	29%	36%	40%	73%	**+65**
Literacy	11%	21%	41%	30%	55%	**+44**

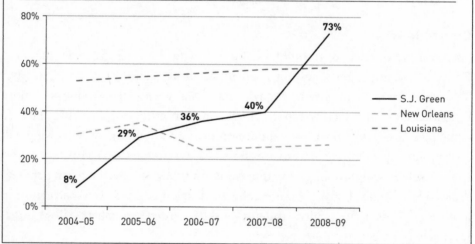

Figure 4.2   Louisiana State Assessment: Percentage of Samuel J. Green Students at or Above Proficiency in Eighth-Grade Math.

The Story

In 2005, Samuel J. Green Middle School had a ten-year history of low performance. The school was surrounded by barbed wire fences and concrete, and dilapidated portable classrooms filled what should have been the playground. The state of Louisiana turned Green into a charter school and handed it over to a local nonprofit organization in an attempt to turn the school around. One week later, the levees broke and the floodwaters of Hurricane Katrina inundated the city. The Green campus collected a few feet of water but was quickly drained and repaired. In January 2006, Samuel J. Green Charter School reopened for former Green students and new students returning to the city after Hurricane Katrina.

As co-founder of Firstline Schools and the leader of the school turnaround, Tony Recasner found himself without a principal—the one who started the year never returned post-Katrina—and so he started to bring order and address the urgent learning needs of students who had missed months of school and whose families were displaced across the country. Two years later, Recasner was rejoined by his fellow co-founder Jay Altman, and they set two primary goals for Green: implement an effective data-driven instructional model and ensure a calm, orderly environment where teaching and learning could thrive. Leaders were trained to work effectively with teachers in individual and group data meetings. Teachers received extensive professional development during summer staff orientation, particularly in how to use assessment data to drive instruction. They launched formal interim assessments, getting feedback from teachers to increase investment and the quality of the tests. They also implemented Data Days, where teachers analyzed students' performance on the assessments. Teachers used tracking sheets to monitor students' performance between interim assessments and adjust their teaching strategies in the moment to meet student learning needs.

The gains from 2005 to 2009 are an inspiring story of rebirth after the hurricane. "We've improved in a lot of areas since taking over the school in 2005," Altman reflects, "but the biggest driver of our success in the past year has been implementing interim assessment and using the data in a systematic way." Expect to see Green hitting 90 percent proficient in the near future!

Key Drivers from the Implementation Rubric

- *Build by borrowing:* Altman traveled the country to pull the best practices from high-achieving urban schools and apply them to Green's improvement strategies.
- *Ongoing assessment:* Tracking sheets enabled teachers to have precise in-the-moment measures of student learning.

How, then, to justify data? Although no one answer will settle this question for all who ask, there are several important basics to keep in mind. First, as suggested earlier, keep your responses short and direct. Beyond this, it is important to connect with the questioner on a personal level; in this regard, stories and analogies are extremely effective. Examples and stories need not come from education; indeed, they can be drawn from entertainment, family life, literature, and even sports. Consider the following argument, originally created by Darlene Merry:

> TEACHER: Listen; this data-driven education thing seems interesting and all but . . . why are we doing it?
>
> PRINCIPAL: Do you watch basketball?
>
> TEACHER: Sure.
>
> PRINCIPAL: During a recent high school basketball playoff game, the scoreboard completely malfunctioned midway through the game. So the refs kept the score and time on the sidelines. As it came close to the end of the game, the visiting team was down by two points, but they did not realize it nor how much time was left. The clock ran out before they took the final shot.
>
> TEACHER: That's not right!
>
> PRINCIPAL: Of course not. If the scoreboard had been working, the entire end of the game could have been different. So you'd agree that a working scoreboard is critical for sporting events, correct?
>
> TEACHER: Of course.
>
> PRINCIPAL: At the end of the day, data-driven instruction is like fixing the broken scoreboard. Relying on state tests is like covering up the scoreboard at the beginning of the game and then uncovering it at the end of the game to see if you won. At that point, there's nothing you can do to change the outcome! We use interim assessments to keep the scoreboard uncovered, so we can make the necessary adjustments to be able to win the game.

Of course, you needn't use this story; indeed, this particular anecdote will only work for someone who is comfortable with a sports metaphor. But others can be drawn from almost any area of life—baking a soufflé with no timer and no thermostat, driving with nothing but a speeding ticket to tell you you're going too fast, shopping with no idea how much money you have or when you'll get more. Regardless of what story you use, creating a short, clear, and accessible explanation for the pursuit of data-driven instruction provides a powerful tool for creating a culture of excellence.

THE LARGEST ROCK OF ALL: EFFECTIVE PROFESSIONAL DEVELOPMENT FOR LEADERS AND TEACHERS

After establishing a calendar, the single most important element of building a data-driven culture is *effective training for both teachers and leaders.* Unless school leaders and teachers are given the opportunity to experience the success of data-driven instruction—and concrete strategies to implement—it is impossible to implement the changes it requires. Unfortunately, much of the existing professional development in the field of data-driven instruction does meet this framework. Part Two attempts to address this critical need in two ways:

Chapter Six, "Leading Professional Development," directly lays the framework for designing effective learning opportunities for teachers and school leaders. Each professional development activity offered in this book follows the model presented in Chapter Six.

Chapters Seven through Eleven include explicit professional development activities for each core principle of data-driven instruction that then can guide leaders and teachers in learning how to implement data-driven instruction effectively. Each of these activities has been thoroughly tested in the field, having been used with thousands of educators nationwide.

With a well-trained leadership in place, seemingly insurmountable obstacles can be overcome; without them, even ideal conditions cannot guarantee success.

APPLICATION: FIRST STEPS FOR TEACHERS AND LEADERS

So what is the most effective way to build a data-driven culture as a classroom teacher, school leader, or multicampus or district office leader? What follows are the first steps that could be taken to put this into action.

Level 1 — Teachers

As a teacher, you have the most influence over the data-driven culture in your own classroom. If your school doesn't have one, set up your own assessment calendar. Visit the classes of the highest-achieving teachers you can find (within your school and in neighboring schools) to identify best practices that could increase your repertoire and make you a stronger teacher. But more than anything, focus on the key steps listed for assessment, analysis, and action (described in Chapters One through Three).

Level 2 — School-Based Leaders

The core drivers listed in this chapter are the basic road map for your work as school leader. Listed here are just some final tips during the implementation of each of these drivers:

- *Professional development for leaders:* It is imperative to train every leader in your building who will lead analysis meetings with teachers (for example, a coach, department chair, grade-level chair, or assistant principal). Plan for a leadership retreat, or gather for a few afternoons over the summer. Take advantage of the professional development activities listed in Part Two, with a particular focus on analysis and action.

- *Professional development for teachers:* In the best timing, you will launch the school year with an introductory training on the core concepts of data-driven instruction. Ideally you can cover the introduction, assessment, analysis, and action. If you have to limit your focus given time constraints, be sure not to skip analysis and the role playing of analysis meetings (these are as valuable for teachers to witness as they are for school leaders).

- *Keep the interim assessment cycle free of other commitments:* Make sure the calendar during interim assessment week and the following week are free of other events and teacher duties. One concrete piece of advice: keep the report card dates far enough away so that teachers don't have to turn in grades anytime near when they turn in action plans from their assessment. This might initially seem counterintuitive as many school leaders think it ideal for the interim assessment to fall at the end of the quarter. However, that timing is unnecessary given that the assessments are cumulative and continue to measure the standards each progressive round. In turn, your teachers will thank you for not creating an unbearable week!

- *Ongoing professional development:* The best agenda for professional development after each round of interim assessments is the results meeting protocol (see Chapter Three and the "Data-Driven Implementation Rubric" section of the Appendix). In addition, one of the most fruitful topics to address after the first round of interim assessment implementation can be "checking for understanding": how a teacher can effectively use in-the-moment assessments to check student learning on a daily basis.

Data-Driven Success Story

Lanier and Riverview Middle Schools: Building by Borrowing Together

The Results

Tennessee State Assessment — Percentage of Students at or Above Proficiency

Year	Riverview Middle School		Lanier Middle School	
	Math	Language Arts	Math	Language Arts
First year as principal	54%	68%	76%	75%
2006–07	71%	82%	89%	84%
Gains	+17	+14	+13	+9

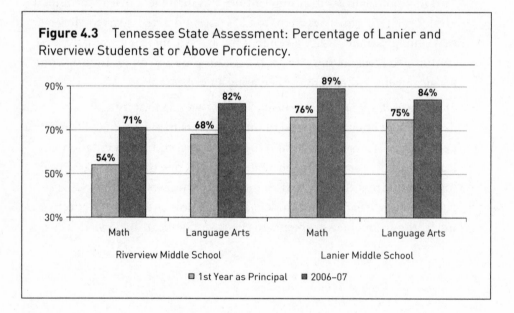

Figure 4.3 Tennessee State Assessment: Percentage of Lanier and Riverview Students at or Above Proficiency.

The Story

When Tiffany Hardrick began her principalship at Lanier Middle School in Tennessee (99 percent African American students with 90 percent free and reduced lunch), she walked into a school that already had the beginnings of a data-driven culture. The previous principal had looked at data, but the analysis had been on a global scale. Hardrick immediately led the teachers to look at student-level and question-level analysis. She launched an opening professional development session using the data-driven workshop materials provided in this book. The teachers analyzed student data from the preceding year, looking at individual student performance and determining the key first steps for that school year. They created small groups within each classroom based on student needs and their Tennessee Value Added Scores (TVAS). When each round of Renaissance interim assessments took place, the teachers dove into the data and created detailed re-teach plans according to the results.

In this process, Hardrick reached out to fellow principal Keith Sanders of Riverview Middle School, who was a graduate of the same principal training program at New Leaders for New Schools (NLNS). They both had attended the Data-Driven Instruction Comprehensive Leadership Workshop (Chapter Twelve) and were eager to put those steps into action. The two of them connected with Mark Murphy, the head of assessment for NLNS. They shared data across their schools, identifying best practices and areas in need of improvement. Hardrick brought her instructional experience in math and science, and Sanders provided leadership in English and language arts, as well as social studies. By relying on each other's expertise, they were able to provide better feedback and support to their teachers. They even brought their teachers together for data analysis work!

One of the most important steps for them was to have the teachers all predict the performance of their own students on each question a few days prior to the actual interim assessment. They then compared predicted performance with actual performance, which allowed teachers to see the disconnect between their perception of student understanding and the reality. When building re-teaching plans, they led teachers to design mini-lessons: ten minutes at the start of every class that would hit one standard with some small check for understanding. Each week, the teachers would assess whether they needed to revisit the same standard or could move on to another one. Each conversation was personalized by focusing on the specific students who were still struggling.

Not only did both schools go on to make gains in 2006–07, but Sanders and Hardrick took those lessons with them as they responded to the call to launch a school in New Orleans in the aftermath of Hurricane Katrina. Miller McCoy Academy will surely benefit from their leadership.

Key Drivers from Implementation Rubric

- *Build by borrowing:* There is no better example of this driver than two principals collaborating across their schools to drive achievement and share best practices.
- *Introductory professional development:* Hardrick and Sanders started each school year with a thorough, engaging introduction to data-driven instruction and the skills of data analysis.

- *Use the Data-Driven Implementation Rubric:* In the Appendix is a rubric you can use to evaluate your overall progress in implementing data-driven instruction. After the first cycle of interim assessments and then midyear, evaluate your school using this rubric. Identify the areas of weakness in your data-driven approach and develop a corresponding action plan for the leadership team. This is a great exercise for schools to do even after implementing data-driven instruction for many years: it keeps you fresh and focused on areas of improvement.

Level 3—District-Level or Multicampus Leaders

If districts have established effective interim assessments and analysis structures, you have done the most important things to set up principals to lead the core elements of action effectively. Your ongoing work here is to block and tackle: keep everything else away from school leaders so they can focus on these elements. Here are some of the most important ways to do that:

- *Professional development for leaders:* It is imperative to train every principal and school leader in each of your schools. Depending on the size of your district and organization, you can train all principals and then have them train their second-tier leaders (coaches, assistant principals, and so on), or you can set up districtwide training for all school leaders. Plan for a leadership retreat, or gather a few afternoons over the summer. Use the professional development activities listed in Part Two, with a particular focus on analysis and action. *If a principal is not fully trained in data-driven instruction, the initiative is likely to fail at that school.*

- *Make a districtwide calendar that prioritizes interim assessments first, everything else second:* Just as the big rocks analogy suggests, make sure the interim assessment cycle drives the rest of the district calendar and meets the criteria established in each chapter. Keep all other events and requests away from leaders during those critical times.

- *Use the Data-Driven Implementation Rubric:* As mentioned for Level 2, in the Appendix is a rubric you can use to evaluate each school's overall progress in implementing data-driven instruction. After the first cycle of interim assessments and then midyear, have school leaders evaluate their school using this rubric and develop a corresponding action plan for the leadership team. Collect the evaluations from all the schools and look for common trends across your district as well as differences from school to school. Are your assessments not seen as aligned by your principals (despite all your best efforts to do so at the district level)? Are schools struggling to lead analysis meetings? This evaluation can give you insight into additional professional development school leaders need and help you create a road map for districtwide improvement.

Chapter Four: Reflection and Planning

Take this opportunity to reflect upon culture at your own school or district. Answer the following questions:

• After reading this chapter, what are the key action steps around culture that you are going to implement in your school (and that you can realistically do)?

_____

_____

_____

_____

• Who are the key people in your school with whom you need to communicate this plan and have on board?

_____

_____

_____

_____

• How are you going to get them on board? What are you going to do when someone says no? (What's Plan B?)

_____

_____

_____

_____

• Set the key dates for each action step, write them here, and then put them in your personal agenda and calendar to hold yourself accountable for implementing these steps.

_____

_____

_____

_____

Overcoming Obstacles

Frequently Asked Questions

ASSESSMENT QUESTIONS

Are interim assessments and formative assessments the same thing?

Kim Marshall has established himself as one of the definitive authors on this topic. At Uncommon Schools, we recommend four to six interim assessments that follow the key drivers outlined in Chapter Two. This definition of interim assessment coincides with Marshall's. Still, teachers assess every day. As Kim Marshall defines them, formative assessments are "in-the-moment" checks for understanding: dipsticking, Do Nows, exit tickets, quizzes, and the like. There is no end to the times when teachers can use such assessments.

The difference between interim assessments and formative, in-the-moment assessments is their scope. Interim assessments cover all material taught up to that point, whereas formative assessments can look at any subset of what has been taught. Therefore, a unit test that only assesses standards from Unit 2 and not the ones from Unit 1 cannot be an adequate interim assessment. In the end, both interim assessments *and* in-the-moment assessments are necessary and important. In this book, in-the-moment assessments are treated as part of the action steps teachers take before and after interim assessment. Thus, look in Chapter Three (Action) for more details on in-the-moment assessments.

Aren't formative assessments enough to drive learning?

Kim Marshall's work is useful here as well. *By not assessing all standards taught up to that point, formative assessments run the risk of not gauging student retention of learning.* Most learning is not like riding a bike: if you stop practicing, you do forget what you've learned. (Poll the room at your next workshop: of all the people who took calculus in high school or college and do not currently use it, how many actually are still proficient at it?) I cannot tell you how many times I have seen a teacher check for understanding in the classroom and see that the students have mastered the material, only to find out that a month later they are no longer able to show the same mastery. Interim assessments make sure not to leave this to chance: you track student progress on *all* standards.

We have so many state and district-mandated assessments being thrown at us, far more than the four to six per year per subject recommended in the assessment section. Don't we reach a point of overassessing? How should we cope with this?

You definitely can reach a saturation point, and unfortunately many districts have done so. At Uncommon Schools, we recommend having a strong school focus on just four to six assessment cycles per year, and giving little emphasis to any other assessments you are required to implement. By *strong,* we mean full scoring, deep analysis, and effective action as outlined by the data-driven model presented here. For the other assessments, don't build in analysis and action focus. More than that can be overwhelming, especially for a staff new to this sort of work. Additionally, *by limiting this to four to six times per year, you keep it manageable from a leadership perspective . . .* and you will be able dedicate the time to leading the analysis and action components.

Schools have used many strategies to deal with overassessing mandated by districts:

- Actively lobby districts to change their assessment policy to meet the principles shown here. (Show them this book!)

- Create a normal class tone for mandated assessments that won't be the focus of the school year: treat them as simply an in-class assignment. That is, don't give these assessments importance for students or teachers; just comply with the mandate.

- (If permitted) you might even assign the district assessment as a homework assignment!

My district only has two or three assessments, and they aren't cumulative. How can we cope with this most effectively?

It is much easier to deal with too few assessments than too many. In this case, simply build an additional assessment that you can put in the largest time gap between district assessments, and make sure it covers all standards up to that point.

My district assessments are poor. They don't follow the key principles; they're not aligned to our sequence, or they're not aligned to the state tests, or they're not cumulative. How do we deal with each of these situations?

Poorly designed mandated interim assessments are among the most common failures of school districts. Until the districts design better assessments, use the following strategies:

- For non-cumulative assessments, *build a supplemental assessment* to give alongside the district assessment that fills in the gaps of all the standards not covered. Give it to the students at the same time as the district assessment so it still feels like only one test administration. Do the analysis of both assessments combined.

- *De-emphasize the district assessments* completely (see strategies for mandated assessments) and use an alternative set of interim assessments.

Data-Driven Success Story

Kingsbury Middle School: Catching the Data Bug

The Results

Tennessee TCAT Math Results

Year:	Seventh Grade	Eighth Grade
2006–07	72%	66%
2007–08	**83%**	**85%**
One -year gains	**+11**	**+19**

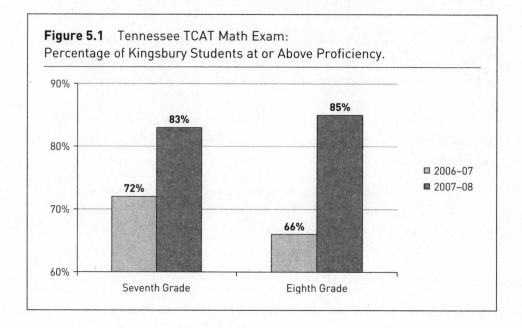

Figure 5.1 Tennessee TCAT Math Exam: Percentage of Kingsbury Students at or Above Proficiency.

The Story

Excitement matters. When Ronnie Mackin took over as principal of Kingsbury Middle School in Memphis, Tennessee, he had to hit the ground running. Up to April 2007 Mackin had thought that he would be working as assistant principal of a six-year high school, but at the end of the summer he was told that the seventh and eighth grade of his school were being spun off into their own building and that he was to start as principal in September. When he arrived, Mackin found a school at which over 70 percent of students were black and Latino and 89 percent of students qualified for free or reduced lunches. Results were dismal, with 78 percent of students reading at below sixth-grade levels in 2006–07. In hopes of boosting student achievement, Kingsbury Middle School decided to put the lessons of the Data-Driven Instruction Comprehensive Leadership Workshop (see Chapter Twelve) into practice and adopt a model of data-driven instruction.

Before data-driven instruction could be put into practice effectively, however, it first had to be accepted by the faculty. As is often the case, the faculty was initially wary of the great changes that were taking place. Rather than require faculty buy-in as a pre-requisite to implementation, however, Mackin used implementation to demonstrate the value of buy-in. Once he presented data as offering specific measures to help specific groups at the school, teachers began to realize that data did not represent a threat to their security but instead represented a tremendous opportunity for their students. Beyond creating a vision of data as a force for the good of students, Mackin also took the important step of ensuring that teachers were prepared for all data conferences before they began. This created a virtuous cycle: teachers who had done their preparation work thoroughly saw better results, and teachers who saw better results bought even further into data-driven instruction.

By the end of the year, a systematic change had taken place. Data-driven instruction had not only pointed the way toward better content and lesson plans, it had also fundamentally altered classroom dynamics; suddenly, lessons became so engaging that students did not *want* to act up, a far cry from the chronic discipline problems of earlier years. Teachers began to know students not only by their names and interests but by their specific areas of weakness on exams and the strategies that were being used to help them. Through data-driven instruction, the focus of Kingsbury had truly become student learning. By creating a compelling vision for data-driven instruction in his school, and by having the results show and not tell, Mackin was able to win over a wary faculty and, in doing so, significantly boost student achievement.

> ## Key Drivers from Implementation Rubric
>
> - *Introductory professional development:* During early professional development sessions it is critical that data-driven instruction is seen not as a bludgeon to punish teachers but instead as a pathway to student achievement. Administrators should take great care to present data conferences not as evaluative and hostile encounters but instead as opportunities to improve learning for everyone.
> - *Ongoing professional development:* Only after teachers saw the potential of data-driven instruction on their own terms did they fully support it. Rather than waste time securing buy-in for the program in advance, Mackin first put data-driven instruction into place and then used its successes to win over others.
> - *Teacher-owned analysis:* Mackin's requirement that teachers be fully prepared before all data conferences was a critical step to ensuring future buy-in. Support will come fastest if data-driven instruction is effective, an outcome predicated on doing things right the first time.

We don't have interim assessments. Creating our own seems like a monumental task. Should we just purchase a commercial set of assessments?

Creating your own interim assessments is indeed a monumental task. If you have the time and personnel to do so, it can be a very valuable experience that increases teacher buy-in. However, it is not essential. The best strategy is to *consult the highest-achieving urban schools in your state* that use interim assessments, and follow their lead. ("Build by borrowing" at its best!) If you choose to look at commercially made assessments, remember that most of these companies are national and design almost identical assessments for every state despite the differences in state assessments. Don't take my word for it (or theirs). Evaluate any product according to the assessment principles presented in Chapter Two. Ask the vendor to give you an actual interim assessment and compare it to your state test. You'll find a template on the CD-ROM to assist you in doing a question-by-question analysis: "Sample Results Grid." If the assessment doesn't meet your specifications, *push the assessment company to improve its product.*

Ideally, you want a product that gives you flexibility to match your school's specific scope and sequence. I see no reason why each school should not make its own decision about the order in which to teach the standards. As long as the final interim assessment is the same (and aligned to state tests and college-ready expectations), the first interim assessments can follow any particular sequence.

What do you do when the students have done poorly on every aspect of an interim assessment? You cannot really re-teach all of it.

An excellent question. When students fail on almost all the questions of an assessment, there are obviously major problems. The reasons behind this performance probably include one or more of the following:

- The test was well above what the students were able to master in the prescribed time period.
- The test doesn't assess what the teacher taught during that time period.
- The students arrived years below grade level, so a grade-level assessment is beyond their reach at the moment.
- The teaching was inadequate.

One of the core premises of assessment is that you must start at the students' learning level. However, if your goal is for all students to be proficient, and in many urban settings students arrive well below grade level, how do you address the need to cover more than a year's worth of learning in one year? *You need to map out an interim assessment cycle that takes students on an accelerated path to grade-level proficiency.* Here are some examples of how the highest-achieving urban schools have accomplished this:

- *Middle Schools:* The initial grade levels have assessments that start with pre-grade-level material and progressively advance to grade-level material, reaching proficiency by the end of the first year or the beginning of the second. For example, at one middle school, the first sixth-grade interim assessment included all pre-sixth-grade content (for example, the fourth- and fifth-grade math standards), the second sixth-grade interim assessment included 25 percent sixth-grade material, and the last sixth-grade interim assessment covered 75 percent of grade-level year-end standards. By the middle of seventh grade, every interim assessment was at or above grade level in terms of its materials.

- *High Schools:* Here, where the gap is even greater, high-achieving high schools have created pre-algebra classes that cover all necessary building blocks to prepare for algebra. They often double up math classes—having students take pre-algebra before school and then a standard algebra class during the school day—so students can complete a standard math sequence by the end of the year.

- *Elementary Schools (K–5):* At this grade level, the highest-achieving urban schools have been able to close the achievement gap almost immediately by using the existing plethora of early literacy assessments effectively.

What about K–2 assessments? Why is there no clear-cut consensus on assessing at this age?

There are a lot of reasons for difficulties here. On one side, people argue that children are too young to be assessed at this age. Ironically, there are more early literacy assessments than for any other age. In fact, when you think about the time it takes to administer individual reading assessments, there is more time spent assessing in K–2 than any other grade span. Often, *these teachers have more data than anyone else and yet don't how to piece it all together in a coherent package that can drive instruction.* Here are some recommendations for K–2 assessment:

- Beware of using an early literacy assessment that does not assess for critical reading comprehension along with more standard fluency and decoding. (Re-visit Chapter One for more details on assessment.)

- Young children do not have to know they're being assessed. They're excited to "read to the teacher"! The key is that we know how they're doing, and that what we assess for is the most effective.

- Kindergartners absolutely can master K–1 math standards, conceptually and procedurally. Design a rigorous assessment of the foundational math skills (counting principles, basic number sense, addition and subtraction, and so on) and give students multiple opportunities to experience the mathematics and practice it. Uncommon Schools (see North Star case study as one example) has developed K–1 math assessments that have led to dramatic achievement results. The assessments are only four times a year, and take only twenty to thirty questions.

- The curriculum chosen isn't what determines student achievement results; it's the data-driven drivers listed in this book. Case in point: both "Saxon Math" and "Investigations" (often considered at two opposite ends of the spectrum of math pedagogy) have led to strong achievement results. By driving yourself via results, you add rigor to whatever curriculum you choose (often by supplementing from other sources!).

- Below second grade, it is almost always necessary to administer the assessment one-to-one or in small groups to ensure you get valid information. Remember, reading difficulties should not impede on your ability to understand a student's math skills . . . therefore, reading the math test to the student is likely to be a good idea.

Is it OK to postpone content on an interim assessment because teachers simply aren't getting enough covered?

Yes. For the moment, let us assume you have control over the content of the interim assessment. *The key is that the content is not eliminated, it is simply postponed until the next interim assessment.* Some might argue that this is lowering the standard. But consider the alternative: you decide not to be flexible and leave the content that the teacher hasn't covered on the interim assessment. The interim assessment results come in, and the teacher's students do very poorly on these questions. Immediately the teacher will fixate on this and protest that the interim assessment wasn't fair. While you can argue with that teacher, you have already set up a resistant analysis conversation. If the students are going to do poorly on the questions anyway, then postponing the questions validates the teacher's concern and forces the teacher to focus on those standards that were covered but that students still didn't master. *Postponed content will still appear on the next assessments, and the teacher will still be held accountable to mastery of those standards.* And even though most districts have eliminated the possibility of making adjustments to the interim assessments, these principles can still apply. If a series of questions measure content that hasn't yet been taught, while you cannot postpone that content, you can focus your analysis with the teachers on the rest of the standards. That's the most important content to analyze.

ANALYSIS QUESTIONS

There's so much data: what should we focus on?

One of the main errors in this world of data is too much information. *As a general rule of thumb, teachers should have only one piece of paper for each classroom of students or subject that they lead.* This flies in direct contrast to most state and commercial data analysis companies. They think more is better. This is far from the truth. In this framework, the single most important driver of student achievement is teacher analysis of specific assessment questions (called item analysis by many). Standards-level and summative analysis won't drive change without looking at individual questions.

These are the three levels of analysis that matter, in this order:

- Question-level analysis
- Standards-level analysis (particularly, how students performed differently on questions measuring the same standard, and on related standards)
- Overall analysis: how students did in one class compared to another, or one school compared to the district

Teachers can do very effective analysis with the first two levels of analysis; leaders benefit the most from adding the third level.

But isn't it important to do a thorough analysis of last year's test data, which normally doesn't include question-level analysis?

Ivor Mitchell, a principal in Baltimore, uses Rick DuFuor's analogy that addresses this question: when someone in your care gets really sick, you probably call a doctor or go to the hospital. You don't wait until the person dies to figure out what is wrong! *Analyzing year-end test data is just that: you are doing an autopsy on last year's data.* The performance of the students is gone: the data is "dead." The students are older, they're in a new grade level, and they have new standards to learn. *It is far better to analyze data from the current year—to go to the hospital right away—rather than wait until the end of the year.* Thus, I argue it's far better to focus efforts on analyzing interim assessment data—or a pre-test at the beginning of the year. This is the analysis that will drive change while there's still something you can do about it. (The one notable exception to this rule is K–5 leveled reading assessments. It is essential to know what reading level a child had in first grade to determine the appropriate reading instruction at the start of second grade.)

What is the best way to begin data analysis when I'm just starting at a school?

Give a quick look at the available test data from the preceding year to see if you can identify any best practices within your school. Then focus on the implementation of your first interim assessment. The best possible thing you can do is give an interim assessment that matches the concepts and skills (standards) that the teachers have been teaching (or were supposed to be teaching) during the first eight or nine weeks. This will provide you with instant information on how the students are doing on material they were taught.

Many districts promote teacher data teams that lead analysis for the entire school. Does that meet the "teacher-owned" criterion?

Not by itself. "Teacher-owned" analysis refers to teachers' owning the data *for their own students.* Another teacher's analysis is *not* a replacement for teachers doing their own analysis. If a school data team is in charge of setting up effective analysis spreadsheets and getting them into the hands of teachers, then the data team is on the right track. If they are trained in facilitating effective analysis meetings (as the Follow-up Workshop provides), then they can be even more effective agents of change! However, a data team that tries to analyze data for the other teachers will fail at making the largest impact it can.

Data-Driven Success Story

E.L. Haynes Public Charter School: Scheduled to Succeed

The Results

District of Columbia Comprehensive Assessment System (DCCAS) Exam: Percentage of Students at or Above Proficiency.

Year	English and Language Arts	Mathematics
2005–06	40%	28%
2006–07	43%	48%
2007–08	60%	67%
2008–09	66%	80%
Three-year gains	+26	+52

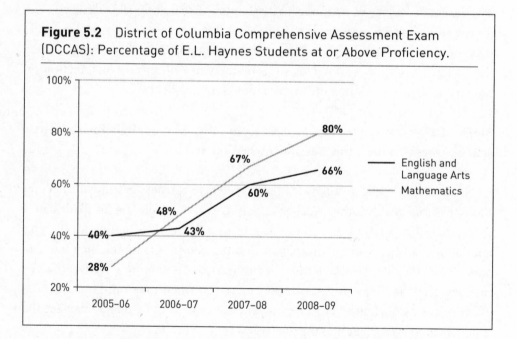

Figure 5.2 District of Columbia Comprehensive Assessment Exam (DCCAS): Percentage of E.L. Haynes Students at or Above Proficiency.

- Winner, $100,000 Fight for Children Quality Schools Initiative Award
- Silver Gain Award Winner, Effective Practice Incentive Community Grant

The Story

E.L. Haynes (ELH) is a diverse school in Washington, D.C., where 80 percent are students of color and 65 percent qualify for free or reduced lunch. Despite having piloted a program of interim assessment in 2005–06, ELH's performance on the citywide DCCAS did not differ from nearby underperforming neighborhood schools. In 2006, founding principal Jennie Niles and NLNS fellow and future middle school principal Eric Westendorf attended the Data-Driven Instruction Comprehensive Leadership Workshop (see Chapter Twelve). Based on that workshop, Westendorf led the systematic implementation of an interim assessment cycle in third and fourth grades. During the fall of 2007, ELH faculty visited high-achieving schools that had successfully implemented data-driven instruction, most notably North Star Academy Charter School of Newark, New Jersey, and Amistad Academy in New Haven, Connecticut. After visiting those schools, the staff further internalized the value of interim assessments to drive student achievement. They also realized that there was no "secret sauce" behind data-driven excellence—just a sound model of assessment, analysis, action, and culture coupled with hard work and creativity. Armed with a newfound proof that success was possible, Westendorf and the ELH faculty put these core systems into place. Although this was a daunting task, they adapted essential tools from the follow-up workshops to get off the ground: effective interim assessment analysis spreadsheets, an action plan, and a comprehensive schoolwide calendar that gave top priority to analysis of interim assessments and related professional development. Math results improved immediately that year, but literacy gains were minimal.

In 2007–08, however, ELH staff truly made data-driven instruction their own. Joined by new school leader Michele Molitor, Westendorf first scheduled four whole days devoted entirely to test analysis and planning in grade-level teams after each interim assessment. Second, they added individual faculty data conferences immediately after the team analysis and planning. Finally, faculty showed their enthusiasm for this data-driven instruction cycle throughout the school by putting up posters with key words like "TRAINED!" everywhere, scheduling time for the entire student body to watch inspirational movies together, and even having faculty wear Rambo-style headbands along with the students on the last day of testing to create a sense of excitement, energy, and urgency.

The work paid off in a major way. In three years, ELH scores on the DCCAS rose by twenty-six points in reading and over fifty points in math.

ACTION QUESTIONS

What are the most effective strategies for action that are not content-specific? Does one strategy fit all teachers?

Clearly not. As Jon Saphier has stated so precisely, teaching is all about matching: choosing the right strategy for the right circumstance. Therefore, creating more effective teachers in their action plans involves two key prerequisites:

- Develop a larger repertoire of strategies from which to choose.

- Build the capacity to understand when it is most effective to use each of these strategies.

To help teachers develop more targeted action strategies, we brought together twenty of the highest-achieving teachers in the country (teachers who have achieved gains of thirty points or more in student achievement or have reached 90 percent or higher proficiency, or both) and generated a list of the most effective techniques to add rigor to any lesson. That document, "Increasing Rigor Throughout the Lesson: Data-Driven Classroom Best Practices," is available on the CD-ROM.

So does that mean that all teachers should be allowed to have their own style and not have to plan together?

Style and effectiveness are two separate things. The power of data-driven instruction is that every decision can be based on the impact on student achievement. What normally happens in a school that implements interim assessments effectively is that best practices rise to the top and are adopted by others in the school (the culture principle "build by borrowing"). *All teachers can have their own style, but that style cannot interfere with student learning.* Therefore, collective planning—especially when using a tight format like the results meeting protocol—is very important.

How do we guide teachers when they choose different strategies?

Simple: Let the results do the talking. At the beginning, allow (even encourage) teachers to choose different strategies. After each round of interim assessments, see which strategies were most effective based on the results shown on the assessments. Over time, clear best practices will emerge. In the case where they don't (that is, no teachers in the school have had success with a particular standard), look to best practices in neighboring schools that have achieved stronger results with similar students.

CULTURE QUESTIONS

You say that data-driven instruction creates buy-in rather than requiring it. So what are effective strategies to deal with initial resistance, especially given how many bad experiences teachers have had with data-driven instruction done poorly?

The best tool you have is quality professional development and formation, which is why that has been the core content of this book. Second, you need to create the ideal conditions for data-driven instruction to succeed, thus using the drivers listed in the summative data-driven rubric here. Third, you need to allow teachers to progress naturally in their acceptance of the power of this model. As highlighted in the follow-up workshop, the Camden County, Georgia,

School District wrote an excellent article describing the phases of acceptance that teachers and leaders go through before embracing this approach to teaching and learning. *What makes the model presented here so effective is that you already start to get results even before staff really believes in its power.* In fact, once data-driven instruction is implemented effectively, it often becomes such a part of the fabric of the school that staff members don't even identify it as one of the drivers of student achievement—it just becomes inherent to the school's DNA!

One final important piece is for everyone to experience little successes. All it takes is identifying how students did better on certain standards on the second interim assessments based on teacher re-teaching, and you create the awareness that this works. Always note what went well even when focusing on standards that need major improvement. (For other ideas, read the answer to the next question as well.)

Why is there no mention of S.M.A.R.T. goals in your list of most important drivers of data-driven instruction?

S.M.A.R.T. goals have reached almost universal acceptance as a driver of change in education. Yet when looking only at the highest-achieving urban schools in the country, there is no consensus on its importance. While some of these schools have found them useful to drive achievement, others have not. Once a culture has been established of driving instructional change via interim assessments, S.M.A.R.T. goals become less important or useful. Thus the drivers listed for data-driven culture do not include S.M.A.R.T. goals.

Our school doesn't need to be convinced of the importance of being data-driven, but we're only doing some of the core drivers listed in this book. Our results are good, but they're not excellent. The good results, however, create a sense of complacency. How can we build urgency about moving from good to great?

The "build by borrowing" driver is essential here. You need to get the school staff to look outside their building at schools that are getting even better results. Use the case studies in this book to identify some of these schools. Read your state's annual report cards and see which schools have similar student populations to yours and are achieving even more strongly. But the single best creator of urgency is to take as many of your leaders and teachers to visit a data-driven high-achieving school. Most of the schools in the case studies in this book describe their visits to schools that were higher-achieving than they were at the time as among the pivotal urgency-creators for the school community. Seeing success in action creates belief that you, too, can succeed at a higher level. Reading case studies is never as powerful as seeing them!

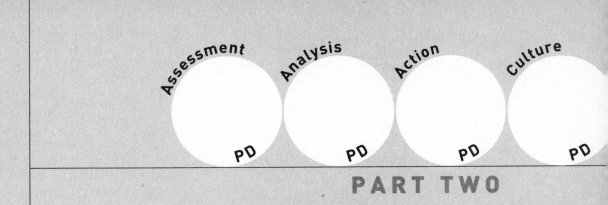

Assessment Analysis Action Culture

PD PD PD PD

PART TWO

Leading Professional Development on Data-Driven Instruction

Leading Professional Development

How Do You Make It Stick?

FOUNDATIONS OF EFFECTIVE ADULT PROFESSIONAL DEVELOPMENT

Up to this point, I have focused entirely on the foundations of data-driven instruction. Once these principles are established, however, it's necessary to confront a different and perhaps more daunting task: training school leaders to put them into practice. Recognizing the decisive role that leadership education plays in harnessing the power of data, the rest of the book offers comprehensive activities to train school leaders and teachers in data-driven instruction. The specifics and rationale of each activity are designed to address the critical challenge of facilitating adults' learning, particularly for adults who are teachers or leaders.

If traditional learning involves listening to a presentation and then acting upon it, "living the learning" involves generating the content yourself and then putting it into action. While successful leaders are always willing to tell you how they succeeded, they often forget that their own success was built not by listening but by living it themselves. Basketball players don't learn from a lecture; they learn on the court, living the directives given by the coach. Likewise, you don't learn to ride a bike by watching someone else do it; you have to get on and ride! Unfortunately, these basic principles are rarely applied to adult professional development. It is much easier to develop a PowerPoint presentation about what we know than to create a lived experience that mirrors our own learning so that others can make the same connections.

Indeed, all too often, those most proficient in an activity are those least able to teach others to follow suit. In the case of data-driven leadership education, this is a particularly salient problem. Although many schools have used data to achieve dramatic gains in student performance, relatively few of these are able to share their model with others in ways that allow it to take root. Put simply, data-driven instruction has not traveled well. Furthermore, even those who are effective at training others are seldom able to teach others how they teach.

FIVE FREQUENT FAILURES ASSOCIATED WITH ADULT LEARNING

The most critical errors in leadership training stem from an incomplete understanding of core principles involved in adult learning.

Teaching by talking: Even though research consistently shows that adults rarely retain what they hear (retaining far more of what they have to use), adult leadership training consistently errs on the side of lecture. PowerPoint can simply be a modernized form of an outdated approach. This may seem counterintuitive; after all, when presenters are chosen to run workshops, surely people expect them to do the talking, right? Not exactly. Think about how few details you can remember even from the most engaging lecture. Trainers who want leaders to walk away with concrete tools to build systems in their schools need to reduce their own talking to a minimum.

Treating adults primarily by "I do—we do—you do": While some leaders err on the side of lecture, others err on the side of leading adult Professional Development in the same way they would in a traditional K–12 classroom: "I do—we do—you do." The leader presents information, models its use, and then asks adults to use it. While this framework significantly increases learning when compared to a standard lecture, it does not address a core tenet of adult education: adults need to generate the content they are learning to be invested in it and to retain it longer. "I do—we do—you do" also sends an implicit message that the participants don't have much to offer on the topic and the presenter is the knowledge-generator. Yet adults learn most when they reach conclusions mostly on their own. Few workshop leaders think about creating the learning experiences that allow for this sort of adult investment.

Not specifically targeting leaders: When presenting data-driven instruction to school leaders, many educators focus primarily on the perspective of classroom teachers. Although this is an intuitive inclination, it is a poor strategy because it ignores the specific role that school leaders must play in implementing any data-based strategy. Rather than focus on the classroom, effective leadership training must emphasize the specific, concrete skills needed by school leaders. If the concerns unique to school leaders are neglected, then not only will the leaders lose focus, when they return to their schools they will be unable to implement data-driven instruction effectively. As a result, it is imperative that every single activity on every day of training is aimed at building effective data-driven *school leaders.*

Struggling to structure large-group sharing: A core element of many workshops is large-group dialogue: question and answer session with the presenter, small-group presentations to each other, conversation around a topic presented, and so on. Allowing for large-group sharing makes sure that participants have a chance to verbalize their learning and share their knowledge with each other, a critical learning component. However, this is also one of the most difficult components to manage, as group participation can vary significantly from one group to the next. Presenters often struggle to know when to let a conversation continue and when to cut it off. Also, when looking for the group to reach a certain conclusion and hearing an incorrect answer, presenters will often state the conclusions themselves rather than allowing more time for participants to unearth these conclusions.

Invariably, some participant will make an off-topic observation or ask an off-task but fascinating question. Without proper management, participants risk going off-track, or if the presenter cuts them off too abruptly, they can decide to shut down.

Poorly planning transitions and time management: When presenting a workshop to a group of up to about fifteen people, leaders do not have to worry as much about the quality of their instructions or the transitions between activities. If a small group didn't understand what they were supposed to do, you can simply walk over to that group and explain the instructions again without pause. If there is any uncertainty about the task at hand in a workshop with a hundred people, however, it will take too long to communicate this message to all the small groups, resulting in significant wasted time. In addition, getting a group of a hundred to "form groups of four" requires far more planning and potentially more structure. Without attention to instructions and transitions between activities, significant learning time can be lost.

THE BEST-KEPT SECRET TO GREAT PROFESSIONAL DEVELOPMENT

Building on the foundations for adult learning, the most effective presentations share one trademark move in common, and it is the foundation upon which the professional development in this book is built:

> ## Core Idea of Leading Adult Professional Development
> - Start by defining the end goal you want adults to reach.
> - Then design activities that can allow people to get there *mostly on their own.*

Table 6.1 Tale of Three Presentations: Fundamentally Different Approaches

Components	Lecture (Sage on Stage)	Guided Practice (I do, we do, you do)	Living the Learning (Act, reflect, frame, apply)
Format	Formal presentation on core principles. Question and answer.	*I do:* Formal presentation on core principles. *We do:* Shared presenter-participant activity modeling the core principles. *You do:* Try it on your own.	*Activity:* Do something that sparks learning. *Reflection:* Use facilitated sharing to identify core principles. *Framing:* Presenter puts formal language around participants' observations. *Application:* Put it into practice.
Approximate percentage of leader talk	90–95%	40–50%	15–30%
Learning Beliefs	We learn best by listening to the expert on the topic.	We learn best by listening to the expert and then having a chance to apply the information.	We learn best by generating the knowledge through experience and then applying it to our context.
Limitation	Adults retain 5–10% of what they hear.	Leader does the heavy cognitive work; participants imitate but don't build their own conclusions, limiting investment and retention.	Requires precisely built activities that lead to the proper conclusions; takes far more time to plan and more work to facilitate.

Table 6.1 sketches what this looks like in three different formats: a traditional lecture with PowerPoint, a Guided Practice lesson (I do—you do—we do), and this Living the Learning model.

One could engage in a debate of the relative merits of each of these models, but growing research support is backing the Living the Learning model.[1] I will not argue from a particular theory but from what I have seen that works. At Uncommon Schools, our observations of fellow practitioners who consistently receive the highest grades from participants for the quality of their workshops and our experience in leading workshops for more than two thousand school leaders lead us to believe that the model of Living the Learning is the most effective at equipping school leaders and teachers with real tools for change. While it requires the most preparation, therein lies the usefulness of this book: all the materials are already designed to embody these principles. By learning the proper facilitation techniques, you can make the greatest impact when launching this in your district or schools.

TALE OF THREE PRESENTATIONS: A SAMPLE PROFESSIONAL DEVELOPMENT SESSION ON ASSESSMENT

To make this clearer, here is an example of a professional development session on the same content delivered in these three different ways. This example makes use of the content from Chapter One, on assessment. Imagine making a presentation about the core principles and key ides around assessment. What follows are the three approaches in action.

The Lecture Approach

In the lecture format, you could take the slides described in this book and present them directly to the participants. You would start by describing the core drivers for assessment—giving a three- to five-minute explanation for each of them beyond what the slide says itself. Then you would show some sample assessment questions to prove your point. The slide deck would look something like this:

Figure 6.1 Opening Slide.

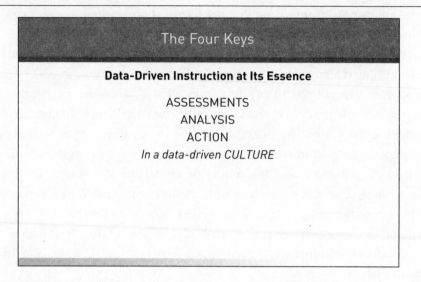

Figure 6.2 Assessment Principles 1.

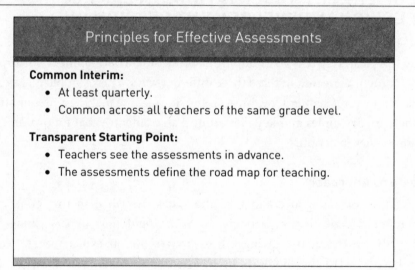

Figure 6.3 Assessment Principles 2.

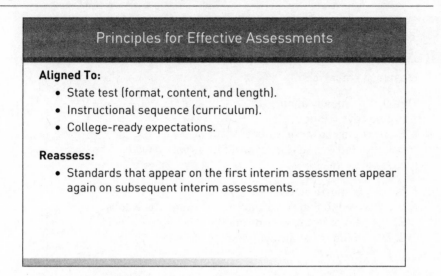

Principles for Effective Assessments

Aligned To:
- State test (format, content, and length).
- Instructional sequence (curriculum).
- College-ready expectations.

Reassess:
- Standards that appear on the first interim assessment appear again on subsequent interim assessments.

Figure 6.4 Types of Assessment Questions: Math.

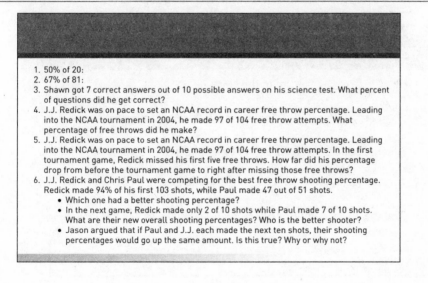

1. 50% of 20:
2. 67% of 81:
3. Shawn got 7 correct answers out of 10 possible answers on his science test. What percent of questions did he get correct?
4. J.J. Redick was on pace to set an NCAA record in career free throw percentage. Leading into the NCAA tournament in 2004, he made 97 of 104 free throw attempts. What percentage of free throws did he make?
5. J.J. Redick was on pace to set an NCAA record in career free throw percentage. Leading into the NCAA tournament in 2004, he made 97 of 104 free throw attempts. In the first tournament game, Redick missed his first five free throws. How far did his percentage drop from before the tournament game to right after missing those free throws?
6. J.J. Redick and Chris Paul were competing for the best free throw shooting percentage. Redick made 94% of his first 103 shots, while Paul made 47 out of 51 shots.
   - Which one had a better shooting percentage?
   - In the next game, Redick made only 2 of 10 shots while Paul made 7 of 10 shots. What are their new overall shooting percentages? Who is the better shooter?
   - Jason argued that if Paul and J.J. each made the next ten shots, their shooting percentages would go up the same amount. Is this true? Why or why not?

Figure 6.5 Types of Assessment Questions: Reading.

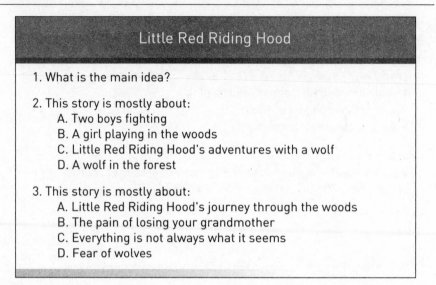

Figure 6.6 Types of Assessment Questions: Language Arts.

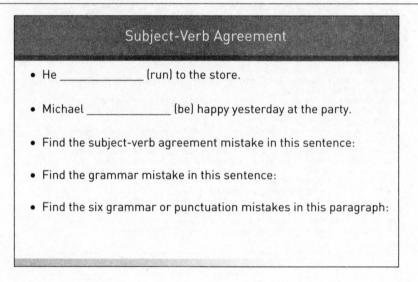

At the end of the presentation, participants would be invited to ask questions.

The Guided Practice Approach

In the guided practice format, you would begin the presentation with the same slide deck, using the first three slides ("I do"). When arriving at the slides with actual assessment questions, you would begin by analyzing the difference among these questions you're to model for the participants, and then you would invite them to do the analysis with you of subsequent assessment questions ("We do").

For the last third of the workshop, the participants would look at a set of questions from their school's or district's interim assessments (or the closest proxy) and their corresponding state test. They would then evaluate each interim assessment question using the worksheet shown in Exhibit 6.1 ("You do").

Participants would reach a conclusion. answering yes or no on the rigor of each sample interim assessment, justifying why they felt that way.

Exhibit 6.1   Assessment Question Evaluation Worksheet.

interim assessment item	THE RIGHT CONTENT Addresses the same standards (and potentially multiple standards in one question if the state test does the same), and addresses the standards as rigorously as the state test. Is both measurable and specific.	THE RIGHT FORMAT Reflects format of and type of questions from state exam; if applicable, reflects format of and types of questions from exam. Rubrics are used, if applicable. Wrong answers illuminate misunderstanding.	THE RIGHT COLLEGE-READY EXPECTATIONS Rigor and content seem appropriate for developing college-bound students. Content is "State test plus" in areas where state test is not college-preparatory. More complex than state tests (require additional critical thinking and application). More standards covered within the test and within the same question.	COMMENTS Comments and suggestions to improve question.
1				
2				
3				
4				
5				

Living the Learning Approach

While the slide deck remains very similar, the order and process change significantly. After making an opening statement that the group would now look at assessment, you would immediately present a state standard, such as this one for the percent of a number:

"Understand and use ... percents in a variety of situations." (New Jersey Core Curriculum Content Standards for Mathematics, Grade 7, 4.1.A.3)

You would then present the questions on percent of a number (Figure 6.7; a repeat of Figure 6.2), arguing that they represent six different teachers trying to assess mastery of this same standard:

Figure 6.7 Types of Assessment Questions: Math.

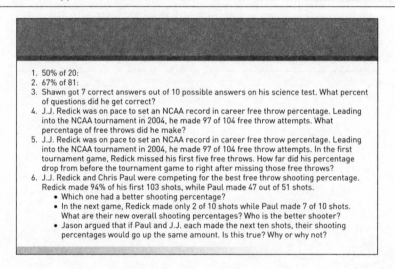

You would ask the participants to read the questions quietly, and then turn to the person sitting next to them to discuss the differences between the questions and what conclusions they could draw from that analysis. Your goal would be to facilitate their sharing, asking scaffolded questions where necessary, until the group has identified all the core principles of assessment that are embedded in the example.

After repeating this process with a few other sets of sample assessment questions, you would put formal language onto the participants' observations by presenting the framework for assessment shown in Figure 6.8, which is a combination of the content of Figure 6.6 followed by that of Figure 6.5:

Figure 6.8   Basic Assessment Principles Total.

> ### Principles for Effective Assessments
>
> **Common Interim:**
> - At least quarterly
> - Common across all teachers of the same grade level
>
> **Transparent Starting Point:**
> - Teachers see the assessments in advance
> - The assessments define the road map for teaching
>
> **Aligned To:**
> - State test (format, content, and length)
> - Instructional sequence (curriculum)
> - College-ready expectations
>
> **Reassess:**
> - Standards that appear on the first interim assessment appear again on subsequent interim assessments.

After reviewing this slide, the participants engage in the same assessment analysis worksheet that was the "You do" activity in the Guided Practice example (shown in Exhibit 6.1). To conclude, participants write down silent reflections on the most important takeaways that they will apply to their school's assessments upon returning from the workshop.

Comparing the Three Approaches

Each of these approaches reaches the same conclusion in the same amount of time, but they do so in decidedly distinct ways. Table 6.2 shows how the time breaks out.

What makes the Living the Learning approach so effective? The percent of a number questions already have embedded in them all the core principles of assessment. When given the opportunity to look at these assessment questions themselves and identify the differences among them, participants will generate almost all the core principles of assessment with minimal scaffolding. Once they've generated the answer, all the leader has to do is put the formal language to it. Because participants have done the cognitive work of generating the content of

Table 6.2 Tale of Three Presentations: Half an Hour on Principles of Assessment

Format	Lecture (Sage on Stage)	Guided Practice (I do, we do, you do)	Living the Learning (Act, reflect, frame, apply)
Part 1	25 minutes: PowerPoint presentation on core principles of assessment (talking through Chapter One).	10 minutes: Presentation on core principles of assessment (talking through basics of Chapter One).	15 minutes: Exercise with Percent of a Number question; in pairs, participants identify differences between the percent questions; share out answers as large group.
Part 2	n/a	10 minutes: Look at sample assessment questions together: jointly identify core principles within those questions.	5 minutes: Leader synthesizes participant answers into the core principles of assessment.
Part 3	5 minutes: Question and answer.	10 minutes: Participants analyze and create other assessment questions to see if they meet the core principles.	10 minutes: Participants analyze and create other assessment questions to see if they meet the core principles.

Chapter One, they will believe in it far more and will be more invested in putting it into practice.

What follows are the strategies that make Living the Learning effective.

THE STRATEGIES THAT MATTER

To develop effective professional development built on the Living the Learning model, the presenter must follow all of the key components shown in the box.

Key Components of Living the Learning: Activity-Reflection-Framing-Applying

- *Design airtight activities* that lead participants to the right conclusions with minimal redirecting by facilitator.
- *Facilitate substantive reflection and sharing* that allows participants to draw the conclusion from the activity.
- *Frame the participants' conclusions* with the formal vocabulary of the associated principles so that participants share one common language.
- Provide ample opportunities to *apply the learning* in simulated and real-world experiences.

Overall, manage time well and inspire by sharing a vision of success: people always want to hear great stories that show it can be done!

The next part of this chapter explores each of these components in depth.

Airtight Activities

High-quality, varied activities are essential to highly effective adult professional development when using the Living the Learning model. In the case of assessment, the activity was fairly simple on the surface: analyze a set of assessment questions. What made the activity powerful, however, was the way it abides by the following guidelines:

- *Align activities to your objectives:* Always start with the end goal in mind: what are the clear outcomes that you want for the participants of this workshop? Then design one or more activities that have these outcomes embedded within them.

- *Make sure your core objectives are well embedded within the activity:* The core question to ask here is: Will the participants be able to reach the proper conclusions from the activity? You might have to facilitate their learning during the reflection time (more on this later in the chapter), but facilitation techniques will be strained if the activity is not well designed.

- *Lesson plan the activity as tightly as a classroom teacher:* Even the best activity will fail without proper attention to detail. Plan each activity with minute-by-minute precision: How will the group move from one activity to the next? What materials will they need? Are the instructions tight enough and clear enough for everyone to work independently without your follow-up? The best way to do this is to script your instructions; the workshop materials presented in this book do exactly that.

- *Address tough situations:* It's important for workshops to offer practice implementing data-driven instruction in tough situations. It is easy to apply new methods with pliable, friendly staff, but how might one approach disgruntled teachers in the midst of a tense moment at school? This is a critical skill; educators must know how to use these methods not only when things are going well but also in difficult situations.

- *Show how to start:* Workshops should also present a coherent and specific perspective on how to make data work, especially at the beginning of the initiative in environments unlike the success stories. Leaders will need a step-by-step plan that leads to success.

A sample set of assessment questions is only one potential activity type. The following activities, when implemented as discussed here, create an intense, creative, and interesting adult learning experience:

- Case studies
- Movie clips
- Video clips of teachers and leaders in action
- Role plays, simulations, games, and modeling

What follows are descriptions of each of these activities and the practices that make their use most effective.

Case Studies   Effective case studies are written intentionally with the end goal objectives embedded thoughtfully and creatively within the story. Case studies most often serve one (or more) of three distinct purposes:

- Solving a problem
- Learning from failure
- Identifying best practices in success

Each purpose is effective for different circumstances, as outlined in Table 6.3.

Making case studies effective: The story must be authentic and realistic, and this is most often accomplished by writing a narrative that includes both positive and negative actions (otherwise the case will feel more like a caricature of reality). For example, in the Springsteen Charter School Case Study, the participants will be able to detect most of the major errors in data-driven instruction within the context of a leader who made genuine effort to improve his school. This sets the stage for discussing effective principles later in the workshop. The Douglass Street Case Study has the purpose of a success story: the most effective drivers of data-driven instruction are subtly embedded in a case study that on the surface appears to be a failure. By discovering principles embedded within a case study, participants develop the capacity to look beyond the superficial in order to focus on the building blocks for effective change. This is a critical skill for any effective school leader!

Table 6.3 Components to Effective Case Studies

Type of Case Study	When to Use	When Not to Use	Positive Example
Solving problems	Participants bring expertise: thus their debate and dialogue will get to a great answer.	Participants do not have significant expertise: solutions generated might not be best practices.	Results Meeting Protocol (Professional Development Activity #8)
Learning from a story of failure	Checking for understanding: allows presenter to see how much participants know about a certain topic. Building comfort zone: critiquing case study errors is a safe way for participants to begin collaborating with colleagues.	Building expertise: critiquing failure does not push students in their understanding of best practices.	Springsteen Charter School Case Study (Professional Development Activity #1)
Identifying key elements of a success story	Building expertise: allows participants to generate proper conclusions connected to formal framework.	Superficial or only positive: case study dwells only on the positives and doesn't highlight how leaders overcame obstacles.	Douglass Street School Case Study (Professional Development Activity #9)

Tips for Strong Case Studies

- When writing a case study, embed every objective participants should learn, and include both positive and negative actions to make case study more authentic.
- Keep group size no more than six people.
- Give participants precise questions to answer before reading the case study in order to focus their reading.
- Have concrete protocol and product to produce during group sharing.

Movie Clips   It is often easier to learn a concept by moving outside the familiarity of your own school and classroom setting. Movie clips afford such an opportunity. However, movie clips are only effective if they are kept very brief and have the core lessons embedded in them (just as in the case study). Framing the right reflection question for each clip can help guide participants as to what to look for while watching.

Making movie clips effective: As with the case study, the movie clip should be directly connected to the overall learning objective. It can be a very effective hook for the audience, but if the clip is unconnected to the objective, then the

> **Tips for Using Movie or Teacher Video Clips**
>
> - Ask a precisely focused framing question to focus participants' observations when watching the movie clip.
> - Keep movie clip short (ideally two to eight minutes).
> - Follow clip with a Think-Pair-Share.

hook does not contribute to participants' learning experience. (This happens far too often!)

Video Clips of Teachers or Leaders in Action   The question you're likeliest to hear in any workshop is, "OK, but what does that look like in action?" Video clips of the teachers and leaders in action at the highest-achieving urban schools strengthen any workshop. Here are some types of video clips that are most appropriate for data-driven instruction workshops:

- Teachers re-teaching students based on assessment analysis
- Leaders running data analysis meetings
- Groups participating in effective results meetings

Making video clips effective: The key for teacher and leader video clips is to have a library of clips that show effective practices and then use targeted questions to focus participants' observations. If the video clip is longer, it can be helpful to have a rubric or observation worksheet where participants can take notes. If the video is of a teacher who will be present at the workshop, the facilitator will need to create an atmosphere where teachers feel safe critiquing each other.

Role Plays, Games, Simulations, and Modeling   The act of simulating a real-world application is useful not only as an opportunity to put theory into practice but also as a vehicle to generate the principles of effective practice. By experiencing the core principles of a given activity, participants deepen their understanding and equip themselves to apply those principles upon return to their school. For example, the Teacher-Principal Role Play highlighted in Activity

> ## Tips for Role Plays, Simulations, and Games
>
> - Have a tight schedule and detailed procedures that make it easy for everyone to follow.
> - Set explicit expectations for the skill or objective participants will be practicing and observing during the activity.
> - Create role plays in which as many people are participating as possible at one time (rather than just one group being observed by the rest of the participants).
> - Keep role plays short to leave time for reflection and feedback.

Five (Chapter Nine) allows participants to experience effective and ineffective analysis meetings in action. Participants first experience the transformative power of using assessments to change the teacher-principal dynamic, and then they use that experience to role play leading effective meetings.

Making role plays, simulations, and games effective: The keys to successful role plays and simulations are detailed instructions, explicit roles for every participant, and properly structured feedback and reflection at the end of the simulation. Too often, role plays are not structured to allow maximum participation or they lack opportunities for participants to receive feedback from their peers.

Reflection and Sharing

If a critical component of adult learning is to have people reach conclusions on their own, then the facilitator's most important role is to manage reflection and sharing time. This occurs in three arenas:

- Individual reflection
- Small-group and pair sharing
- Large-group sharing

Each one deserves special attention.

Independent Reflection One of the most underused techniques in adult professional development is silent, individual reflection time. Yet an opportunity to write down core thoughts solidifies learning, taking it a step beyond listening and doing. Independent reflection and work time is most effective when you

- *Keep it short:* Most adults need only a few minutes to capture their thoughts on a particular topic.

- *Provide materials for writing:* Large multicolored note cards, creatively designed colorful handouts, or a formal reflection template can all be effective tools to make the written reflection stick.

Small-Group and Pair Work   Never underestimate the value of pair sharing in a workshop with adults. Large-group sharing is most often dominated by gregarious, enthusiastic personalities. Participants who are less comfortable in such settings will be reluctant to speak. Having people answer a question in pairs is the most effective way to make sure that *all* participants do the cognitive work asked by a particular reflection question. It also can build confidence that empowers more people to participate in the large-group discussion. In fact, it is often best to stick to pairs unless you have a specific reason why a larger group is necessary. When doing pair work, remember to keep it short (just as with written reflections). Two people can share their thoughts with each other rather quickly.

Small groups are especially effective for generating ideas to share with the large group, or in a role play or simulation that requires more than just two roles. Effective techniques include

- *Having explicit instructions and protocol:* The main error with small-group work is a lack of complete information that prevents the group from working independently. The instructions for small groups presented in the workshops in this book have been tested and have worked consistently.

- *Making sure each member has a concrete role:* Defining roles for group members (recorder, facilitator, observer, and so on) keeps meetings productive and keeps everyone engaged. The Results Meeting Protocol listed in Chapter Three is a classic example of well-defined roles efficiently producing useful results.

- *Keeping a finger on the pulse of group progress to extend or reduce the allotted time as needed:* The best way to avoid downtime in a workshop is to float between the groups and to pay close attention to how they're progressing. If groups are falling behind the rest, encourage them to move forward so as to catch up. If a few groups are about to finish, give a time warning to the other groups to start to wrap up as well.

- *Form intentional groups as often as possible:* Adults will often enter a workshop sitting with the people they are closest to socially, but not necessarily the people that would add most value to their workshop experience. Intentionally creating groups is an especially effective tool for building a valuable workshop. Decide when a homogenous group will benefit the participants (for example, putting all fifth-grade literacy teachers together to analyze literacy questions, or all elementary school principals together to analyze K–2 STEP assessments). When there is no value to homogeneous grouping, try to make groups as heterogeneous as possible.

Large-Group Sharing—Using Effective Questioning Techniques One of the most challenging aspects of leadership training can be managing large-group sharing and participation. Yet this skill is crucial because it is where one guides participant reflections toward the key principles of that activity.

The most effective tools for this process are thoughtful, purposeful questioning from the presenter. The importance of choosing the right questions cannot be overstated. Jon Saphier, author of *The Skillful Teacher,* notes that when a struggling teacher is sent to observe a better teacher, they often fail to draw the right conclusions because they don't know what they're supposed to be looking for. The same effect occurs in the use of video, role plays, or activities during a workshop. Participants might come to very different conclusions without targeted questions and well-guided group sharing. The following guidelines should drive questioning as the facilitator:

1. *Start from the end goal—identify what you want the participants to say during the sharing:* The best presenters have a clear idea of the big ideas that participants should be able to articulate, and they design activities and ask questions that take the participants to each of those ideas. To that end, the workshop materials in this book identify the key ideas that participants should reach. This is notably different from lecturing and presenting these core ideas. Remember: adults need to come to the conclusions on their own for long-lasting impact!

2. *Precisely word the questions to guide the participants to the big ideas:* Many lessons can be drawn from an activity or video clip. However, at any given

moment, you probably only want to focus on some of those lessons. Thus, target your question toward that end goal. For example, after watching a video clip from *Man on Fire*, there is a big difference between "What were your impressions?" and "What made his analysis effective?" The latter question focuses the participants on what you want them to observe.

3. *Give participants the questions before beginning the activity:* If precise questions help participants to focus, then offering the questions in advance focuses their observation as well as their participation. Without this additional focus, the activity or video clip can lead to other conclusions that might detract from the core objective of the workshop.

4. *Nudge; don't drag:* Adults are much more likely to remember the conclusions they draw on their own. For this reason, rather than dragging participants to foregone conclusions, it is much more effective to use scaffolded questions and audience participation to elicit the responses needed. Although it is not easy to strike the ideal balance between saying too little and saying too much, this skill pays tremendous dividends in effective leadership training. Restrain yourself from stating the key takeaways to see if participants can unearth them, elaborating only to provide a common language about the key principle.

5. *Think volleyball, not ping-pong:* Doug Lemov, managing director of Uncommon Schools and author of the *Teach Like a Champion* uses a volleyball versus ping-pong analogy to describe effective questioners. A ping-pong presenter feels the need to respond to and summarize every participant response before calling on another participant. Thus the dialogue is always presenter-participant-presenter-participant. A volleyball presenter allows multiple participants to share before responding—just like teammates working together in a volleyball match.

6. *When the purpose of showing a video clip is to demonstrate effective practices, ask only for strengths:* When shown a clip of actual teachers and school leaders, the first reaction of most participants is to look for weaknesses. Unless the intent of the clip is to show what *not* to do, ask participants to look only for the positives. Looking for the strengths can change a participant's impressions; it creates a more positive learning environment.

If this seems daunting, remember that trying to facilitate a new activity for the first time often does seem like hard and risky work. Fortunately, the professional development activities in this book have tested activities and concrete guidelines for facilitation in "Large-Group Participation" boxes. These will include guidelines, scaffolded questions, and the ideal group responses that you are trying to build. Here is the Large-Group Participation box associated with the activity based on the "Percent of a Number" questions:

Large-Group Participation

Continue audience participation until every key observation listed here has been brought up. Normally, if you allow adequate time for large-group sharing, each of these points will be identified without additional scaffolding required.

Question Prompts

What are the differences between these six assessments of the same standard?
What conclusions do you draw about assessments when looking at these examples?

- *Key Observation 1:* The questions get progressively more difficult. You can answer the first with common knowledge (50% = $^1/_2$), but the last question requires literacy, multiple steps, and a deep conceptual understanding of percents.
- *Key Observation 2:* Questions 3–6 are all open-ended word problems, which is supposedly the measure of "critical thinking" in math class. However, the levels are vastly different. The students in teacher 3's classroom will not be prepared to answer question 6 based on what they're seeing in class.
- *Key Observation 3:* If you used only question 6 in your class, you might not know where the mistake occurred. Having questions of multiple levels on the same assessment (for example, questions 2, 4, and 6) could help you identify where each student starts to struggle.
- *Key Observation 4:* If a teacher designs lessons to get students to master question 4 and no one says that the students must master question 6, it's not the teacher's fault that the students are not ready! The standard by itself is not enough guidance for the teacher to know how deeply to teach.

Framing—Building a Common Language

The process of framing the conversation at the end of the reflection and sharing time allows the facilitator to take the ideas that have been shared and provide a common language for all to use. Sometimes the participants will generate the exact language for you (which is great!), but in most cases you will want to restate their observations. The common language is most often presented on the PowerPoint slides themselves, and in the cases where it is not, the workshop materials provide you with boxes of "Core Ideas" just like those you have seen throughout these first six chapters. Here is an example based on the assessment activity:

> ## Core Ideas
>
> - Standards are meaningless until you define how you will assess them.
> - When you define how you'll assess a standard, you are defining your expectations.
> - Assessments, then, are the *starting point*, not the end point, of teaching and learning.
> - If you don't define the assessment first, teachers will teach to their own level of expectation, with wide variation.
> - Assessments drive standards, not the reverse.
> - Curriculum standards scope and sequences documents are not enough; teachers need assessments to guide them as to the rigor of their teaching.

Making Framing Most Effective

- Use PowerPoint to set up the "Living the Learning" situation; use it for directions.

- Leave it to the end, to crystallize what has been learned.

- Keep each statement brief.

- Keep the text as bullets.

- Provide more visuals than words.

- Use interactive handout.

- Use the PowerPoint as guided practice.

Pitfalls

- Presenting too much text.

- Presenting the framing too early.

This is the sort of information that a traditional lecturer or guided practice presenter would put at the *beginning* of the presentation. Note here that this is the concluding, culminating act of an activity and reflection time. There is not much magic here: simply state the language and give the participants time to digest it.

Apply the Learning

It is no secret that learning is not complete until it is put into action (in the example presented here, the participants applied the learning by analyzing their own actual interim assessments in comparison to their state test using the Interim Assessment Reflection Sheet). However, this principle is often the first to be sacrificed in a workshop because "there is so much material to cover!" Never remove time for application. If you are short on time, reduce the number of points you are going to make so participants still have a chance to apply what they have learned.

Ideally the workshop is a springboard for a real-life application. The best learning experiences are built by having practice on a simulated situation in a safe environment and then an assignment that must be done in school once the workshop is completed. Ideally, someone is holding each participant accountable for that assignment! Because every school district is different, the concrete areas of focus will be different. However, the workshops are set up to meet these differentiated needs by letting participants and school teams identify their areas of growth and make action plans to address those needs.

The Appendix has the most significant documents of the workshop, from the Data-Driven Implementation Rubric to the Entry Plan for Data-Driven Instruction: New School Start-Up task list. Each of these documents can be used by the participants during the workshop and can serve as helpful tools for accountability in implementation in a real school situation.

MANAGE TIME

One of the most important tasks you're apt to face in executing your workshop involves managing the length and quality of large-group sharing. That includes making decisions about whether to respond to audience questions on the spot or to hold them for later, and when to intervene, redirect, or act to extend a conversation or cut it short.

No two large-group sharing sessions will be exactly alike, even when looking at the same content. Some conversations will be more on target, others will raise excellent points, and some will have a consistent outlier participant who attempts to take the whole group off-task. How do you deal with these situations?

Here are some key guiding principles to follow when managing a large-group sharing:

Never sacrifice your core objective: Whenever you evaluate the progress of large-group sharing, always ask yourself: Is this supporting my objective? Does allowing the conversation to go longer than I anticipated strengthen my objective? Make all decisions based on the answer to these questions.

Keep your eye on the clock, and know where you'll cut if you run over: The best-planned workshops have minute-by-minute agendas that allow a facilitator to see whenever the group is falling behind schedule. Know in advance what you'll cut if you run over, because that allows you to decide in the moment whether to stop a conversation or continue.

If the rest of the workshop will answer the question, tell the questioner to hold it: The ideas people observe and learn for themselves are better understood and retained than the ones they are simply told; if a question will be answered naturally by another part of the workshop, it should be held for later. For example, you could be discussing the principles of running great principal-teacher analysis meetings, and a participant asks, "When is the best time to plan for re-teaching standards the students didn't master?" Simply say that you will answer that question during the session on action.

If the question or comment is not directly tied to the topic of the moment, tell the questioner to write it down and save it until the end: Participants often ask great questions that are slightly off task or are very specific to just their own personal situation. (For example: "I'm on maternity leave right now, but I'll be coming back in January and I'll launch data-driven instruction at that point. What tips would you have for me launching in January?") While you might be tempted to answer the question right there, you will slow down the workshop. Ask the participant to write down the question and either ask you during a break or save it for the final question-and-answer session.

If you don't know the answer, admit it: Participants can tell when a presenter is faking it. If you are confronted by a question that is beyond your expertise, be humble and admit that you do not know. For example, if you are asked about how a lesson could be applied to the kindergarten level but have no experience in the area, a great response could be, "Well, I could give you my instincts now, but truth be told elementary school is not my area of expertise. I will find someone with more experience in the field to get you a good answer; track me down after this workshop is over so I can get your e-mail address to send it to you."

INSPIRE

Having a model of workshop in which participants are actively reaching the conclusions on their own will greatly increase investment and excitement in itself. Still, don't be afraid to inspire your audience even further. The impact of this work on schools nationwide is nothing short of astonishing. Sharing stories of that success—and its impact on students, faculty, and leaders—is very important to reinforce the urgency of learning all the systems described within the workshop.

Repeatedly tell stories of success: People rarely tire of hearing stories of success: Why else is the audience for championship games far larger than for the first round of a tournament? This book puts that to practice by including many case studies of schools that have had dramatic success. Tell those stories, and share your own as well. The more people hear that something works, the more they believe it.

Make personal connections: During the presentation, it's important to take steps to establish a personal connection with your audience. Speakers should remind the audience that they share similar aspirations, mention their family and their background, and let them know that they are real people. Remember that in this regard, stories stick much better than speeches.

Be authentically yourself: Speakers should be themselves, and must be willing to adjust the agenda to match their style. Your warmth and sincerity are much more important than a forced public persona!

Learn from mistakes: Finally, it is important to remember that nothing works perfectly the first time around. Keep notes on what succeeded and what did not so you can change behaviors the next time around.

CONCLUSIONS

Effective professional development is the fundamental driver of school change. Trying to implement all these components effectively from scratch is very daunting. This is where the rest of the book fills the need. Each of the workshop activities presented here fully reflects the principles of this chapter. They fill a critical need for school leaders who never have enough time to plan every professional development session perfectly. By employing the workshops and principles in the book, you will have the strongest possible tools to make dramatic student achievement occur at your school or district. We eagerly look forward to news of your success!

Core Concepts: Effective Adult Professional Development

- Design *airtight activities* that lead participants to the right conclusions with minimal redirection by facilitator.
- Facilitate substantive *reflection and sharing* time that allows participants to draw the conclusion from the activity.
- *Frame the participants' conclusions* with the formal vocabulary of the associated principles so that participants share one common language.
- Provide ample opportunities to *apply the learning* in simulated and real-world experiences.
- Overall, *manage time well* and *inspire* by sharing a vision of success: people always want to hear great stories that show it can be done!

Holabird Academy: Coaching to Achievement

The Results

Maryland State Assessments: Percentage at or Above Proficiency — Third Through Sixth Grade Aggregate

Year	English and Language Arts	Mathematics
2005–06	56%	37%
2006–07	71%	76%
2007–08	79%	81%
2008–09	85%	89%
Three-year gains	+29	+52

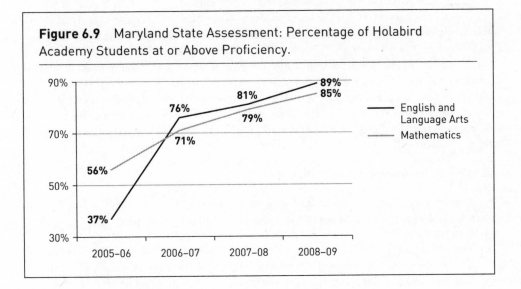

Figure 6.9   Maryland State Assessment: Percentage of Holabird Academy Students at or Above Proficiency.

The Story

Lindsay Krey began her principalship at Holabird Academy after a year of great turmoil: the school had 85 percent staff turnover, and it was serving 81 percent free or reduced lunch students. Krey had attended three data-driven workshops presented by the author prior to beginning the principalship: Comprehensive Data-Driven Instruction (see Chapter Twelve), follow-up, and start-up workshops, and she had had success in her residency site prior to beginning at Holabird. She quickly put that experience to work.

Given the staff turnover, almost all the teachers in Krey's opening year were first-year teachers. To address this issue, Krey divided her school into three learning communities (Grades PreK–1, 2–4, and 5–6) and assigned a coach to each group. She trained the coaches in the use of Excel data spreadsheets so that they could likewise train the teachers in data analysis in the first weeks of school. Weekly professional development meetings were devoted to building instructional capacity and using data to track student progress. The leaders tapped into the successful districtwide Mathworks professional development program, which looked closely at math test items to determine the most effective teaching strategies, whereas literacy professional development focused on the components of Balanced Literacy. Every leadership team meeting started by looking at the spreadsheets of student results on the latest interim assessment, and Krey trained her coaches to run the same conversations with their teams. Twice a year, they did a "full school run-through": a targeted look at every child's individual progress and needs for growth according to data collected for the past six months. A large data wall in the staff room highlighted the performance of each student on each round of benchmark assessments, and intervention groups were created based on that data.

A core component of Krey's success came when the staff looked closely at open-ended responses. They realized that students were not writing effectively within the time constraints of the assessment. They put special focus on this aspect of student learning, creating anchor papers and posting student writing in all the classrooms. Students whose writing was not proficient were immediately put to the task of rewriting their answers until they reached proficiency. The staff designed constructed-response tasks that were significantly above the rigor of the state tests—so far above that when the students finally took the Maryland State Assessment it felt very easy for them. The results speak for themselves.

Key Drivers from Implementation Rubric

- *Aligned beyond assessments:* By focusing on writing that was beyond the rigor of the state assessment, students were even more prepared for the rigor of the state assessments.
- *Plan new lessons:* The use of coaches for each learning community allowed teachers to have support in planning lessons that embodied the best practices of math and literacy while also focusing in on the areas where students most needed to improve.

7

Framework

Professional Development Agendas and Activities

ACTIVITY 1—SETTING THE RATIONALE
Purpose of Data-Driven Instruction
Time 0:00–0:15 (15 minutes)

Objectives		Materials and Handouts
Core Objectives (participants):		**Materials:**
• Identify the core challenges facing urban education.		• PowerPoint
• Identify schools that have succeeded despite the odds.		**Handouts:**
• Agree on common goal for the workshop: drive student achievement upward.		• None
Differentiation and Adjustments		
• Adapt to your own personal leadership story.		

Doug Lemov Graphs (0:05–0:15)

Present a slide based on Figure 7.1.

Context: Educator Doug Lemov wanted to track the relationship between students' free or reduced lunch status and achievement. To do this, he plotted the elementary schools of New York State on this chart. On the horizontal axis, the chart measures the percentage of students who qualify for free or reduced lunch, which is a good indicator of students' socioeconomic level. On the vertical axis, the chart measures the percentage of students who were proficient on New York State's fourth-grade English and language arts assessment.

Every dot on the graph represents a school. For example, if a school is in the top-left corner, then that school had few free or reduced lunch students and high student achievement.

Figure 7.1   New York State Public School ELA Fourth-Grade Performance Versus Free or Reduced Lunch Rates.

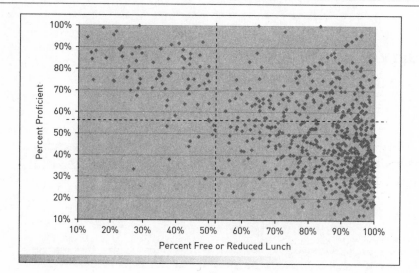

Large-Group Participation

Continue participation until each key observation listed here has been brought up. Note that the audience does *not* need to say the exact line as printed—the substance of the observation is enough. If the audience is lost, use the question prompts to get them back on track, but try to do so as little as possible.

Question Prompts
What do you notice about this graph?
What else do you notice?

- *Key Observation 1:* In general, the more students who qualify for free or reduced lunch, the lower the percentage of students who are proficient. In mathematical terms, we call this the "line of best fit," which is drawn in on the second slide. You tell me what your free or reduced lunch status is, and I'll tell you your test scores.
- *Key Observation 2:* The performance of schools with high free or reduced lunch populations is incredibly varied: there are schools well below anticipated performance and others well above it. In contrast, schools with low free or reduced lunch populations are closely grouped around the line of best fit.
- *Key Observation 3:* Despite the trend, some schools appear in the upper right-hand corner: both high percentage of free or reduced lunch students and high student achievement. These are referred to in the literature as 90/90/90 schools: 90 percent free or reduced lunch, most often 90 percent students of color, and 90 percent proficient on state assessments.

Present a slide based on Figure 7.2.

Core conclusions to share with group:

- What are those schools in the upper right-hand corner doing that those at the lower right aren't?

- If those schools can do it, then so can I. [Emphasize this point!]

Figure 7.2   New York State Public School ELA Fourth-Grade Performance Versus Free or Reduced Lunch Rates: Line of Best Fit.

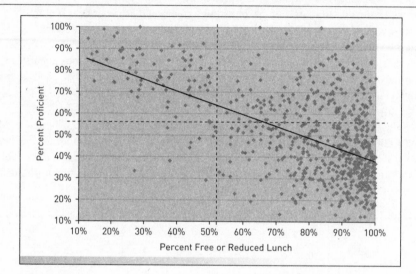

State focus of workshop:

- Focus on the most effective, efficient level in improving student achievement in our schools: data-driven instruction.

ACTIVITY 2 — HIGHLIGHTING PITFALLS

Springsteen Charter School Case Study
Time 0:15–1:35 (1 hour 20 minutes)

Objectives	Materials and Handouts	
Core Objectives (presenter): • Pre-assess participants for prior knowledge of data-driven instruction. **Core Objectives (participants):** • Analyze a case study on failed implementation of data-driven instruction and identify false drivers of student achievement. • Understand that even with the best of intentions, data-driven instruction can still fall short.	**Materials:** • PowerPoint • Poster paper (one pad per 8–10 people) • Large markers (one set per 8–10 people) • Method to put up posters (tape, tacks, or whatever suits the room) **Handouts:** • Springsteen Charter School (Use Grade 5–12 version or K–5 version as appropriate)	
Differentiation and Adjustments for Group Size and Type		
• There are two versions of the Springsteen case study: one targeted to K–5 schools, the other targeted to Grade 5–12 schools. If you have a mixed group, use the 5–12 case study for everyone. • You can save workshop time by assigning this case study for homework: in that case you can adjust the opening to having the group summarize the case study, and then move immediately into the role play with Marc Jones. • If you have a large group (seventy people or more), you can save time by setting up the small groups in advance. Try to mix up all groups for this case study: there is no value to having people in their normal teams.		

Case Study Introduction (0:15–0:20)

Display a slide based on Figure 7.3.

Set expectations: Begin with an example of a charter school that tried to use effective data-driven decision making:

- Dive into each level of analysis as if this were your school.

- Always have one part of your mind focused on what connections this district has with yours.

- In essence, then, you should find commonalities between this case and your own and think through how you can apply these lessons to your city.

Figure 7.3 Springsteen Case Study Introduction.

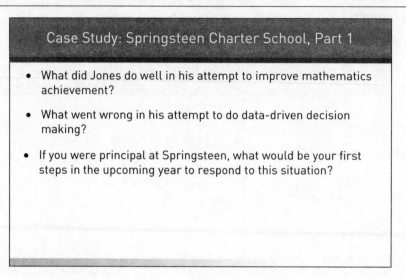

Case Study: Springsteen Charter School, Part 1

- What did Jones do well in his attempt to improve mathematics achievement?

- What went wrong in his attempt to do data-driven decision making?

- If you were principal at Springsteen, what would be your first steps in the upcoming year to respond to this situation?

Set context for case study:

- Marc Jones, the principal of Springsteen Charter School, has tried unsuccessfully to launch data-driven instruction.

- Jones has hired you to come to school, analyze what went wrong, and explain what he should do about it.

Key questions to answer while reading case study:

- What did Jones do well?

- What went wrong?

- What would be your first steps to improve math achievement?

Read Case Study (0:20–0:35)

Marc Jones Role Play (0:35–0:50)
Take the role of Marc Jones and let participants ask questions about the case (use "Large-Group Participation" box as guidance).

Large-Group Participation

Read the case study carefully so you can embody Marc Jones as well as possible. The key is to choose answers that are *not* the key drivers that make data-driven instruction effective. You can refer back to the Introduction—particularly the sections titled "Eight Mistakes That Matter" and "Roadside Distractions: False Drivers"—as a review. Almost all the common errors are explicitly embedded within the case study. Allow the group to ask questions for fifteen minutes total. With a minute left, warn them when you can only take one or two more questions.

Likely audience questions: Why did you switch to the TerraNova but not include the open-ended questions? OR Why did you choose the TerraNova?

Marc Jones response: Like I said in the case, adding the open-ended questions would have delayed the scoring by an additional month, and I didn't want to wait that long to do analysis with the teachers. Besides, the TerraNova test representative told me that the Multiple Choice version was still a good predictor of state test performance, so we did that version for the sake of being able to do analysis right at the beginning of the school year.

Likely audience question: It shows here that your students struggled with problem solving on the Stanford Nine. How did your teachers address critical thinking and problem solving in your class?

Marc Jones response: Every one of my teachers created mini-assessments for their class, and all of them included open-ended word problems that were focused on critical thinking. We spent a lot of time talking about that, and my teachers responded—every one of them cares deeply about teaching critical thinking.

Likely audience question: It says that you didn't classify special education students except in extreme cases. Why?

Marc Jones response: I had seen in my previous schools how special education students had been relegated to isolated classrooms where expectations were lower for them than for anyone else. I had also experienced how our African American males were disproportionately labeled "Emotionally Disturbed" and put into isolated classrooms. I didn't want to repeat this discrimination, so we built a full inclusion model where all students took classes together.

Likely audience questions: How did you verify that students were actually learning? OR Did you actually track how students were doing?

Marc Jones response: Of course we tracked how students were doing. That's why we had the giant data wall in the teachers' room: we didn't just track overall student performance, we tracked how each student was doing on every standard. Teachers would constantly change the status of a student when they had reached proficiency in their classroom. I tell you—we are *very* data-driven!

Likely audience questions: How were the teacher mini-assessments aligned to the state test? OR How did you make sure that teachers created quality assessments?

Marc Jones response: Since our state tests are secret, we cannot see them, and no past copies have been released. So we looked at the TerraNova data reports and created assessments that address the standards that the report listed as weaknesses for our students. The teachers all created their own assessments according to their students' needs.

Likely audience questions: What was the quality of the teaching? OR How did you work to make your teachers better?

Marc Jones response: I worked hard to improve my teachers. I observed them and gave them lots of feedback; that's the most important thing you can do to develop your teachers. My fifth-grade math teacher is especially strong, and I always praised her strong teaching.

Likely audience questions: Did you provide any support for students that were struggling? How did you deal with all the different learning needs in one classroom?

Marc Jones response: We talked a lot about differentiated instruction so that teachers tried to design activities that allowed students to learn at their own pace.

Small-Group Work (0:50–1:10)

Record answers on chart paper and designate one person who will present answers to the large group.

Answer the three questions on the slide:

- What did Jones do well in his attempt to improve mathematics achievement?

- What went wrong in his attempt to do data-driven decision making?

- If you were principal at Springsteen, what would be your first steps in the upcoming year to respond to this situation?

Large-Group Presentations (1:10–1:30)

Share out: each group has a minute to say their conclusions. Subsequent groups are not allowed to say anything that has already been said.

Review your checklist of important points to see if they have been addressed.

Large-Group Presentations — Key Points

Continue participation until each key observation listed here has been brought up. Note that the audience does *not* need to say the exact line as printed — the substance of the observation is enough. If the audience is lost, use the question prompts to get them back on track, but try to do so as little as possible.

Key points to make sure groups mention (or mention yourself during conclusion):

- Jones accepted the test representative's description without checking the test himself. What's a test representative's goal? To sell more tests! Everyone is going to claim that their tests are aligned, but the truth is that standards vary wildly from state to state. So you need to check the test for yourself.
- Jones asked students how they felt about themselves and not what they knew and how they knew it.
- Teachers subjectively decided when students achieved mastery without looking to actual performance. The charts in the teachers' room tracked student performance, but they were entirely based on teacher opinion of whether students had mastered the standard or not.
- Standards-based report cards are good in theory, but they can easily fall into the trap of stating their opinion for each standard's mastery rather than having concrete assessment of each standard (because of the sheer volume of standards that had to be filled out for each student).

Big Ideas (1:30–1:35)

State any key points that weren't given by a small group, or points that you want to give greater emphasis to than what the group gave.

So in conclusion:

- Year-end results are not enough to make an action plan that will work.
- Lists of standards are not enough.
- "Power Standards," "professional learning communities," or any other single bell or whistle will not be enough either.

So the question, then, is what will be enough? What has to happen at the classroom level to create genuine change?

Core Conclusions Stated by Facilitator

- "Alignment" means different things to different people.
- I've never met a teacher who didn't think he taught "critical thinking."
- Using "open-ended questions" does not guarantee achievement or rigor.
- Year-end results are not enough.
- Lists of standards are not enough.
- So what has to happen to lead to genuine change?

8

Assessment

Professional Development Agendas and Activities

ACTIVITY 3 — PRINCIPLES OF ASSESSMENT
The Power of the Question
Time 0:00–0:50 (50 minutes)

Objectives	Materials and Handouts
Core Objectives (participant): • Analyze assessment questions to understand that standards are meaningless until you define how to assess them. • Identify the key principles of assessment.	**Materials:** • PowerPoint **Handouts:** • None
Differentiation and Adjustments for Group Size and Type	
• The assessment questions used here are middle school questions: ideal for a mixed audience of K–12 school leaders. If you are leading a workshop primarily for K–5 school leaders or high school leaders, keep the percent of a number and Little Red Riding Hood questions, as they set the stage for the drivers of assessment. Then cut the grammar question and instead choose the elementary question or high school questions that are in the Appendix.	

Introduction to the Power of the Question: Math (0:00–0:05)

The first key principle is assessment. Quality interim assessments are where the rubber meets the road; if we don't create good tests, then we won't have useful data and, as a result, won't be able to identify our weaknesses.

Context for questions slide on "Percent of a Number":

- Six different teachers of seventh-grade math all have to teach the same state standard.

- The standard (while a little different in each state) basically looks like this: "Students should be able to understand and use the percent of a number in a variety of real-world situations."

Look at the six assessment questions on the slide.
Display a slide based on Figure 8.1.

Figure 8.1 Review of Assessment Questions: Math.

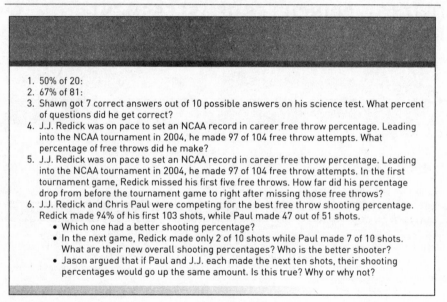

1. 50% of 20:
2. 67% of 81:
3. Shawn got 7 correct answers out of 10 possible answers on his science test. What percent of questions did he get correct?
4. J.J. Redick was on pace to set an NCAA record in career free throw percentage. Leading into the NCAA tournament in 2004, he made 97 of 104 free throw attempts. What percentage of free throws did he make?
5. J.J. Redick was on pace to set an NCAA record in career free throw percentage. Leading into the NCAA tournament in 2004, he made 97 of 104 free throw attempts. In the first tournament game, Redick missed his first five free throws. How far did his percentage drop from before the tournament game to right after missing those free throws?
6. J.J. Redick and Chris Paul were competing for the best free throw shooting percentage. Redick made 94% of his first 103 shots, while Paul made 47 out of 51 shots.
   - Which one had a better shooting percentage?
   - In the next game, Redick made only 2 of 10 shots while Paul made 7 of 10 shots. What are their new overall shooting percentages? Who is the better shooter?
   - Jason argued that if Paul and J.J. each made the next ten shots, their shooting percentages would go up the same amount. Is this true? Why or why not?

Think-Pair-Share (0:05–0:20)

- Look at questions on screen quietly.

- Talk in pairs for two minutes about the Large-Group Participation question prompts.

- Share answers as large group.

Large-Group Participation

Continue audience participation until every key point listed below has been brought up. Normally, if you allow adequate time for large-group sharing, each of these points will be identified without requiring additional scaffolding.

Question Prompts

What are the differences between these six assessments of the same standard?

What conclusions do you draw about assessments when looking at these examples?

- *Key Observation 1:* The questions get progressively more difficult. You can answer the first question with common knowledge (50% = ½), but the last question requires literacy, multiple steps, and a deep conceptual understanding of percents.
- *Key Observation 2:* Questions 3–6 are all open-ended word problems, which is supposedly the measure of "critical thinking" in math class. However, the levels are vastly different. The students in teacher 3's classroom will not be prepared to answer question 6 based on what they're seeing in class.
- *Key Observation 3:* If you used only question 6 in your class, you might not know where the mistake occurred. Having questions of multiple levels on the same assessment (for example, questions 2, 4, and 6) could help you identify where each student starts to struggle.
- *Key Observation 4:* If a teacher designs lessons to get students to master question 4 and no one says that the students must master question 6, it's not the teacher's fault that the students are not ready! The standard by itself is not enough guidance for the teacher to know how deeply to teach.

State conclusions and core ideas:

> ## Core Ideas
>
> - Standards are meaningless until you define how you will assess them.
> - When you define how you'll assess a standard, you are defining your expectations.
> - Assessments, then, are the *starting point*, not the end point, of teaching and learning.
> - If you don't define the assessment first, teachers will teach to their own level of expectation, which will vary widely from room to room.
> - Assessments drive standards, not the reverse.
> - Curriculum standards scope and sequences documents are not enough; teachers need assessments to guide them as to the rigor of their teaching.

Power of the Question: Reading Think-Pair-Share (0:20–0:35)

- Have audience look at questions on screen quietly.

- Talk in pairs for two minutes about the Large-Group Participation question prompts.

- Share answers as large group.

Display a slide based on Figure 8.2.

Large-Group Participation

Continue audience participation until every key point listed below has been brought up. Normally, if you allow adequate time for large-group sharing, each of these points will be identified without requiring additional scaffolding.

Preemptive Strike (Make comment before starting sharing)
Before anyone starts protesting that #3 is a tricky question that isn't fair, let me just establish that if I fill this room with all advanced proficient readers, 99 percent of them will choose letter C. They might not like that the other answers also have some validity, but they will know that answer C is the best option. Something about their critical reading

preparation allows them to answer that question effectively. So focus on what makes the difference between that question and the others.

Question Prompts

What are the differences between these three questions on main idea and theme?

Which question is most rigorous?

What conclusions do you draw about assessment in general?

- *Key Observation 1:* Question 3 is harder than question 2 because the options are more difficult. The answer is no longer a summary but an identification of the core message of the story.
- *Key Observation 2:* Whether question 1 is more rigorous than question 3 depends completely on the way that the teacher grades it. If a one-line answer is accepted, then question 3 is more rigorous. If students must write a complete essay with evidence from the story, question 1's rigor increases dramatically.

Figure 8.2   Review of Assessment Questions: Reading.

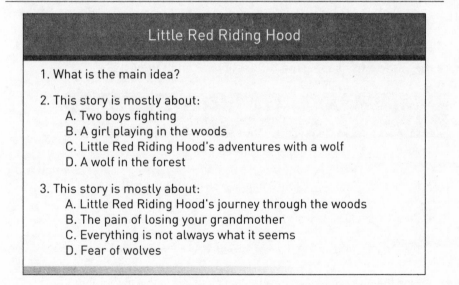

Little Red Riding Hood

1. What is the main idea?

2. This story is mostly about:
    A. Two boys fighting
    B. A girl playing in the woods
    C. Little Red Riding Hood's adventures with a wolf
    D. A wolf in the forest

3. This story is mostly about:
    A. Little Red Riding Hood's journey through the woods
    B. The pain of losing your grandmother
    C. Everything is not always what it seems
    D. Fear of wolves

State conclusions and core ideas:

> ## Core Ideas
>
> - In a multiple-choice question, the options define the rigor.
> - In an open-ended question, the rubric defines the rigor.
> - Multiple-choice and open-ended questions are complementary forms of assessing the same standard, and you need *both* to assess mastery completely.

Power of the Question: Differentiated (0:35–0:45)

- If middle school focus, use the grammar question given here.
- Insert elementary or high school questions here if group has that grade-level focus.
- Have audience look at questions on screen quietly, talk in pairs, and then share in large group.

Display a slide based on Figure 8.3, using questions appropriate to the grade level.

Figure 8.3   Review of Assessment Questions: Language Arts.

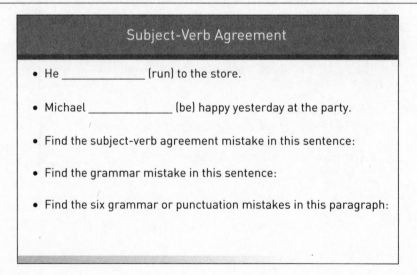

Subject-Verb Agreement
• He _____ (run) to the store.
• Michael _____ (be) happy yesterday at the party.
• Find the subject-verb agreement mistake in this sentence:
• Find the grammar mistake in this sentence:
• Find the six grammar or punctuation mistakes in this paragraph:

Large-Group Participation (Grammar Question)

Continue audience participation until every key observation listed here has been brought up.

Question Prompts

What are the differences between these three questions?

What conclusions do you draw about assessments?

- *Key Observation 1:* The first three questions address the grammar standard in isolation; students who answer correctly still might not be able to correct similar errors in the last question when other grammar errors are included.
- *Key Observation 2:* The last question is the closest to being authentic in that you have to edit and correct a passage for multiple grammar errors. However, it is still easier to correct someone else's errors than it is to find your own.
- *Key Observation 3:* While it is often necessary to teach grammar skills, we should always strive to embed these assessments in the writing and editing process.

Keys of Assessment (0:45–0:50)

State key principles of assessment, giving context for each one.

Display a slide based on Figure 8.4.

Figure 8.4 Assessment Principles Total.

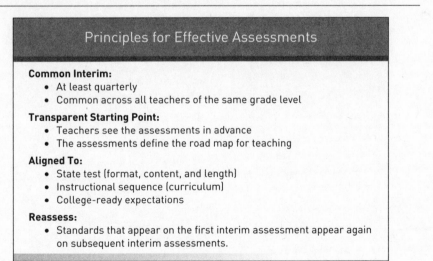

Principles for Effective Assessments

Common Interim:
- At least quarterly
- Common across all teachers of the same grade level

Transparent Starting Point:
- Teachers see the assessments in advance
- The assessments define the road map for teaching

Aligned To:
- State test (format, content, and length)
- Instructional sequence (curriculum)
- College-ready expectations

Reassess:
- Standards that appear on the first interim assessment appear again on subsequent interim assessments.

9

Analysis

Professional Development Agendas and Activities

ACTIVITY 4—INTRO TO ANALYSIS
Film Clip: Analysis
Time 0:00–0:15 (15 minutes)

Objectives	Materials and Handouts
Core Objectives (presenter): • Hook the audience with the core principles of data-driven instruction in a non-traditional classroom. **Core Objectives (participants):** • Identify the key foundations that make data-driven instruction powerful.	**Materials:** • PowerPoint • Movie clip illustrating effective analysis, such as *Man on Fire* **Handouts:** • None.
Differentiation and Adjustments	
• Choose any movie clip that captures the essential message of data-driven instruction.	

Movie Clip (0:00–0:05)
Display a slide along the lines of Figure 9.1.

Give context for movie clip.

Answer the following questions:

• What were the key moments in Creasy's attempt to help Pita?

• What makes Creasy's analysis effective?

Figure 9.1 Movie Clip Questions.

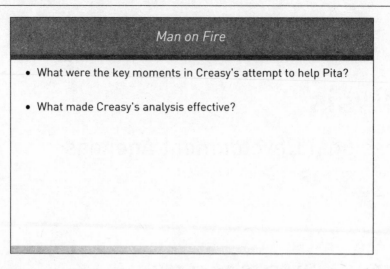

> ### Man on Fire
>
> - What were the key moments in Creasy's attempt to help Pita?
>
> - What made Creasy's analysis effective?

Sample Movie Clip — *Man on Fire*, Scene 1

Action: Bodyguard Creasy watches Pita swim in a race. The gun goes off and the girl hesitates slightly. The race proceeds, and Pita finishes in third place. They have a conversation about what happened after the race.

CREASY: You're a strong swimmer.
PITA: I never win.

[*Change scene.*]

PITA: So what do I do?
CREASY: What do you think you should do? You're the fastest one in the water and the slowest one off the blocks. What do you think you should do?
PITA: Get faster off the blocks.
CREASY: That's right.

Think-Pair-Share (0:05–0:15)

Reflect and share:

- Talk in pairs for two minutes about the Large-Group Participation question prompts.

- Share answers as large group.

Large-Group Participation

Continue participation until each key observation listed here has been brought up. Note that the audience does *not* need to say the exact line as printed — the substance of the observation is enough. If the audience is lost, use the question prompts to get them back on track, but try to do so as little as possible.

Question Prompts

What were the key moments?
What made Creasy's analysis effective?

- *Key Observation 1:* Creasy actually saw the race himself. He paid close attention to Pita's swimming, looking for what went well and what needed to be improved.
- *Key Observation 2:* Creasy asked Pita a targeted, scaffolded question that presented the data in a form that allowed her to come to the right analysis herself

Scaffolded question (if they're not hitting this answer directly): How did Creasy get her to see the error? He could have said, "You have to get better off the blocks!" Or he could have just asked her, "Well, what do you think you should do?" What did he do instead?

- *Key Observation 3:* Creasy established a positive relationship with Pita by using honest praise.

Follow-up question (to highlight this point): When Creasy said, "You're a strong swimmer," was that false praise? No. It was accurate about what she did well. Students can always distinguish between unsubstantiated flattery and true praise.

State core ideas:

Core Ideas

- If you're not at the pool, you cannot do the analysis.
- The heart of the matter is presenting the data so clearly that the student or teacher can come to the right conclusion on their own.

ACTIVITY 5 — TEACHER-PRINCIPAL ROLE PLAY

Assessment Analysis

Time 0:15–2:00 (1 hour 45 minutes)

Objectives		Materials and Handouts
Core Objectives (participants):		**Materials:**
• Implement the key principles of deep analysis.		• PowerPoint
• Read and correctly interpret an assessment data report.		**Handouts — Choice of (depending on group):**
• Identify effective and ineffective assessment analysis.		• Third-grade literacy assessment and results
• Compare the differences between traditional post-observation teacher conferences and interim assessment analysis meetings.		• Fifth-grade literacy assessment and results
		• Sixth-grade math assessment and results
		• Ninth-grade algebra assessment and results
• Identify the ways in which interim assessments drive change.		• Teacher One and Teacher Two Sheet (Not for full group; make one for every 20 workshop participants)

Differentiation and Adjustments for Group Size and Type
• Plan on making groups of four to six participants that will analyze the results on either a K, third-, fifth-, sixth-, or ninth-grade assessment. Choose the appropriate assessments based on the grade level and subject area expertise of the members in the group. When you have a diverse group or a set of school leaders that will be looking at all grade levels, choose fifth-grade literacy, sixth-grade math, and ninth-grade algebra.
• For every subject assessment beyond one, you'll need one volunteer who can role play being the teacher (you'll be the teacher in one of the role plays). You can have twenty to thirty people observing a single role play, so choose enough volunteers accordingly. However, the quality of the volunteer is *critical* for the success of the role play. Ideally, choose people who have done the workshop before (or ask people from earlier sessions to attend this part to help you). The preparation for these volunteers is discussed later in the chapter.

Introduction to Assessment Analysis Project (0:15–0:20)

Give context: participants will be playing the role of a school leader who is getting ready to meet with two teachers about their results on the latest interim assessment.

- In order to get ready, they will analyze the interim assessment data that they have, and then actually role play this conversation.

Model Interim Assessment Data Analysis (0:20–0:35)

Have participants turn to their binders and pull out the appropriate assessment, results template, and action plan.

Model how to do the appropriate analysis by explaining all aspects of the spreadsheet illustrated in Table 9.1.

Slowly walk through each part of the spreadsheet, highlighting each component:

- Top row: Number of the assessment question.

- Next row: Name of the standard covered by that test questions.

- Left-hand side: Name of each student.

- Next columns: Percent correct on multiple-choice questions; percent correct on open-ended responses; total percent correct.

- Middle section where there are lots of blank spaces and letters:

    - Blank space means the student answered that particular question *correctly*.

    - Letter means the *wrong* letter choice on a multiple-choice question.

    - Number equals the *points earned* on an open-ended question.

- Gray boxes at bottom: how students did on all the questions measuring a certain standard:

    - Repeated 6–1 standards = standards introduced in first quarter and reassessed on the subsequent interim assessments.

    - 6–3 standards = the material that is being assessed for the first time here.

    - Numbers in parentheses are the test questions that assessed that given standard.

- Bottom: overall performance of the class on the assessment.

- Color-coding: Above 75 percent correct is green font, between 60 percent and 75 percent is yellow, and less than 60 percent correct is red (differences that show as shades of gray on a black-and-white printer).

- Sorting: Students are arranged by results, with the highest-achieving students at the top of the chart.

Table 9.1 North Star Interim Assessment Results Analysis Template

TEAM NAME / Student	MULT. CHOICE: % CORRECT	OPEN-ENDED: % CORRECT	COMBINED PROFICIENCY SCORE	1 — (1) Computation: add and subtract decimals and money	2 — (NSA) Fractions in Context: +/−	3 — (2) Computation: 3 × 2 multiplication	4 — (3) Computation: division by 1–2 digits	5 — (4) Fractions: add/subtract mixed numbers	6 — (5) Computation in Context: multiplication	7 — (6) Computation with money: subtraction	8 — (5) Computation in Context: division	9 — (5) Computation in Context: division	10 — (7) Estimation and rounding: division	11 — (8) Estimation and rounding; addition of decimals
Moet	82%	81%	81%											
Jaleel	82%	62%	76%									C		
Terrell	79%	42%	69%					C					B	
Aniya	79%	38%	68%					C						B
Juwan	68%	58%	66%					A						
Aziz	74%	42%	65%					A				D	B	D
Juan	63%	58%	62%					D		E			D	B
Shannon	71%	31%	60%											B
Maniyah	71%	31%	60%		C									B
Kabrina	63%	38%	56%		C			A		C		D	B	D
Keshawn	55%	54%	55%		B		B	A						B
PERCENTAGE CORRECT:	95%	47%		95%	85%	100%	95%	40%	90%	90%	90%	80%	60%	45%

PERCENTAGE CORRECT: **TOTAL:** 85%

Repeated 6–1 Standards:

Comp: +/− decimals/money (1):	95%
Comp: 2 × 2 multiplication (3):	100%
Comp: divide by 1–2 digits (4):	95%
Multiply/divide in context (6,8,9):	87%

Estimation/Rounding (10,11):	53%
Charts: missing element (23):	75%
Add/subtract with money (7):	90%

	Multiple-Choice	Open-Ended	COMBINED
TEAM NAME	69%	47%	63%

Describe the first level of analysis to be done.

Display a slide based on Figure 9.2.

Figure 9.2 Assessment Analysis 1.

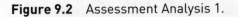

Part 1—Global Impressions

- How well did the class do as a whole?

- What are the strengths and weaknesses in the standards: Where do we need the most work?

- How did the class do on old versus new standards? Are they forgetting or improving on old material?

- How were the results in the different question types (multiple-choice versus open-ended, reading versus writing)?

- Who are the strong and the weak students?

Describe the second level of analysis—dig in—and go deeper into the data:

Display a slide based on Figure 9.3.

Mention each step on the PowerPoint slide and then model this process.

Model what this looks like by looking at specific questions on the math assessment connected to rates:

Ratio-Proportion Results Overall:	70%
Ratio-Proportion — General (Questions #12,13, 21):	82%
Ratio/Proportion — Rates (Questions #22, 30):	58%

Look more closely at the two Rate questions:

Student Performance on Rates Questions:

Question #22:	35%
Question #30:	80%

Figure 9.3   Assessment Analysis 2.

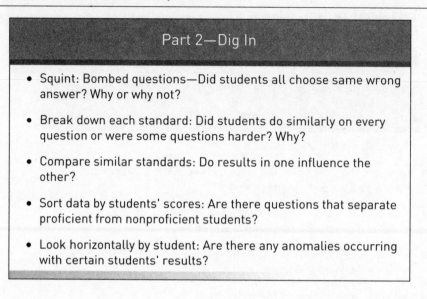

Part 2—Dig In

- Squint: Bombed questions—Did students all choose same wrong answer? Why or why not?

- Break down each standard: Did students do similarly on every question or were some questions harder? Why?

- Compare similar standards: Do results in one influence the other?

- Sort data by students' scores: Are there questions that separate proficient from nonproficient students?

- Look horizontally by student: Are there any anomalies occurring with certain students' results?

Go back to the test and look at the questions themselves.

22. Jennifer drove 36 miles in an hour. At this rate, how far would she travel in 2 ¼ hours?
A) 72 miles (most commonly chosen wrong answer)
B) 80 miles
C) 81 miles
D) 90 miles

Elicit audience answer: Students are struggling with multiplying mixed numbers, *not* with rates.

Look at similar standards to see if they verify this idea:

Student Performance on Mixed Numbers Questions:

Operations: Mixed Numbers (Question #5):   40%

Describe final two steps:

- Search for questions on which the generally stronger academic students outperform their weaker peers. Such questions are relevant because they reveal areas where smaller group focus or pullout groups would be highly effective at targeted instruction.

- Look at individual students, as in the example here:

Question:	1	2	3	4	5	6	7	8	9	10	11	12	13	14	15	16	17	18	19	20	21	22	23
Kenyatta				A				D						C	D	A	B	D	D	D	C	D	A

Audience answer: She fell asleep, got distracted, was a slow test-taker, or the like. Key point: she's not the lowest performing student in the class: something else happened that we'll need to address.

Walk through each part of the Assessment Analysis Template (see CD-ROM); focus on the section "Whole-Class Instruction: Which standards warrant more time for whole-class instruction" and the correlating "Why did the students not learn it?"

Small Groups: Complete Data Analysis (0:35–1:15)

Main group works for forty minutes; while they work, meet with the "teachers" group and hand out teacher one and teacher two sheets.

To the Teachers Group: Share context of Teacher One and Teacher Two.

Teacher One is the "good teacher" in this exercise. When you play Teacher One, you will play a teacher who is

- Frustrated by poor results but driven to improve them.

- Aware that mistakes are a teacher's own fault.

- Very willing to talk, but at the same time respectful: If the principal drives conversation, Teacher One won't say much or interrupt, but will talk as much as principal allows.

- In terms of analysis, Teacher One has done a great deal of independent work and has made some important insights.

Teacher Two, by contrast, is

- Reluctant to converse: produces the minimal answers required without appearing passive-aggressive; if principal asks for a more detailed answer, this teacher will attempt to give one, though the longer answer will often be one of the excuses discussed here.

- Inclined to think the current results are OK, not great, and is frustrated that the students didn't do a better job.

- Apt to blame students for shortcomings and to say things like "they just make mistakes!" "They know this stuff!" or "I did this in class and tested them on it! I explained it again when they got it wrong. There's not much more I can do."

- Resistant if pushed to make major changes. Teacher Two will challenge the rationale behind data-driven instruction, declaring, "This stuff worries me. From what you're saying, I'm going to have to cut a lot of important projects to do this. I don't think we should be taking away any opportunity for real understanding of how this subject is applied in the real world."

To play Teacher One effectively, volunteers must do deep analysis of the data. Give them a cheat sheet on the analysis, and let them spend the rest of the time analyzing the data in preparation for the role play.

To play Teacher Two effectively, in addition to making the sample comments noted in the list here, volunteers should say something to make it clear that they don't have any materials and need to use the principal's.

Role Play Introduction (1:15–1:20)

Form clusters of twenty to thirty participants gathered around one role play, depending on how many different case studies you chose and how many participants you have.

Give participants selected to play the principal's part guiding points for the role play:

- First, get the teacher to do the talking. Your goal is not to show how much you know; it is to get the teacher to do the analysis.

- Second, go back to the text of the tests whenever possible. This ensures that the focus of the conference will always be on results.

The rest are observers. They should develop answers to the questions listed in Figure 9.4 while observing the role play.

Display a slide based on Figure 9.4.

Figure 9.4 Teacher-Principal Role Play.

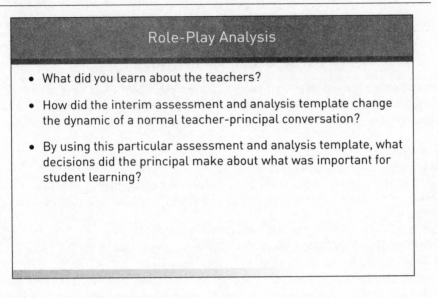

The principal should begin the role play with the phrase, "How did the students do?"

Role Play, Teacher One (1:20–1:25)
Introduce Teacher One. Allow five minutes for the role play. Everyone should be observing and taking notes.

Individual Reflection (1:25–1:27)
Give the group time for silent reflection, asking people to jot down their observations on that meeting. The second principal should step into the role play.

Role Play, Teacher Two (1:27–1:32)
Introduce Teacher Two. Allow five minutes for the new role play. Again, everyone should be observing and taking notes.

Individual Reflection (1:32–1:35)
Silent reflection: have people write observations on that meeting.

Small Groups: Observations and Reflections on Role Play (1:35–1:45)

In small groups of six to eight debrief the two role plays, answering the questions given as prompts in the large-group participation discussion.

Large-Group Sharing (1:45–1:55)

Large-Group Participation

Continue audience participation until every key point listed below has been brought up. Use the following leading questions if needed, and given limited time state the main ideas if you can't get the audience to identify them.

Question Prompts

What did you learn about the teachers?

How did the interim assessment and analysis template change the dynamic of the conversation from a normal teacher-principal conversation in a post-observation conference?

- *Key Observation 1:* The assessment and analysis template shifts the focus from what the teacher taught to what the students learned.
- *Key Observation 2:* In a teacher observation, the conversation is centered around the principal's or teacher's opinion about what happened and whether learning was effective. In this data analysis meeting, the conversation centered around the actual results of student learning. Having the assessment data makes the conversation more objective: there's no debate about whether the students learned something or not.
- *Key Observation 3:* Whereas an observation looks at one small portion of teaching, the interim assessment results look at much more. Even if the assessment doesn't assess everything students have learned, it's still the equivalent to looking at 80 percent of the student learning instead of 2 percent. (Only 2 percent? Kim Marshall notes that if you observe every teacher for fifteen minutes once a week for the entire year—a noble goal—you will have observed only 1–2 percent of the teaching of that teacher.)
- *Key Observation 4:* Looking at student results together immediately puts the principal and teacher in a place to collaborate. It's not about talking about what went wrong; it's about immediately moving to what to do better.
- *Key Observation 5:* For the resistant teacher, you find out about their excuses or resistance in October, rather than waiting until June (or whenever the state test results come in) when it's too late to do anything about it.

During large-group sharing, add the meta-analysis questions shown in Figure 9.5 at the end.

Display a slide based on Figure 9.5.

Figure 9.5 Analyzing the Teacher-Principal Role Play.

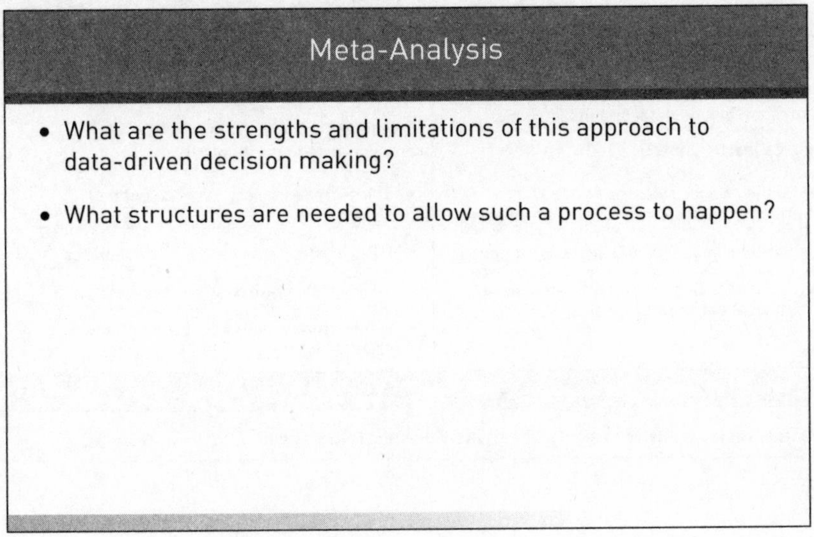

Meta-Analysis

- What are the strengths and limitations of this approach to data-driven decision making?

- What structures are needed to allow such a process to happen?

Video of Actual Teacher-Principal Conference (1:55–2:00)

Watch an example of an actual teacher-principal conference if possible. You can videotape conferences at your own school, or you can look for examples that are available from organizations such as the Effective Practice Incentive Community (EPIC) at New Leaders for New Schools.

ACTIVITY 6—LEADING EFFECTIVE ANALYSIS MEETINGS

What Makes a Meeting Effective
Time 2:00–2:55 (55 minutes)

Objectives	Materials and Handouts
Core Objectives (presenter): • Introduce the teacher-principal data conference as a critical system behind data-driven instruction. **Core Objectives (participants):** • Understand the specific systems needed for teacher-principal analysis meetings to be effective. • Lead effective teacher-principal analysis meetings. • Overcome obstacles that are likely to arise during teacher-principal data conferences.	**Materials:** • PowerPoint **Handouts (same as from assessment analysis meeting role play):** • Third-grade literacy assessment and results • Fifth-grade literacy assessment and results • Sixth-grade math assessment and results • Ninth-grade algebra assessment and results
Differentiation and Adjustments for Group Size and Type	
• Use the same handouts that you used for the analysis meeting role play earlier in the workshop.	

Role Play: Ineffective Analysis Meetings (2:00–2:10)

The teacher-leader analysis meeting represents a crucial component of effective data-driven implementation.

Revisit the role play of the principal-teacher data meeting. Focus on what it takes to lead those meetings effectively.

As seen in the last role play, teacher buy-in is by no means guaranteed at the beginning. This session will look at ways to overcome this obstacle, what works, and what doesn't.

Ask for a volunteer to do a role play with you in front of the group, playing a teacher while you play the role of the principal. Brief the volunteer publicly, explaining that whenever you ask why the students got bad results, the volunteer should respond that they "just made stupid mistakes." Tell the volunteer that you will make a follow-up comment, and the volunteer should act as they imagine a resistant teacher might act.

Ineffective Role Play: Group Participation

Presenter and volunteer do each role play listed here, then pairs discuss what went wrong. At that point, the large group shares their answers.

Role Play #1

TEACHER: They just made stupid mistakes.
LEADER: Why do you think they made silly mistakes?

[Teacher acts according to instinct. Most likely the response will be a litany of excuses.]

Why This Approach Fails
Asking why just legitimizes the assertion about stupid mistakes, and allows the teacher to mention every other sort of excuse. It leaves the teacher unaccountable for the problem and just pulls you further and further away from analyzing the problem.

Role Play #2

TEACHER: They just made stupid mistakes.
LEADER: You know, that sort of language [referring to *stupid*] is unacceptable. I will not let you talk about the students that way. [Continues with a lecture on the importance of student learning.] Is that understood?

[Teacher acts according to instinct, most likely getting defensive or shutting down.]

Why This Approach Fails
By fighting the teacher about word choice, all the principal is doing is offering the sort of challenge that only makes people shut down or launch into an ideological debate. In the long run, the participants have just pulled themselves further away from real analysis, and it is doubtful the teacher will be engaged during the rest of the meeting.

Role Play #3

TEACHER: They just made stupid mistakes.
LEADER: Well actually, if you look to questions 22 and 30, you'll notice that they got #30 right but they struggled with #22. As you look more closely, you can see that the students actually had problems with multiplying mixed numbers. You can re-teach that concept to them.

[Teacher acts according to instinct, likely nodding or saying "OK."]

Why This Approach Fails

Although the principal does point directly to the data, the statement includes all the analysis, thus cutting the teacher out of the process. If analysis is to be effective, it must be teacher-owned; teachers must reach conclusions by looking at the data themselves.

Role Play #4

> TEACHER: They just made stupid mistakes.
> LEADER: Let's look specifically at question 17; why do you think so many students got this question wrong?

Why This Approach Is More Successful

By guiding the teacher back to the data and offering the opportunity to do the analysis, the leader makes sure the teacher will own the analysis process and draw independent conclusions about the data, making it more likely that the teacher will remember the analysis when it's time to re-teach the standard.

Principles for Leading Effective Analysis Meetings (2:10–2:25)

Review the key steps to leading an effective analysis meeting.

Display a slide based on Figure 9.6.

Figure 9.6   Analysis Meeting Principles.

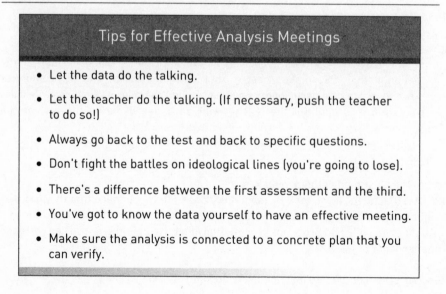

Tips for Effective Analysis Meetings

- Let the data do the talking.
- Let the teacher do the talking. (If necessary, push the teacher to do so!)
- Always go back to the test and back to specific questions.
- Don't fight the battles on ideological lines (you're going to lose).
- There's a difference between the first assessment and the third.
- You've got to know the data yourself to have an effective meeting.
- Make sure the analysis is connected to a concrete plan that you can verify.

Highlight precursors that can help make these steps happen.

Talk through slides based on Figures 9.7 and 9.8.

Figure 9.7 Precursors for Analysis Meetings 1.

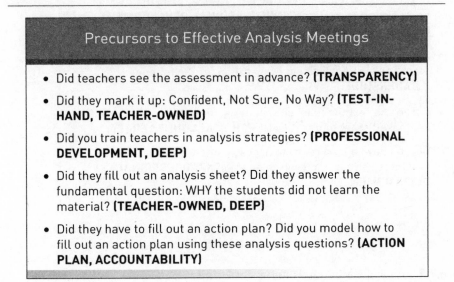

Precursors to Effective Analysis Meetings

- Did teachers see the assessment in advance? **(TRANSPARENCY)**
- Did they mark it up: Confident, Not Sure, No Way? **(TEST-IN-HAND, TEACHER-OWNED)**
- Did you train teachers in analysis strategies? **(PROFESSIONAL DEVELOPMENT, DEEP)**
- Did they fill out an analysis sheet? Did they answer the fundamental question: WHY the students did not learn the material? **(TEACHER-OWNED, DEEP)**
- Did they have to fill out an action plan? Did you model how to fill out an action plan using these analysis questions? **(ACTION PLAN, ACCOUNTABILITY)**

Show helpful phrases to use during such meetings. Each of these phrases returns focus to the question and to the data and the concrete actions a teacher needs to take.

Talk through slides based on Figures 9.9 and 9.10.

Role Play: Leading Effective Analysis Meetings (2:25–2:55)

Have the group pull out their first-round data sheets from yesterday (the fifth-grade, sixth-grade, and ninth-grade results) and reassemble in the groups they were in.

Figure 9.8   Precursors for Analysis Meetings 2.

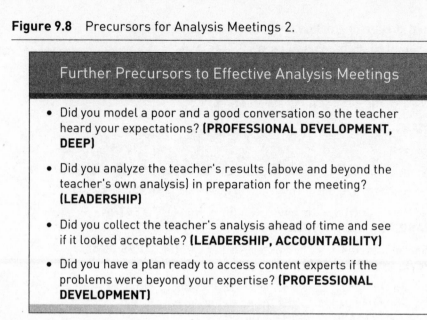

Further Precursors to Effective Analysis Meetings

- Did you model a poor and a good conversation so the teacher heard your expectations? **(PROFESSIONAL DEVELOPMENT, DEEP)**

- Did you analyze the teacher's results (above and beyond the teacher's own analysis) in preparation for the meeting? **(LEADERSHIP)**

- Did you collect the teacher's analysis ahead of time and see if it looked acceptable? **(LEADERSHIP, ACCOUNTABILITY)**

- Did you have a plan ready to access content experts if the problems were beyond your expertise? **(PROFESSIONAL DEVELOPMENT)**

Figure 9.9   Analysis Meeting Helpful Phrases 1.

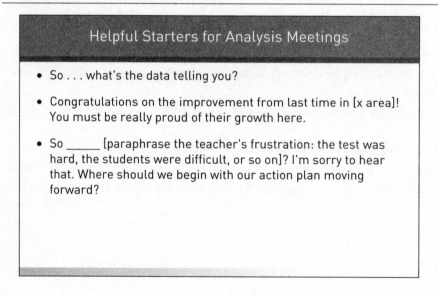

Helpful Starters for Analysis Meetings

- So . . . what's the data telling you?

- Congratulations on the improvement from last time in [x area]! You must be really proud of their growth here.

- So _____ [paraphrase the teacher's frustration: the test was hard, the students were difficult, or so on]? I'm sorry to hear that. Where should we begin with our action plan moving forward?

Figure 9.10 Analysis Meeting Helpful Phrases 2.

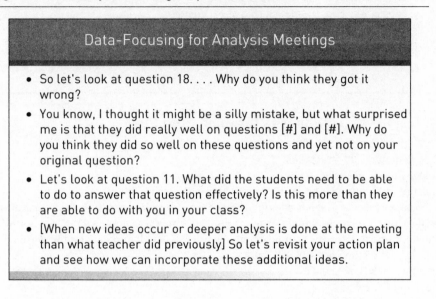

> ### Data-Focusing for Analysis Meetings
>
> - So let's look at question 18. . . . Why do you think they got it wrong?
> - You know, I thought it might be a silly mistake, but what surprised me is that they did really well on questions [#] and [#]. Why do you think they did so well on these questions and yet not on your original question?
> - Let's look at question 11. What did the students need to be able to do to answer that question effectively? Is this more than they are able to do with you in your class?
> - [When new ideas occur or deeper analysis is done at the meeting than what teacher did previously] So let's revisit your action plan and see how we can incorporate these additional ideas.

Announce that the focus today will be on building more effective practices in dialogue.

Analysis Meeting Role Play

Walk around during the role plays and listen to what is being said: take the opportunity to praise best practices and offer feedback.

Process

1. Participants: Pull out the assessment analyzed in the role play yesterday and pick one or two questions that you will analyze during the role play (two questions that you have a good understanding of why the students made errors). Use those questions when you are the principal in the role play.
2. Form groups of three: one principal, one teacher, and one observer.
3. Presenter gives a phrase to the group; the teacher starts the role play by repeating the phrase.
4. The principal's goal is to get the teacher back to the analysis as effectively as possible. Use the phrases that have been given to you as well as the tips about leading meetings.
5. Each role play will last one minute.

6. Then groups debrief the role play, beginning with the observer's notes.
7. The group rotates roles, and next role play begins.
8. Presenter: After the first few role plays and every third thereafter, have large-group sharing about what is working most effectively.

Phrases for Each Role Play

- They just made silly mistakes.
- That's a dumb question.
- This test isn't helpful; I know what students *really* need to know.
- I'm really concerned about adding all these SAT and state test questions that aren't really a part of what we should be teaching. This is just test prep; it's not real learning.
- We don't use this format and terminology in our class. If you change the wording to _____, then the students will get it.
- I taught it and they knew it.
- We'll just review it.
- Students will never be able to master all of this — it's too hard.
- I just don't know how to teach any better.

10

Action

Professional Development Agendas and Activities

ACTIVITY 7—INTRO TO ACTION

Movie Clip: Action with Analysis

Time 0:00–0:45 (45 minutes)

Objectives	Materials and Handouts
Core Objectives (participants):	**Materials:**
• Generate conclusions as to how effective analysis goes beyond ''what'' is happening and into ''why'' it has happened.	• PowerPoint
	• Movie clip showing effective analysis, such as *Man on Fire*
• Make the connection between deep analysis and effective action.	**Handouts:**
	• None
Differentiation and Adjustments for Group Size and Type	
• Choose any movie clip that highlights analysis.	

Movie Segment (0:00–0:05)

Give context to movie segment and focus questions.

Display a slide based on Figure 10.1.

Figure 10.1   Movie Clip Analysis 1.

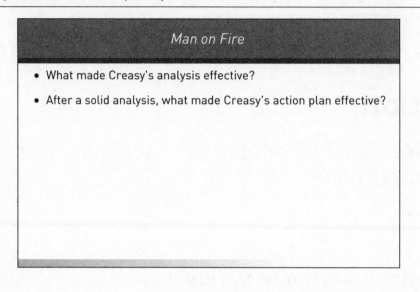

Man on Fire

- What made Creasy's analysis effective?
- After a solid analysis, what made Creasy's action plan effective?

Movie Clip — *Man on Fire*, Scene 2

Bodyguard Creasy works with Pita to improve her start off the blocks. As the scene opens, Creasy is slamming two bricks together to simulate the gun shot, and Pita flinches.

CREASY: What happened?
PITA: I flinched.
CREASY: You flinched. The gunshot holds no fear.
PITA: [Repeats this phrase three times.]
CREASY: That's good. Now you listen for that sound, and that sound will set you free. You are a prisoner on this block until the gunshot sets you free. Are you ready? Go!

[Change scene: Creasy gives little advice while Pita practices, then Pita does a simulated race where she sets a new best time.]

PITA: Yes. I'm tough, Creasy!
CREASY: There's no such thing as tough. Either you're trained, or untrained. Now what are you?
PITA: Trained!
CREASY: Good. Let's get out of the water and try it again.

Think-Pair-Share (0:05–0:15)

- Look at questions on screen.

- Talk in pairs for two minutes about the Large-Group Participation question prompts.

- Share answers as large group.

Large-Group Participation

Continue audience participation until every key observation listed here has been brought up. Ask guiding questions when necessary.

Question Prompts

What made Creasy's analysis effective?
After a solid analysis, what made Creasy's action plan effective?

- *Key Observation 1:* Creasy went from "what" was wrong (slow off the blocks) to "why" (Pita flinched when she heard a gunshot): the analysis was deep.
- *Key Observation 2:* All of the practice targeted the exact problem Pita had: he taught her motivational phrases to stop her from being afraid of the gunshot, and then they practiced getting off the blocks repeatedly.
- *Key Observation 3:* At the end, Creasy made sure to have her practice getting off the blocks in the simulation of the real race, making sure she could put the individual piece back in the larger objective.
- *Key Observation 4:* The action was effective because the analysis was effective.

View Film Clip (0:15–0:25)

Give context:

- Assessments, analysis, and culture are great and necessary things, but unless they are coupled with real, concrete action, they will not bear fruit.

- Focus on the concrete strategies needed to move from theory to reality in the classroom.

To give context to video clip and focus questions, display and discuss a slide based on Figure 10.2.

Figure 10.2   Movie Clip Analysis 2.

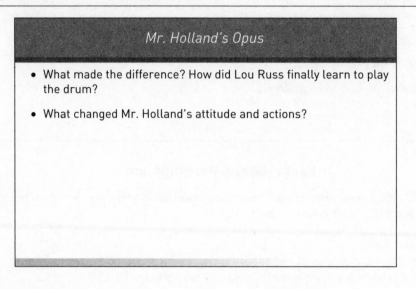

Movie Clip — *Mr. Holland's Opus*

Glen Holland, a music teacher, tries to teach an athlete, Lou Russ, to play the drums. While most of the clip consists of concrete actions, there is one core piece of dialogue between Holland and his friend the gym teacher and wrestling coach.

COACH: So, Lou Russ: is he going to make it?

MR. HOLLAND: I don't think so.

COACH: What do you mean? Glen, I need this guy.

MR. HOLLAND: If he can't wrestle, it's not the end of the world!

COACH: For him it is. Listen, it's not just about wrestling. I care about the kid. You're telling me you cannot teach a willing kid how to play to drum or something?

MR. HOLLAND: I tried, and I can't!

COACH: Then you're a lousy teacher! [Pause.] Look: I was a kid just like him once. And if someone hadn't given me a chance, I never would have become the gum-chewing coach that I am. [Laughter]

Think-Pair-Share (0:25–0:35)

- Look at questions on screen.

- Talk in pairs for two minutes about the Large-Group Participation question prompts.

- Share answers as large group.

Large-Group Participation

Continue audience participation until every key observation listed here has been brought up. Ask guiding questions when necessary.

Question Prompts

What made the difference? How did Lou Russ finally learn to play the drum? What changed Mr. Holland's attitude and actions?

- *Key Observation 1:* Even for the most developed teacher, there will come a time when nothing that you currently do can reach a certain student and teach certain standards. In times like this, it takes trying something new. Each time you try something new, you expand your repertoire of strategies to use for the next teachable moment.
- *Key Observation 2:* Mr. Holland did not succeed with his first attempts, but he kept trying. Teacher perseverance is crucial.
- *Key Observation 3:* Mr. Holland devoted extra one-to-one time to Lou Russ to help him succeed.
- *Key Observation 4:* The fact that his friend (the coach) challenged him to be a better teacher was instrumental in Mr. Holland's trying to teach effectively. Our goal is to create school communities where peers can push each other in this way. It doesn't work nearly as well coming from the principal!
- *Key Observation 5:* Even when Mr. Holland started to try new approaches, he still wasn't convinced he would succeed. Buy-in comes after success!

Keys of Action (0:35–0:45)

Present keys to action steps in a slide based on Figure 10.3.

Figure 10.3 Principles of Action.

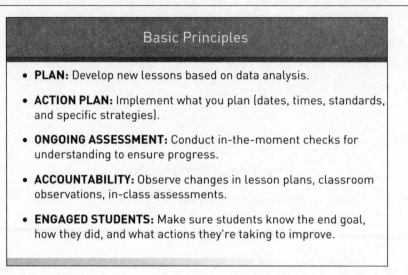

> **Basic Principles**
>
> - **PLAN:** Develop new lessons based on data analysis.
>
> - **ACTION PLAN:** Implement what you plan (dates, times, standards, and specific strategies).
>
> - **ONGOING ASSESSMENT:** Conduct in-the-moment checks for understanding to ensure progress.
>
> - **ACCOUNTABILITY:** Observe changes in lesson plans, classroom observations, in-class assessments.
>
> - **ENGAGED STUDENTS:** Make sure students know the end goal, how they did, and what actions they're taking to improve.

Review North Star analysis sheets and action plans as a sample. Discuss examples of how leaders can review lesson plans and use observations to check for action:

- Make sure that in their lesson plans teachers refer directly to the six-week plan in their action plan.

- In observations, look to see that teachers are teaching the right standards to the right rigor.

- Review the rigor of the Do Nows: Do the questions of the Do Nows match the rigor of the assessment?

- Review the in-class activities and homework assignments with the same lens.

- Review the questions the teacher is asking: Are they targeting the learning needs identified in the action plan?

Ongoing assessment is where we make sure that the students are actually learning the material. You can check for that in observations as well:

- How are students doing on the Do Nows? Does the teacher note which students are doing well and which are struggling? Is that information driving actual teaching in the classroom?
- Is the teacher using an exit ticket? Tracking that data?
- Does the teacher cold call and use other effective questioning techniques to check for understanding?

ACTIVITY 8 — RESULTS MEETING PROTOCOL

Re-Teaching Challenging Standards
Time 0:45 -1:55 (1 hour 10 minutes)

Objectives	Materials and Handouts
Core Objectives (participants): • Learn the results meeting protocol system for effective team meetings. • Implement the results meeting protocol. • Develop an explicit action plan to address a challenge facing their school during implementation of data-driven instruction.	**Materials:** • PowerPoint. **Handouts:** • None
Differentiation and Adjustments for Group Size and Type	
• The topics for the results meetings presented here are ideal for school leadership teams to address the core issues around implementation of data-driven instruction. These topics should be changed to difficult standards if working with teacher teams, and can be changed to any particular challenge you want your school team to face. Choose the topics based on the needs of the group.	

Introduce Results Meeting Protocol — Model It (0:45–1:00)

Introduce effective protocol for group meetings—the results meeting protocol:

- The original inspiration behind the results meeting protocol comes from the Brazosport (Texas) School District as highlighted in Mike Schmoker's *Results Fieldbook*.

- The action-results protocol is designed to be run over the course of fifty minutes, and can work in any group greater than three people. The protocol is shown in Figure 10.4.

Model each step with a group of participants, highlighting protocols for brainstorming, reflection, and action planning. Display slides based on Figures 10.5 and 10.6 as appropriate.

School Teams: Results Meeting (1:00–1:50)

Break off into groups and practice.

Give groups a choice of topics for this exercise, such as the ones listed in Figure 10.7. (See "Differentiation" for potential different topics.)

Figure 10.4 Results Meeting Protocol.

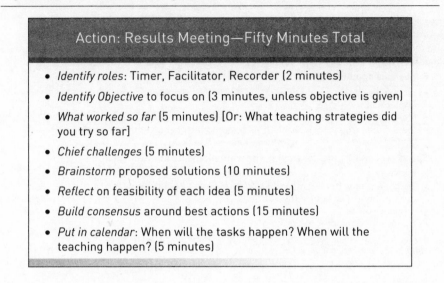

Action: Results Meeting—Fifty Minutes Total

- *Identify roles*: Timer, Facilitator, Recorder (2 minutes)
- *Identify Objective* to focus on (3 minutes, unless objective is given)
- *What worked so far* (5 minutes) [Or: What teaching strategies did you try so far]
- *Chief challenges* (5 minutes)
- *Brainstorm* proposed solutions (10 minutes)
- *Reflect* on feasibility of each idea (5 minutes)
- *Build consensus* around best actions (15 minutes)
- *Put in calendar*: When will the tasks happen? When will the teaching happen? (5 minutes)

Figure 10.5 Results Meeting Brainstorming and Reflection.

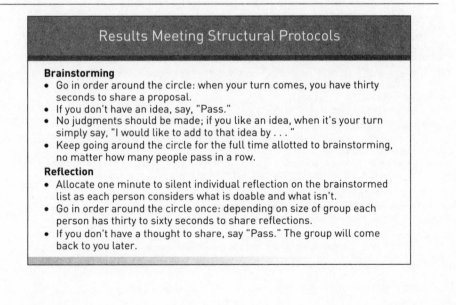

Results Meeting Structural Protocols

Brainstorming
- Go in order around the circle: when your turn comes, you have thirty seconds to share a proposal.
- If you don't have an idea, say, "Pass."
- No judgments should be made; if you like an idea, when it's your turn simply say, "I would like to add to that idea by . . . "
- Keep going around the circle for the full time allotted to brainstorming, no matter how many people pass in a row.

Reflection
- Allocate one minute to silent individual reflection on the brainstormed list as each person considers what is doable and what isn't.
- Go in order around the circle once: depending on size of group each person has thirty to sixty seconds to share reflections.
- If you don't have a thought to share, say "Pass." The group will come back to you later.

Figure 10.6   Results Meeting Consensus and Action Planning.

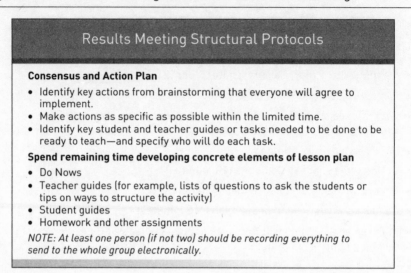

Results Meeting Structural Protocols

Consensus and Action Plan
- Identify key actions from brainstorming that everyone will agree to implement.
- Make actions as specific as possible within the limited time.
- Identify key student and teacher guides or tasks needed to be done to be ready to teach—and specify who will do each task.

Spend remaining time developing concrete elements of lesson plan
- Do Nows
- Teacher guides (for example, lists of questions to ask the students or tips on ways to structure the activity)
- Student guides
- Homework and other assignments

NOTE: At least one person (if not two) should be recording everything to send to the whole group electronically.

Figure 10.7   Results Meeting Topics.

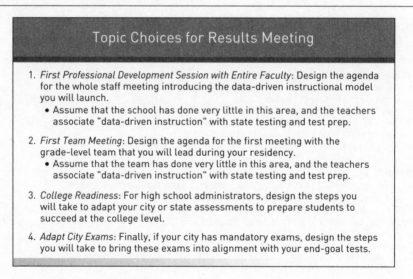

Topic Choices for Results Meeting

1. *First Professional Development Session with Entire Faculty*: Design the agenda for the whole staff meeting introducing the data-driven instructional model you will launch.
   - Assume that the school has done very little in this area, and the teachers associate "data-driven instruction" with state testing and test prep.

2. *First Team Meeting*: Design the agenda for the first meeting with the grade-level team that you will lead during your residency.
   - Assume that the team has done very little in this area, and the teachers associate "data-driven instruction" with state testing and test prep.

3. *College Readiness*: For high school administrators, design the steps you will take to adapt your city or state assessments to prepare students to succeed at the college level.

4. *Adapt City Exams*: Finally, if your city has mandatory exams, design the steps you will take to bring these exams into alignment with your end-goal tests.

Reminder: Tell participants to give the protocol a chance and follow it strictly for now. The last part of the meeting will include a discussion of its strengths and weaknesses.

Launch the protocol in groups of four to ten participants.

Reflection on Use of the Protocol (1:50–1:55)

Allow two minutes of audience participation on what was effective about the protocol.

Follow up with two minutes of audience participation on potential limitations and pitfalls that need to be avoided.

Large-Group Participation

Continue audience participation until every key observation listed here has been brought up. Ask guiding questions when necessary.

Question Prompt

What was effective about the protocol?

- *Key Observation 1:* The protocol forces you to stay on point and not get distracted. You can accomplish a great deal in a short amount of time.
- *Key Observation 2:* The protocol allows the facilitator to cut someone off or redirect them without being seen as rude.
- *Key Observation 3:* Participants leave the meeting with concrete activities and strategies to implement immediately.
- *Key Observation 4:* The "What Worked so Far" section acknowledges the teachers' efforts up to this point. This creates a less judgmental environment and makes the participants more willing to share their challenges and struggles.
- *Key Observation 5:* The protocol can make the decision feel rushed, but it is better to leave with a somewhat imperfect action plan than to leave with no action plan at all!

Core Ideas for Results Meetings

- Don't stop the brainstorming early; the best ideas come after the group feels like there's very little more to say.
- Make sure the meeting ends with clear action steps, and who's responsible for creating each student or teacher guide or document.
- Follow the protocol strictly, even if it feels uncomfortable at first.
- As a school leader, lead the first results meetings yourself until you can identify other members of the school community who can facilitate the meetings effectively.

11

Culture

Professional Development Agendas and Activities

ACTIVITY 9 — BUILDING A DATA-DRIVEN CULTURE

Douglass Street School Case Study

Time 0:00–1:20 (1 hour 20 minutes)

Objectives	Materials and Handouts
Core Objectives (participants): • Analyze a second case study on data-driven instruction. • Distinguish the core drivers of data-driven success from false drivers. • Understand that complete faculty buy-in is not needed for data-driven instruction to be effective. • Identify the key principles of data-driven culture.	**Materials:** • PowerPoint • Pad of poster paper • Large markers (one set per eight to ten workshop participants) **Handouts:** • Douglas Street Case study (See "Culture" section of CD-ROM.)
Differentiation and Adjustments for Group Size and Type	
• None needed.	

Introduction to Douglass Street Case (0:00–0:05)

Hand out Douglas Street case study.

Give context:

- This is a fact-based case study, based on the real experience of two public schools.

• The principal of the Douglass Street School, Krista Brown, is a friend of Marc Jones from the Springsteen case study. She has tried to learn from his struggles and has made a bet that she can get 15 percent improvement or better in every single class using data-driven instruction. Your task is to determine whether she succeeds. While reading, focus on answering the questions shown in Figure 11.1. (Display a slide based on the figure.)

Figure 11.1 Case Study Questions.

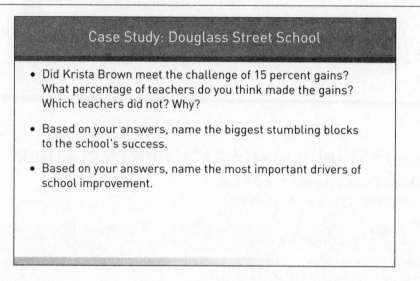

Case Study: Douglass Street School

- Did Krista Brown meet the challenge of 15 percent gains? What percentage of teachers do you think made the gains? Which teachers did not? Why?

- Based on your answers, name the biggest stumbling blocks to the school's success.

- Based on your answers, name the most important drivers of school improvement.

Have participants spend the next fifteen minutes reading through this case study, but do not reveal the results; instead, have the audience make predictions about what they think will happen and list what they consider to be the key factors and power actions behind the outcome at Douglass Street. Tell everyone to write down their own prediction without consulting anyone else.

Make sure people write down the key drivers and stumbling blocks.

Individual Reading of Case Study (0:05–0:25)
Have the participants read the case study, which can be found in the "Culture" section of the CD-ROM.

Share Predictions, Reveal Actual Results (0:25–0:30)
Write 100%, 77–99%, 51–75%, 26–50%, and 0–25% on a piece of block paper. Have people raise hands revealing what percentage of teachers they thought made

the gains. Write their answers down. In most cases, the answers will either be largely negative (less than 50 percent) or a diverse sample all over the place.

Reveal the real answer. In this school, *every single teacher* made fifteen-point gains in achievement.

Small-Group Sharing: Real Drivers and "Not Really" Stumbling Blocks (0:30–0:50)

Divide the participants into groups of six to eight, and ask people to spend twenty minutes answering the following on flip-chart paper:

- What were *not really* stumbling blocks to achievement gains?
- What are the *true drivers* for the achievement gains?

Break (0:50–1:05)

Before the break, identify three volunteers; tell them that while the others are on break, you and the volunteers will go through the responses recorded by the groups and highlight common answers across all groups as well as the unique responses.

Case Study Conclusions: Keys to Data-Driven Culture (1:05–1:20)

Discuss the traditional but ineffective ways to measure teacher effectiveness, showing a slide based on Figure 11.2.

Present a summary of what all the groups identified, or have a volunteer do so.

Point out that in a data-driven culture, five things drive everything else. Display a slide based on Figure 11.3 to underscore this point.

Notice that buy-in is not listed as one of the drivers. That's deliberate—it's an effect, not a cause. You *create* teacher buy-in by doing these things.

Core Ideas

- In traditional school systems, the focus of quality is on how the teacher teaches.
- In a data-driven culture, the focus shifts to how the students are learning.

Figure 11.2   Traditional Systems: Principal-Centered Evaluation.

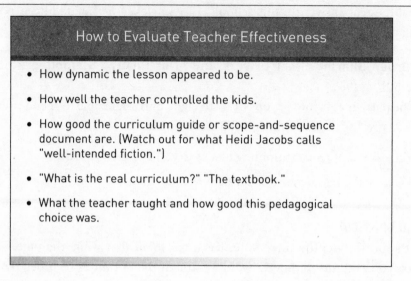

How to Evaluate Teacher Effectiveness

- How dynamic the lesson appeared to be.

- How well the teacher controlled the kids.

- How good the curriculum guide or scope-and-sequence document are. (Watch out for what Heidi Jacobs calls "well-intended fiction.")

- "What is the real curriculum?" "The textbook."

- What the teacher taught and how good this pedagogical choice was.

Figure 11.3   Drivers of Data-Driven Culture.

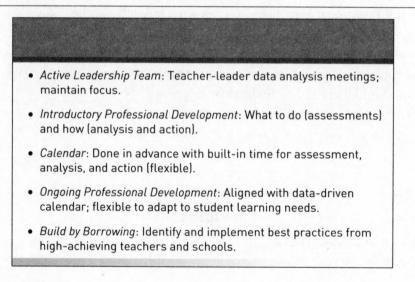

- *Active Leadership Team*: Teacher-leader data analysis meetings; maintain focus.

- *Introductory Professional Development*: What to do (assessments) and how (analysis and action).

- *Calendar*: Done in advance with built-in time for assessment, analysis, and action (flexible).

- *Ongoing Professional Development*: Aligned with data-driven calendar; flexible to adapt to student learning needs.

- *Build by Borrowing*: Identify and implement best practices from high-achieving teachers and schools.

Language of Leadership
Time 1:20–1:35 (15 minutes)

Objectives	Materials and Handouts
Core Objectives (participants): • Practice explanations and responses to faculty prepared the night before.	**Materials:** • PowerPoint **Handouts:** • None
Differentiation and Adjustments for Group Size and Type	
• Note: The "elevator speech" can be given as a homework assignment prior to this part of the workshop.	

Introduction to the Power of Language (1:20–1:25)

This segment sets the context.

No matter how well you've established all your systems and how effective the professional development you have done, at the end of the day, you will still have some teachers who say, "That was nice, but . . . what's this all about? Why data-driven instruction?" In responding to this, I've found that what works best are simple, vivid analogies like the hidden scoreboard.

It's also useful to share a set of examples. (Refer to the Success Stories sprinkled throughout this book for good material to use.)

To prepare, write out an analogy or anecdote that you feel can simply and effectively explain just why we are using data-driven instruction.

Practice Responses to Faculty (1:25–1:35)

Form groups of three. Give each member one minute to deliver a message.

Colleagues give the speaker feedback about what was effective and ineffective about the message.

At the end of role plays, elicit responses from the large group on the most effective stories and analogies that emerged.

Walk around during the deliveries and listen to what is being said: take the opportunity to praise best practices and offer feedback.

ACTIVITY 10 — START-UP SCENARIOS

Confronting Obstacles

Time 1:35–2:00 (25 minutes)

Objectives	Materials and Handouts
Core Objectives (participants): • Overcome obstacles likely to arise in the start-up stages of implementing data-driven instruction.	**Materials:** • PowerPoint **Handouts:** • None

Differentiation and Adjustments for Group Size and Type
• The start-up scenarios presented reflect some of the challenges that have been most common in the schools that have launched the processes described in this book. Adjust these scenarios as needed to match the challenges you anticipate your participants will be facing. • If you are running overtime at this stage of the workshop, you can speed things up here by allowing just the pair sharing and then stating the right answer (rather than letting the large group share their ideas after each challenge). This can recover fifteen minutes from the agenda.

Start-Up Scenarios (1:35–2:00)

Give context:

- Focus on some of the start-up challenges you might face as you put data-driven instruction into practice.

- After presenting the challenge, spend one minute with the person next to you discussing what you would do, and then spend a few minutes discussing the ideas as a group.

Present each scenario—one at a time.

Go through the pair sharing process, allowing one minute each.

Then, if time allows, do the large-group sharing—up to two minutes per scenario (see "Differentiation" for guidance)

Display slides based on Figures 11.4, 11.5, and 11.6.

Figure 11.4 Entry Scenarios: Dealing with Challenging Situations 1.

Dealing with Challenging Situations 1

YOUR TEACHER TEAM HAS NO INTERIM ASSESSMENTS
You are placed with a teacher team at a grade level for which there are no citywide interim assessments, and the school doesn't have any either. What do you do?

YOUR DISTRICT HAS POOR MANDATED INTERIM ASSESSMENTS
Your district has an interim assessment in November and April, and your state test is in June. Not only are the interim assessments too far apart, as you review them you realize that they address only about half the standards that will be on the state assessment, and they don't include any open-ended responses. What do you do?

Figure 11.5 Entry Scenarios: Dealing with Challenging Situations 2.

Dealing with Challenging Situations 2

JADED LEAD TEACHER
You are working with a team of teachers. When you do your opening professional development work with them around data-driven instruction, the younger teachers seem very interested in working on it. But the oldest teacher on the team (who has a great deal of influence on everyone else) makes dismissive comments about how this is a waste of time. You give your one-minute response about the importance of this work, but you can see the newer teachers' enthusiasm drop. What do you do?

Figure 11.6 Entry Scenarios: Dealing with Challenging Situations 3.

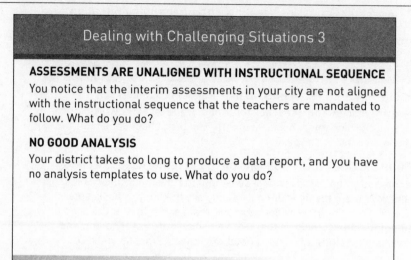

Dealing with Challenging Situations 3

ASSESSMENTS ARE UNALIGNED WITH INSTRUCTIONAL SEQUENCE
You notice that the interim assessments in your city are not aligned with the instructional sequence that the teachers are mandated to follow. What do you do?

NO GOOD ANALYSIS
Your district takes too long to produce a data report, and you have no analysis templates to use. What do you do?

Core Idea

- Build by borrowing: Whenever you face a struggle, find a school that has made significant gains in achievement and employ systems that they have already built. There is no need to reinvent the wheel!

Large-Group Participation

These are ideal answers for each of these scenarios. Other answers could also be plausible. Use your best judgment on the plausibility of each idea generated by the group based on the core principles of the Data-Driven Implementation Rubric.

Start-Up Scenario 1 (No Interim Assessments)

- Easiest solution: Find a school in your state that already has great results using interim assessments and ask to use its assessments. Most states have schools that have developed interim assessments aligned to state assessments that can serve as a model for your own school.
- Harder solution: Create a teacher team that will write assessments for the school.

Start-Up Scenario 2 (Poor District-Mandated Interim Assessments)
Answers will vary depending on the flexibility of the district. Here are some potential solutions:

- Supplement the district assessments with an additional set of questions that add the standards that will be on state assessments or are college-ready. Have students answer that set of questions at the same time as the district assessment. Combine the results to see how the school did.
- De-prioritize the district assessment and implement school-specific interim assessments that will be the drivers of instruction. Students can view the district tests as simply an in-class or even homework assignment so as to reduce the feel of overtesting.
- If the mandated assessments are far enough apart, add a school-based interim assessment between two district assessments.

Start-Up Scenario 3 (Jaded Lead Teachers)
Answers could vary depending on the teacher. Here are some potential solutions:

- Ask jaded lead teacher to lead the initiative within your framework. (Remember the Douglass Street case: It's harder to undermine something if you are charged with leading it!)
- Separate out the work of your teachers with a positive reaction from those who are resistant. Work one-to-one with resistant teachers in the data analysis process.
- There are phases of acceptance of data-driven instruction: be patient with people's attitudes. (See Follow-up Workshop for School Leaders.)

Start-Up Scenario 4 (Assessments Unaligned with Instructional Sequence)
If the city interim assessments are *good* (as defined by the implementation rubric), then find creative ways to change the instructional sequence to match:

- Revisit the pacing guide. Embed missing standards in appropriate places within the pacing guides: plan for embedding them in Do Nows, learning centers, homework assignments, mini-lessons, and so on.
- Reduce the time on certain standards to add the additional standards that are missing from the instructional sequence.

If the city interim assessments are not good, you're back with Scenario 2.

Start-Up Scenario 5 (No Good Tools for Analysis)
Select tools from this book to use in your school!

Agenda for Leadership Workshop

Putting All the Pieces Together in a Comprehensive Workshop

COMPREHENSIVE LEADERSHIP WORKSHOP

Designed to form the foundation of data-driven leadership training, this comprehensive leadership workshop agenda organizes the activities from preceding chapters to provide a thorough introduction to the key principles of data-driven education and its practical application. Although it ideally serves as a preface to additional follow-up workshops, this workshop can also serve independently as a complete crash course on the theory and practice of making data work.

On the agenda, each session is labeled either "targeted" or "flexible." For the "targeted" sessions, I recommend you use the activity precisely as presented in this book. For the "flexible" sessions, you should tailor and adapt to the particular needs and context of each school.

Target Audience and Time Frame

This workshop is designed for school leaders of all types: principals, assistant principals, school leadership teams, coaches, department chairs, grade-level team leaders, and anyone else interested in schoolwide systems of data-driven instruction.

This workshop is designed to be delivered over the course of three four-hour sessions of professional development. This can be a day and a half straight or three half-days.

Materials

To deliver this workshop effectively, you will need access to

- Laptop or other computer and DVD player (ideally built into laptop)
- LCD projector and screen
- Microsoft PowerPoint
- One large pad of poster paper and set of markers for every six to eight participants
- Method to put post chart paper where it can be widely viewed (Post-it paper, tape, tacks, or whatever will work in the room)
- Video of an actual Teacher-Principal Assessment Analysis Conference (from your own school or from another resource)
- Short film clip illustrating effective analysis, such as *Man on Fire*
- Short film clip illustrating effective action, such as *Mr. Holland's Opus*
- Short film clip illustrating hope and perseverance, such as *Shawshank Redemption*

Handouts

Note: The best way to distribute handouts is to make packets for each audience member that include all handouts in a three-ring binder with corresponding tabs. This way, you will save time handing out copies and waiting for participants to shuffle through them. If copy resources are limited, participants can experience the workshop adequately without having a hard copy of the PowerPoint presentation.

Materials for every participant:

- PowerPoint slide show
- Springsteen Charter School case study
- Selected interim assessments with accompanying results (selection criteria follow this list)

- Assessment analysis sheet
- Douglass Street case study
- Implementation calendar
- Implementation rubric
- North Star assessment calendar—elementary, middle school, or high school, depending on audience
- Results meeting protocol

Choose one case study per participant based on grade level and subject area that would be closest to their subject. When you have a diverse group or a set of school leaders who will be looking at all grade levels, choose fifth-grade literacy, sixth-grade math, and ninth-grade algebra. Each participant will analyze *only one assessment,* so they don't necessarily need to receive copies of every grade level you choose.

- K–12 assessment materials:
  - Third-grade literacy assessment results
  - Fifth-grade literacy assessment
  - Fifth-grade literacy results
  - Sixth-grade math assessment
  - Sixth-grade math results
  - Ninth-grade algebra assessment
  - Ninth-grade algebra results
- Teacher One and Teacher Two Sheets (not for full group; make one for every four or five workshop participants)

Logistics   This workshop uses the "Comprehensive Leadership Workshop" PowerPoint from the attached CD-ROM.

To deliver this workshop most effectively, you will need a room with tables that can accommodate six to eight people each. The room should have a central projector screen and, if needed for acoustics, a microphone.

WORKSHOP OVERVIEW: FIRST HALF-DAY

Workshop Session:	Timing:	Format:
Activity 1—Setting the Rationale:	0:00–0:15	Flexible
Introduction and Ground Rules	0:00–0:05	
Tales of Newark and Lemov Graph	0:05–0:15	
Activity 2—Springsteen Charter School Case Study:	0:15–1:35	Targeted
Case Study Introduction	0:15–0:20	
Read and Review Case Study	0:20–0:35	
Marc Jones Role Play	0:35–0:50	
Small-Group Work	0:50–1:10	
Large-Group Presentations	1:10–1:30	
Big Ideas	1:30–1:35	
Activity 4—Intro to Analysis:	1:35–1:50	Flexible
View Film Clip	1:35–1:40	
Pair-Share	1:40–1:50	
Break	1:50–2:05	—
Activity 5—Teacher-Principal Role Play	2:05–3:50	Targeted
Introduction to Assessment Analysis Project	2:05–2:10	
Model Interim Assessment Results Analysis	2:10–2:25	
Small Groups: Complete Data Analysis (Presenter prepares for role play during this period.)	2:25–3:05	
Role Play Introduction	3:05–3:10	
Role Play, Teacher 1	3:10–3:15	
Individual Reflection	3:10–3:15	
Role Play, Teacher 2	3:17–3:22	
Individual Reflection	3:22–3:25	
Small Groups: Observations and Reflections on Role Play	3:25–3:35	
Large-Group Sharing	3:35–3:45	
Video of Actual Teacher-Principal Conference	3:45–3:50	
Impact:	3:50–4:05	Flexible
Share North Star Story (or Other Data-Driven Success Story from book)	3:50–4:00	
Conclusions	4:00–4:05	

WORKSHOP OVERVIEW: SECOND HALF-DAY

Workshop Session:	Timing:	Format:
General Introduction:	0:00–0:10	Flexible
Introduction to the Framework:	0:10–0:20	Targeted
Quick-Write: Most important things needed to launch a data-driven instruction	0:10–0:12	
Large-Group Sharing	0:12–0:15	
Present the Framework for Data-Driven Instruction	0:15–0:20	
Activity 3—Principles of Assessment:	0:20–1:10	Flexible
Introduction to the Power of the Question: Math	0:20–0:25	
Think-Pair-Share	0:25–0:40	
Power of the Question: Reading	0:40–0:55	
Power of the Question: Differentiated	0:55–1:05	
• K–5: Early Literacy Assessment questions		
• Middle School: Grammar questions		
• High School: Quadratic equations questions		
Keys to Assessment	1:05–1:10	
Activity 9—Building a Data-Driven Culture	1:10–2:30	Targeted
Introduction to Douglass Street Case Study	1:10–1:15	
Individual Reading	1:15–1:35	
Share Predictions, Reveal Actual Results	1:35–1:40	
Small Groups: Real Drivers and Not Really Stumbling Blocks	1:40–2:00	
Break	2:00–2:15	
Case Study Conclusions: Keys to Data-Driven Culture	2:15–2:30	
Activity 7—Intro to Action (Part 1):	2:30–2:55	Flexible
View Film Clip	2:30–2:35	
Pair-Share	2:35–2:45	
Keys of Analysis	2:45–2:55	
Activity 6—Leading Effective Analysis Meetings:	2:55–3:45	Targeted
Role Play: Ineffective Analysis Meetings	2:55–3:05	
• Large Group: Identify Leadership Errors		
Principles to Leading Effective Analysis Meetings	3:05–3:20	
Role Play: Leading Effective Analysis Meetings	3:20–3:50	
Intro to Activity 9—Language of Leadership:	3:50–3:55	Targeted
Give preview for next day's activity		
Conclusions:	3:55–4:00	Flexible
Tales of success	3:55–4:00	

WORKSHOP OVERVIEW: THIRD HALF-DAY

Workshop Session:	Timing:	Format:
General Introduction: Recap learning from previous session	0:00–0:05	Flexible
Activity 9—Language of Leadership:	0:05–0:20	Targeted
Introduction to Power of Language	0:05–0:10	
Practice Responses to Faculty	0:10–0:20	
Activity 7—Principles of Action (Part 2):	0:20–0:50	Flexible
View Film Clip	0:20–0:30	
Pair-Share	0:30–0:40	
Keys of Action	0:40–0:50	
Review the Entire Framework: Key Drivers for Assessment, Analysis, Action, and Culture	0:50–1:00	Targeted
Calendar, Entry Plan, and Rubric:	1:00–1:45	Flexible
Present Sample Assessment Calendars—Differentiated by Elementary School, Middle School, or High School (depending on group)	1:00–1:10	
Tools for Launch: Implementation Calendar	1:10–1:20	
Tools for Evaluation: Implementation Rubric	1:20–1:30	
Break	1:30–1:45	—
Activity 8—Results Meeting Protocol:	1:45–2:55	Targeted
Introduce Results Meeting Protocol—Model	1:45–2:00	
School Teams: Results Meetings	2:00–2:50	
Reflection on Use of Protocol	2:50–2:55	
Activity 10—Start-up Scenarios—Confronting Obstacles: Present Case Studies and Pair-Share	2:55–3:20	Flexible
Answer Burning Questions from Participants:	3:20–3:45	Flexible
Conclusions:	3:45–4:00	Flexible
Move Clip	3:45–3:55	
Workshop Conclusions and Inspiring Stories	3:55–4:00	

Highlights from
the CD-ROM

DATA-DRIVEN IMPLEMENTATION RUBRIC

Data-Driven Instruction and Assessment

The rubric is intended to be used to assess the present state of data-driven instruction and assessment in a school. The rubric specifically targets interim assessments and the key drivers leading to increased student achievement.

Rating codes: 4 = Exemplary Implementation 3 = Proficient Implementation 2 = Beginning Implementation 1 = No Implementation

Data-Driven Culture	Rating
1. *Highly active leadership team:* Facilitate teacher-leader data analysis meetings after each interim assessment and maintain focus on the process throughout the year.	__/4
2. *Introductory professional development:* Teachers and leaders are introduced to data-driven instruction effectively—they understand how interim assessments define rigor and experience the process of analyzing results and adapting instruction.	__/4
3. *Implementation calendar:* Begin school year with a detailed calendar that includes time for assessment creation and adaptation, implementation, analysis, planning meetings, and re-teaching (flexible enough to accommodate district changes and mandates).	__/4
4. *Ongoing professional development:* Professional development calendar is aligned with data-driven instructional plan: includes modeling assessment analysis and action planning and is flexible enough to adapt to student learning needs.	__/4
5. *Build by borrowing:* Identify and implement best practices from high-achieving teachers and schools: visit schools and classrooms; share and disseminate resources and strategies.	__/4

Assessments	Literacy Rating	Math Rating
1. *Common interim assessments:* Assessments conducted four to six times per year.	__/4	__/4
2. *Transparent starting point:* Teachers see the assessments at the beginning of each cycle and use them to define the road map for teaching.	__/4	__/4
3. *Aligned to state tests and college readiness.*	__/4	__/4
4. *Aligned to instructional sequence* of clearly defined grade-level and content expectations.	__/4	__/4
5. *Re-assessed* previously taught standards.	__/4	__/4

Analysis	Rating
1. *Immediate turnaround* of assessment results (ideally within forty-eight hours).	__/4
2. *Data reports* provide user-friendly, succinct item-level analysis, standards-level analysis, and bottom-line results.	__/4
3. *Teacher-owned* analysis facilitated by effective leadership preparation.	__/4
4. *Test-in-hand* analysis between teacher and instructional leader.	__/4
5. *Deep* analysis moves beyond what students got wrong to answer why they got it wrong.	__/4

Action	Rating
1. *Planning:* Teachers plan new lessons collaboratively to develop new strategies based on data analysis.	__/4
2. *Implementation:* Explicit teacher action plans are implemented in whole-class instruction, small groups, tutorials, and before- or after-school support sessions.	__/4
3. *Ongoing assessment:* Teachers use in-the-moment checks for understanding and in-class assessment to ensure student progress between interim assessments.	__/4
4. *Accountability:* Instructional leaders review lesson and unit plans and give observation feedback driven by the action plan and student learning needs.	__/4
5. *Engaged students:* Students know the end goal, how they did, and what actions they are taking to improve.	__/4

TOTAL: ____/100

RESULTS MEETING PROTOCOL

Agenda for Teacher Teams When Looking at Interim Assessment Data

- *Identify roles:* Timer, facilitator, recorder (2 minutes)
- *Identify objective* to focus on (3 minutes unless objective is given)
- *What worked so far* (5 minutes) [Or: What teaching strategies did you try so far?]
- *Chief challenges* (5 minutes)
- *Brainstorm* proposed solutions (10 minutes)
- *Reflection:* Feasibility of each idea (5 minutes)
- *Consensus* around best actions (15 minutes)
- *Put in calendar:* When will the tasks happen? When will the teaching happen? (10 minutes)

(TOTAL TIME: 55 minutes; can be adjusted for more or less time)

Brainstorming Protocol	Reflection Protocol
Go in order around the circle: each person has 30 seconds to share a proposal	1 minute—silent personal/individual reflection on the list: what is doable and what isn't for each person
If you don't have an idea, say "Pass."	
No judgments should be made; if you like the idea, when it's your turn simply say, "I would like to add to that idea by . . . "	Go in order around the circle once: depending on size of group each person has 30-60 seconds to share their reflections.
Even if 4-5 people pass in a row, keep going for the full brainstorming time.	If a person doesn't have a thought to share, say "Pass" and come back to him/her later.

Consensus and Calendar Guidelines

- Identify key actions from brainstorming that everyone will agree to implement.
  - Make actions as specific as possible within the limited time.
- Identify key student-teacher guides or tasks needed to be done to be ready to teach.
  - Identify *who* will do each task.
  - Identify *when* each task will be done.
- Put date for re-teaching on *calendar*.
- Spend remaining time developing concrete elements of lesson plan:
  - Do Nows
  - Teacher guides (for example, what questions to ask the students or how to structure the activity)
  - Student guides, homework, and so on.

Results Meeting Protocol copyright © 2010 by Paul Bambrick-Santoyo. Adapted from Brazosport Texas School District Program.

INCREASING RIGOR THROUGHOUT THE LESSON: DATA-DRIVEN CLASSROOM BEST PRACTICES

1. Objectives: Rewrite and tighten with assessments in mind:

   - Connect objective to how the students will be assessed.

   - Write "know/do" objectives: Students will know _____ by doing _____ .

   - Look at test questions beforehand to be sure the skills assessed on the test were worked into the daily lesson.

   - Write an assessment of the skills immediately after the objective, at the top of the lesson plan.

   - First write assessment questions that align to obective; then break the objective into smaller chunks that will ensure mastery of all the skills needed to answer each question correctly.

   - Use verbs from Bloom's taxonomy to ensure that the objective is rigorous.

2. Do Now (five- to ten-minute individual exercise to start class):

   - Use Do Now as a re-teach tool: Write questions that students struggled to master on the last interim assessment.

   - Use mixed-format questions for a skill: multiple-choice, short answer, open-ended, and so on.

   - Organize questions sequentially according to difficulty.

   - Spiral objectives, skills, and questions from everything previously learned to keep student learning sharp.

   - Develop Do Now tracking sheet for teachers and students that shows student performance on the skills in each Do Now.

   - Make Do Nows that look like test questions and make sure they are reviewed in class.

Increasing Rigor Throughout the Lesson: Data-Driven Classroom Best Practices copyright © 2010 by Paul Bambrick-Santoyo.

- Observe students' answers during Do Now and note kids with wrong answers to follow up with them during oral review.

- Add multiple-choice questions to Do Now to allow real-time assessment.

- Add why and how questions (for example, Why did you choose this answer? How do you know your answer is correct?) for different levels of learners and to push thinking.

- Revisit yesterday's objectives in the Do Now.

- Collect and grade four straight Do Nows, and for the fifth day let students correct their first four Do Nows for extra points toward their Do Now grades.

3. Questioning to check for understanding and increase engagement:

- Develop whole class responses to student answers (for example, snap if you agree, stomp if you don't) to engage 100 percent participation.

- Use cold call: Avoid just calling on students with hands raised.

- Move from ping-pong to volleyball: Instead of responding to every student answer yourself, get other students to respond to each other: "Do you agree with Sam?" "Why is that answer correct (or incorrect)?" "What would you add?"

- Script questions in advance of the lesson to make sure they scaffold appropriately and address rigor at varied levels.

- Have an observer record teacher questions: highlight where students are succeeding and where they can grow.

3a. Student error (techniques for helping students encounter the right answer):

- Have a student who struggled initially repeat the correct answer eventually produced by the class.

Increasing Rigor Throughout the Lesson: Data-Driven Classroom Best Practices copyright © 2010 by Paul Bambrick-Santoyo.

- Use whiteboards to have every student write down a response to question: whole class shows answers simultaneously so teacher can immediately check to see how many students answered correctly.

- Write questions in plan to specific students who are struggling with a standard; jot down their responses in the plans during class.

- Note in your book or lesson plan what questions students answer incorrectly; call on them again when you revisit that sort of question later in the week.

- Choose "No opt out": do not let students off the hook when struggling with an answer.

3b. Think ratio (techniques to reduce teacher talk and push student thinking):

- Require students to support answers with evidence from the text.

- Feign ignorance (for example, write wrong answer that student gives on the board, let students find the error rather than correcting it yourself; pretend you don't even know that the answer is wrong).

- Ask students: "put it in your own words" about a classroom definition, concept, and so on.

- Reword question to force students to think on their feet about the same skill.

- Use Wait Time to give more students the chance to think through the answer.

- Model "Right is right": press to get the 100 percent correct answer.

- Check for student use of specific strategies and not just correct answers.

- Ask "what if" question: "What if" I took away this information from the problem, how would you approach it?

Increasing Rigor Throughout the Lesson: Data-Driven Classroom Best Practices copyright © 2010 by Paul Bambrick-Santoyo.

4. Differentiated instruction (teaching students at different levels):

- Create leveled questions for assessments.

- Include a bonus section of challenging questions.

- Prepare different Do Nows, worksheets, and so on for students at different levels.

- Use data (tracking sheets, interim assessment results, exit tickets) to determine the degree of scaffolding and extra support each student needs.

- Group students according to the skills they need to develop.

- Communicate and collaborate with skills room and special education teachers to develop appropriate scaffolding for special needs students.

- Implement station work.

- Create individual "work contracts" so students have a clear path of what they are working on.

- Use Do Now, exit tickets, and interim assessment data to drive small-group re-teach sessions.

- Create assignments with menu options by level (easy, medium, hard)—students can choose or teacher can assign.

- Have observers sit by lower-achieving students during an observation to provide extra support.

5. Peer-to-peer support strategies:

- Observe student work carefully during independent work—enlist strong students to help weaker students determine right answer during review of assignment.

- Have students teach parts of the lesson to small groups of their peers.

- Have students run stations.

- Train peer tutors—teach student tutors how to ask questions instead of giving answers and how to get tutee to do most of the talking.

Increasing Rigor Throughout the Lesson: Data-Driven Classroom Best Practices copyright © 2010 by Paul Bambrick-Santoyo.

- Think, pair, share: Have students think of the answer, talk with a partner, and then share as a large group.
- Turn and talk: students turn toward a partner and explain answers to a question.
- Peer to group: student models think-aloud.
- Implement peer editing and revision.
- Develop study groups that jigsaw activities and content.
- Create mentoring relationships: twelfth to tenth grade, eleventh to ninth grade, and so on.

6. Student self-evaluation:
- Create weekly skills check with a tracking chart: students track their own progress on each skill.
- Go over tests after grading them, discussing "Why is choice A wrong?" and similar questions.
- Have students grade their own papers based on a rubric.
- Give students independent practice worksheets with answers on the back so that students can check their own work once completed.
- Create a cumulative rubric (adding skills as taught): have students do periodic self-evaluations with the rubric.

7. Exit tickets (brief class-ending activity to check for understanding of that day's lesson):
- Create a tracking sheet to match the exit ticket.
- Assess the same skills through varied methods.
- Align format to interim assessment.
- Grade immediately.
- Immediately follow up (breakfast, lunch, home-room).
- Answer essential questions on exit ticket.

Increasing Rigor Throughout the Lesson: Data-Driven Classroom Best Practices copyright © 2010 by Paul Bambrick-Santoyo.

- Follow up data from exit ticket with next day's Do Now.
- Use exit ticket to determine small-group re-teach.
- Engage instructional leaders to design effective exit tickets for newer teachers.
- Monitor whether exit tickets reflect scope and sequence.

8. Homework:
- Develop homework center targeting specific skills identified by interim assessments.
- Review problem areas within homework assignment in class soon after assignment.
- Have students fix homework errors and teach them how to scrutinize errors.
- Make tracking sheet by skill.
- Incorporate spiraled review in homework assignments: include questions and tasks from previously learned standards.
- Create leveled homework (student-specific).
- Design homework that is aligned with interim assessments, state test, SAT.
- Use homework for open-book quizzes.
- Encourage homework completion with classwide or schoolwide competition.
- Include above-grade-level challenge problems.

STUDENT ASSESSMENT REFLECTION TEMPLATE
Williamsburg Collegiate Charter School

Name: _____ Assessment/Subject: _____ Date: _____

Question	Using the essential. . . . What skill was being tested?	Did you get the question right or wrong? Check the correct column.		Why did you get the question wrong? Be honest.	
		Right	Wrong	Careless mistake	Didn't know how to solve
1	Algebra substitution: add				
2	Algebra substitution: add 3 numbers				
3	Algebra substitution: subtract				
4	Translate word problems				
5	Solve equations				
6	Elapsed time—find end time				
7	Elapsed time—find elapsed time				
8	Elapsed time—word problem				
9	Elapsed time—word problem				
10	Elapsed time—word problem				
11	Switch out				
12	Switch out				
13	Switch out				
14	Switch out				
15	Switch out				
16	2 by 1 multiplication				
17	2 by 1 multiplication				
18	2 by 1 multiplication				
19	2 by 1 word problem multiplication				
20	2 by 1 word problem multiplication				
21	Choose the correct operation				
22	Choose the correct operation				
23	Choose the correct operation				
24	Choose the correct operation				
25	Choose the correct operation				

Reflection

1. Which test did you do the best on? Why do you think you do well on this test?

   _____

   _____

   _____

2. Which test are you not proud of? Why not?

   _____

   _____

   _____

3. How many checks do you have in the column marked careless errors?

   √ Are you happy with this number? If yes, why? If no, why not?

   _____

   _____

   _____

4. How many checks do you have in the column marked didn't know how to solve?

   √ What should you have done before the test?

   _____

   _____

   _____

   √ What do you plan to do in the future?

   _____

   _____

   _____

5. Name three skills you need extra help on before moving into the next unit.

   _____

   _____

   _____

- Now begin making corrections on both quiz 5 and quiz 6.
- You will make corrections on the exam.
- If you do not know how to solve a problem, star it on the table you just filled out.

To prepare for our next unit, we want to help you find out a little more about yourself, your test taking style and how you can SHINE on assessments.

Using your test reflections, please fill out the following table.

Type of Error	Careless Errors	Did Not Know How to Solve
Number of Errors		

On the following grid, plot this data in a bar graph.

_____

(title)

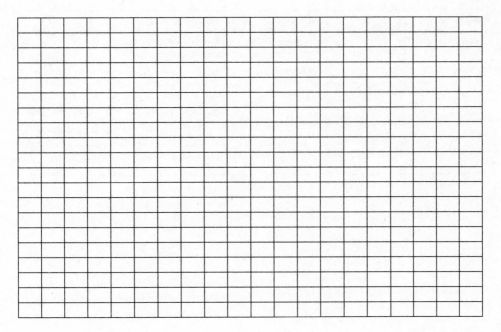

Based on the information on the graph, you will be able to learn more about your learning and test-taking style.

If you have …	You are a …	In class you …	During class you should …	During assessments you should …
More careless errors than "don't know's" …	RUSHING ROGER	Are one of the first students to finish the independent practice Want to say your answer before you write it Often don't show work Get assessments back and are frustrated	SLOW DOWN! Ask the teacher to check your work or check with a partner Push yourself for perfection, don't just tell yourself "I get it." Take time to slow down and explain your thinking to your classmates Keep track of your mistakes, look to see if you keep making the same ones over and over	SLOW DOWN. You know you tend to rush, so make yourself slow down. REALLY double-check your work (since you know you tend to make careless errors) Use inverse operations when you have extra time
More "don't know's" than careless errors	BACK-SEAT BETTY	Not always sure that you understand how to do independent work Are sometimes surprised by your quiz scores	Ask questions about the previous night's homework if you're not sure it's perfect Do all of the problems with the class at the start of class Use every opportunity to check in with classmates and teachers to see if you're doing problems correctly	Do the problems you're SURE about first Take your time on the others and use everything you know Ask questions right after the assessment while things are still fresh in your mind

Are you a Rushing Roger? **Then answer question #1**

1. In your classwork and homework, if you notice you keep making similar careless errors, what you should you do?

_____

_____

_____

Are you a Back-Seat Betty? **Then answer question #2**

2. When you get a low score on a quiz, what should you do?

_____

_____

_____

DATA-DRIVEN ANALYSIS MEETINGS

Leading Effective One-to-One Assessment Analysis Meetings Around Interim Assessment Results

---

Precursors for Effective Analysis Meetings

Before Giving Interim Assessment

- *Six weeks prior:* Teachers review assessment and plan toward the rigor of those assessments.
- *A few weeks prior:* Teachers predict student performance on each assessment question, choosing one of three options:
  a) Confident they'll get it right
  b) Not sure
  c) No way they'll get it right
- *Professional development (timing flexible):* Teachers receive model of how to do assessment analysis and complete action plan, and they see model of effective and ineffective analysis meetings.

Immediately Following Interim Assessment Administration

- *Teacher analysis:* Teachers do analysis of results prior to meeting, trying to answer fundamental question: *Why* did the students not learn it?
- *Teacher action plan:* Teachers complete action plans.
- *Leader analysis:* Leader analyzes teacher results personally in preparation for the meetings.
- *Review of teacher plans:* Instructional leader collects each teacher's action plan and analysis in advance and makes sure it meets pre-established expectations.
  Content expertise: If the subject in the assessment is beyond the expertise of the instructional leader, the leader identifies an expert within or outside of school to call on for extra support.

Data-Driven Analysis Meetings copyright © 2010 by Paul Bambrick-Santoyo.

Conversation Starters and Re-Directors
During Analysis Meetings

Starters

- "Congratulations on the improvement on _____ from last time!"
- "So . . . what's the data telling you?"

Re-Directors for Resistant Comments

- "Let's look at question ___. Why did the students get it wrong?"
- "What did the students need to be able to do the get that question right? How was this more than what they are able to do with you in class?"
- "What's so interesting is that they did really well on question #___ but struggled on question #___ on the same standard. Why do you think that is?"

Synthesizer for Quality Analysis

- "So what you're saying is . . . [paraphrase and improve good responses]."

Action Triggers

- "So let's review your action plan and make sure we have all these ideas incorporated."
- [When new analysis and action is proposed during the meeting] "Let's go back to your action plan and add these new actions."

Key Principles for Leading Analysis Meetings

- Let the data do the talking.
- Let the teacher do the talking. (Or if necessary, push the teacher to do so!)
- Always go back to specific questions on the test.
- Don't fight the battles on ideological lines. (In the larger picture, you'll lose.)
- You've got to know the data yourself to lead an analysis meeting effectively.
- Keep in mind the difference between the first assessment and the third.
- Make sure the analysis is connected to a concrete action plan you can verify.

Data-Driven Analysis Meetings copyright © 2010 by Paul Bambrick-Santoyo.

ENTRY PLAN FOR DATA-DRIVEN INSTRUCTION: NEW SCHOOL START-UP

Implementation Calendar

As Soon as Possible (Spring or Summer)—Assessment *Adopt and apply rubric metrics to ensure completion (all in "Assessment" section): Common, Aligned, Reassesses, Wrong Answers, and Transparent.*

Build a full plan for interim assessments for the following school year:

- Acquire quality interim assessments, build your own, or supplement existing assessments using the Interim Assessment Checklist as guide.

- Change curriculum scope and sequence to match interim assessments that will be used (or vice versa).

- Identify who will help you complete the assessment and curriculum adjustment process to be ready for launch by the beginning of the school year.

Grade your school with the implementation rubric in the category of "assessment," identifying where the school stands and where you need to be before the school year begins.

Support Materials: "Interim Assessment Review" checklist (see Appendix and CD-ROM).

Summer—Culture *Adopt and apply rubric metrics to ensure completion (all in "Culture" section): Calendar, Leadership Team Training, Professional Development Plan, Vision.*

The following items should be completed:

- Create a detailed Assessment Calendar that includes assessment creation, assessment implementation, scoring and analysis dates, teacher–instructional leader meetings, and re-teaching time (see Assessment section of CD-ROM for prototypes to follow).

Entry Plan for Data-Driven Instruction: New School Start-Up copyright © 2010 by Paul Bambrick-Santoyo.

- Create a skeletal Professional Development Calendar that includes launch of data-driven model, training for staff in analysis, time for scoring and analyzing, training staff to develop new lesson plans, and other key meetings (see professional development ideas in Part 2).
- Create a detailed plan for the training of the school's leadership team.
- Have the first professional development session planned for launch.

Plan training for your leadership team (your formal leadership team and the informal staff leaders).

Support Materials: Assessment Calendars (see Appendix and CD-ROM).

September—Assessment and Culture *Evaluate all the rubric metrics in "Assessment" and "Culture."*

You should have evidence of each of the following:

- An opening professional development session has been held with the faculty, presenting the data-driven instructional model.
- The first interim assessments (or the closest proxy) are finalized and comply with each aspect of the assessment rubric in reading, writing, and math.
- The teachers have already seen the first interim assessments (or the closest proxy) so that they can plan for mastery ("Transparency").

Review your protocols for lesson plan supervision and walk-throughs or observations.

- Improve the lesson plan reviews and observations to support the data-driven instructional model.

Develop plan to determine how test scoring and analysis will be completed.

- Use all staff to accomplish this task.

Support Materials: See Part Two of *Driven by Data* (Chapters Six through Twelve).

Entry Plan for Data-Driven Instruction: New School Start-Up copyright © 2010 by Paul Bambrick-Santoyo.

October — Analysis   *Evaluate all the rubric metrics in "Analysis" and two metrics in "Action"—new lesson plans and teacher action plans.*

Prior to first interim assessment, have teachers predict performance, marking each question as follows:

- "Confident" (sure that the students will get it right)
- "Not sure"
- "No way" (students will definitely get it wrong)

Administer the first interim assessment.

Make sure Teacher Analysis and Action Plan templates are in place.

Principal and instructional leaders run test-in-hand analysis meetings with teachers.

- Principal runs meetings or observes other instructional leaders in action.
- After the meetings, principal gives feedback to other instructional leaders about how to facilitate the meeting more effectively in the future Principal makes point to attend team meetings where teacher teams plan new lessons.

Support Materials: See Appendix and CD-ROM: "Data-Driven Analysis Meetings" and "Assessment Analysis Sheet and Instructional Plan" template.

November — Action   *Evaluate all the rubric metrics, with focus on "Action."*

The second assessment is in the hands of the teachers, so they can plan backward from it.

Run Results Meetings to plan to re-teach challenging standards.

Have teachers add rigor to their lesson using "Increasing Rigor Throughout the Lesson: Data-Driven Classroom Best Practices."

The principal does a formal school review and walk-through with other instructional leaders.

Entry Plan for Data-Driven Instruction: New School Start-Up copyright © 2010 by Paul Bambrick-Santoyo.

- Review lesson plans: Is there evidence of implementation of teacher action plans from the assessment analysis meetings?
- Observe classes: Is there evidence of implementation of teacher action plans? Can you identify examples of changed teaching practices?

The leadership team completes full mid-semester evaluation of the school based on the entire data-driven instruction implementation rubric.

Support Materials: See Appendix and CD-ROM: "Results Meeting Protocol," "Increasing Rigor Throughout the Lesson: Data-Driven Classroom Best Practices," and "Data-Driven Implementation Rubric."

December — June *Repeat interim assessment cycle mentioned above:*

- Teachers see interim assessment in advance
- Teachers predict performance
- Administer interim assessment
- Teachers complete Assessment Analysis Instructional Plans
- Instructional leaders and teachers participate in test-in-hand analysis meetings
- Run Results Meetings
- Teacher implement action plans
- Leaders observe for implementation

Entry Plan for Data-Driven Instruction: New School Start-Up copyright © 2010 by Paul Bambrick-Santoyo.

ENTRY PLAN FOR DATA-DRIVEN INSTRUCTION: NEW PRINCIPAL IN EXISTING SCHOOL

Implementation Calendar

As Soon as Possible (Spring or Summer)

Perform a culture, power, and networking audit.

- Interview as many staff members and leaders as possible and acquire answers to the following questions:
    - Who are the people you most admire in the school?
    - Who are the teachers who you look to the most as model teachers?
    - Who do you work most closely with/trust the most?
    - (Indirectly) Who on the staff do you spend time with outside of school activities?
    - Who do you turn to for advice?
- Create a networking map with your answers.
- Create a web: put first teacher's name on board and note the names of the others that teacher goes to for advice.
- Create a second web: teachers the first one most trusts.
- As you add more teachers to the board, connect them as they mention the people they work with most or are closest to.
- Upon completion, identify the *hubs*: the teachers and staff members who are most connected to others and could have the biggest pull when launching a project.

Make a list of teachers most identified for their high-quality teaching.

(If possible) Do a walk-through of the school in session.

- Visit as many classrooms as you possibly can.
- Based on your gut reaction to these thirty-second classroom visits, identify the teachers who seem to be the strongest and those who will need the most support.

Entry Plan for Data-Driven Instruction: New Principal in Existing School copyright © 2010 by Paul Bambrick-Santoyo.

Gather a teacher group of the hubs identified in the school and present your plan for the upcoming school year.

- State that you want their feedback but that you will make the final decision.
- Invite those who are willing to help you launch the project.

Support materials: "Informal Networks: The Company Behind the Chart." (Purchase from *Harvard Business Review*.)

Summer—Assessment *Adopt and apply rubric metrics to ensure completion (all in "Assessment" section): Common, Aligned, Re-assesses, Wrong Answers, and Transparent.*

Build a full plan for interim assessments for the following school year:

- Acquire or develop city-specific assessments to replace or supplement the assessment you are currently using.
- Change curriculum scope and sequence to match interim assessments that will be used (or vice versa).
- Identify who will help you complete the assessment and curriculum adjustment process to be ready for launch by the beginning of the school year.

(If possible) Grade your school with the implementation rubric in the category of "Assessment," identifying where the school stands and where you need to be before the school year begins.

Support materials: "Interim Assessment Review" checklist in Appendix and CD-ROM.

Summer—Culture *Adopt and apply rubric metrics to ensure completion (all in "Culture" section): Calendar, Leadership Team Training, Professional Development Plan, Vision.*

Entry Plan for Data-Driven Instruction: New Principal in Existing School copyright © 2010 by Paul Bambrick-Santoyo.

Complete the following items:

- Create a detailed assessment calendar that includes assessment creation, assessment implementation, scoring and analysis dates, teacher–instructional leader meetings, and re-teaching time (coaches are given a prototype to follow—based on models in this Appendix).
- Create a skeletal professional development calendar that includes launch of data-driven model, training for staff in analysis, time for scoring and analyzing, training staff to develop new lesson plans, and other key meetings.
- Create a detailed plan for the training of the school's leadership team.
- Have the first professional development session planned for launch.
- Based on the size of your school staff, plan how to have effective face time with teachers (you or one of your other instructional leaders).

Plan training for your leadership team (your formal leadership team and the informal staff leaders identified in your network audit).

Grade your school with the implementation rubric in the categories of "Culture" and "Assessment," identifying where the school stands and where you need to be before the school year begins.

Support Materials: See Part Two of *Driven by Data* (Chapters Six through Twelve).

September—Assessment and Culture *Evaluate all the rubric metrics in "Assessment" and "Culture."*

You should have evidence of each of the following:

- An opening professional development session has been held with the faculty, presenting the data-driven instructional model.

Entry Plan for Data-Driven Instruction: New Principal in Existing School copyright © 2010 by Paul Bambrick-Santoyo.

- The first interim assessments (or the closest proxy) are finalized and comply with each aspect of the assessment rubric in reading, writing, and math.

- The teachers have already seen the first interim assessments (or the closest proxy) so that they can plan for mastery ("Transparency").

Review your protocols for lesson plan supervision and walk-throughs or observations.

- Improve the lesson plan reviews and observations to support the data-driven instructional model.

Develop a plan to determine how test scoring and analysis will be completed.

- Use all staff to accomplish this task.

Support Materials: See Part Two of *Driven by Data* (Chapters Six through Twelve).

October — Analysis *Evaluate all the Rubric metrics in "Analysis," plus two metrics in "Action"—new lesson plans and teacher action plans.*

Prior to first interim assessment, have teachers predict performance, marking each question as follows:

- "Confident" (sure that the students will get it right)

- "Not sure"

- "No way" (students will definitely get it wrong)

Administer the first interim assessment.

Make sure Teacher Analysis and Action Plan templates are in place.

Principal and instructional leaders run test-in-hand analysis meetings with teachers.

- Principal runs meetings or observes other instructional leaders in action.

- After the meetings, principal gives feedback to other instructional leaders about how to facilitate the meeting more effectively in the future.
- Principal makes point to attend team meetings where teacher teams plan new lessons.

Support Materials: See Appendix and CD-ROM: "Data-Driven Analysis Meetings" and "Assessment Analysis Sheet and Instructional Plan" template.

November — Action *Evaluate all the rubric metrics, with focus on "Action."*

- The second assessment is in the hands of the teachers, so they can plan backward from it.
- Run Results Meetings to plan to re-teach challenging standards.
- Have teachers add rigor to their lessons using "Increasing Rigor Throughout the Lesson."
- The principal does a formal school review and walk-through with other instructional leaders.
  - Review lesson plans: Is there evidence of implementation of teacher action plans from the assessment analysis meetings?
  - Observe classes: Is there evidence of implementation of teacher action plans? Can you identify examples of changed teaching practices?
- The leadership team completes full mid-semester evaluation of the school based on the entire data-driven instruction implementation rubric.

Support Materials: See Appendix and CD-ROM: "Results Meeting Protocol," "Increasing Rigor Throughout the Lesson," and "Data-Driven Implementation Rubric."

Entry Plan for Data-Driven Instruction: New Principal in Existing School copyright © 2010 by Paul Bambrick-Santoyo.

December Through June — Repeat *Continue to run through the interim assessment cycle:*

- Teachers see interim assessment in advance.
- Teachers predict performance.
- Administer interim assessment.
- Teachers complete Assessment Analysis Instructional Plans.
- Instructional leaders and teachers participate in test-in-hand analysis meetings.
- Run Results Meetings.
- Teachers implement action plans.
- Leaders observe for implementation.

MIDDLE SCHOOL INTERIM ASSESSMENT CALENDAR

Time Frame:	Unit or Assessment:	Notes:
8 weeks (8/25–10/10)	Unit 1	
3 days (10/13—10/15)	North Star Assessment #1	Approximately 1 hour per assessment. Aligned State Test objectives for 8 weeks
1 week (10/20—10/24)	RE-TEACH Objectives from interim assessment #1	Re-teach based on test results analysis
7 weeks (10/24—12/8)	Unit 2	
4 days (12/11–12/14)	Interim Assessment #2	Cumulative: all objectives from Units 1 and 2 (@ 1:20 hours per exam)
1 week (12/15—12/19)	RE-TEACH Objectives from interim assessments 1 and 2	Re-teach based on test results analysis
6 weeks (1/2—2/9)	Unit 3	
4 days (2/9–2/13);	Interim Assessment #3	Cumulative: All objectives from units 1–3 (@ 1:40 hours/exam)
1 week (2/16—2/20)	RE-TEACH Objectives from NSA 1–3	Re-teach based on test results analysis
6 weeks (2/20—4/3)	Unit 4	
1 week (4/6-4/10);	North Star Assessment #4	Cumulative: all objectives from units 1–4 (about 2 hours/exam)
2-3 weeks (4/13—4/27)	Re-teach of Units 1–4, and Test Preparation	
STATE TEST (4/28-5/1)	STATE TESTING	
5 weeks (5/5—6/10)	Unit 5	
1 week (6/12-6/19)	Final Performance Task Preparation	
1 week (6/22–6/26)	Final Performance Tasks	Oral presentations and large math projects

Middle School Interim Assessment Calendar copyright © 2010 by North Star Schools.

ELEMENTARY SCHOOL INTERIM ASSESSMENT CALENDAR

Time Frame:	Unit or Assessment:	Notes:
12 days (9/10–9/21)	Math and STEP Pre-Tests	STEP assessments done during reading blocks
6 weeks (9/24–11/2)	Unit 1	
1 week (11/5–11/9); 6 weeks after preceding assessment	STEP Assessment #1 and NSA Math #1	STEP Individual Assessment Math: 10 Questions
1 week (11/12—11/16)	MATH RE-TEACH Objectives from NSA 1	Re-teach based on test results analysis
3 days (11/12–11/21)	Sight Word Assessment	
4 weeks (11/19—12/14)	Unit 2 (re-teach sight words for 1 week)	
1 week (12/10–12/14)	Sight Word Assessment	
1 week (12/10–12/14) 6 weeks after preceding assessment	STEP Assessment #2 and NSA Math #2	STEP Individual Assessment Math: 15 Questions
1 1/2 weeks (1/3—1/11)	MATH RE-TEACH Objectives from NSA 1 and 2	Re-teach based on test results analysis
1 week (1/14–1/18)	Sight Word Assessment	
5 weeks (1/14—2/15)	Unit 3	
1 week (2/18–2/22)	STEP Assessment #3 and NSA Math #3	STEP Individual Assessment Math: 20 Questions
4 days (2/25–2/28)	Sight Word Assessment	
6 weeks (2/22—4/11)	Unit 4	Re-teach based on test results analysis
1 week (4/5–4/11)	Sight Word Assessment	
1 week (4/14–4/18) 6 weeks after preceding assessment	STEP Assessment #4	STEP Individual Assessment
6 weeks (4/21—5/30)	Re-teach of Units 1–4, and Test Preparation	
1 week (4/28–5/2)	Practice TerraNova Assessment (ELA and NSA Math #4)	ELA: 40 Questions, 50 minutes; Math: 30 Questions, 40 minutes
4 weeks (5/5—5/29)	Unit 5	Preparation for all objectives and TerraNova testing
1 week (6/9–6/13)	TerraNova Testing	
1 week (6/16–6/20) 8 weeks after preceding assessment	STEP Assessment #5	STEP Individual Assessment
1 week (6/23–6/27)	Rising Stars Ceremony	Oral presentations and large math projects

Note: This calendar does not provide dates for writing compositions, which are often done concurrently with sight word or STEP assessments.

Elementary School Interim Assessment Calendar copyright © 2010 by North Star Schools.

Living the Learning Model

An Effective Approach for Leading Adult Professional Development

- Design *airtight activities* that lead participants to the right conclusion with minimal redirecting by facilitator.
- Facilitate substantive *reflection* and *sharing* time that allows participants to draw the conclusion from the activity.
- *Frame* the participants' conclusions with the formal vocabulary of the associated principles so that participants share one common language.
- Provide ample opportunities to *apply* the learning in simulated and real-world experiences.

Overall, *manage time well* and *inspire* by sharing a vision of success: we always want stories that show it can be done!

AIRTIGHT ACTIVITIES Align to Objective, Plan Tightly, Relevant	
Teaching Video Clips	**Movie Clips**
Focus on the positive.	Make sure clip is explicitly connected to learning objective.
Provide Precise focus questions *before* showing clip.	Provide precise focus questions *before* showing clip.
Keep clips short.	Keep clips short.
Case Studies	**Role Plays and Simulations**
Embed every professional development objective in well-written case:	Keep a tight schedule and follow detailed procedures.
• Type 1: Solving problems — for participants with expertise. (Results Meeting)	Set explicit guidelines for skills participants will be practicing and observing during activity.
• Type 2: Learn from failure — to check for understanding and to set the stage for positive learning.	Have as many people directly participating as possible.
• Type 3: Success story: build expertise by identifying the key drivers of success.	Keep role plays short; include time for feedback.

Living the Learning Model copyright © 2010 by Paul Bambrick-Santoyo.

| AIRTIGHT ACTIVITIES | |
Align to Objective, Plan Tightly, Relevant	
Teaching Video Clips	**Movie Clips**
Large-Group Sharing	Reflection and Framing
Start from the end goal: identify what you want participants to say.	Keep reflection brief and written in one place
Ask questions that lead participants to goal. (Offer scaffolding, nudge rather than drag, play volleyball and not ping-pong.)	Wait until the end for framing; let participants do the cognitive work.
	Limit the words; be succinct and precise.
Small-Group Sharing	Application
Have explicit instructions and protocol.	Make it as directly connected to participants' work as possible (lesson plans, teaching role play).
Be intentional about grouping participants; simple affinity groups are rarely most effective.	Combine with follow-up activities after the workshop to guarantee effective implementation.
Track group progress; check for understanding and adjust times as needed.	

Living the Learning Model copyright © 2010 by Paul Bambrick-Santoyo.

INTERIM ASSESSMENT REVIEW

State Test Being Used as Reference Point: _____ State: _____ Subject: _____ Grade level: _____

Interim Assessment Being Reviewed: _____ Source: _____ Subject: _____ Grade level: _____
Time of Year (#1, #2, etc.): _____

- "Yes" indicates item is aligned in this category
- "No" and a comment indicate a concern (add as long a comment as you feel necessary to address the concern with the question)

Interim Assessment Item	The Right Content	The Right Format	The Right College-Ready Expectations	Comments
	Addresses the same standards, and addresses the standards as rigorously as the state test.	Reflects format and type of questions from state exam. If applicable, reflects format of and types of questions from exam. Rubrics are used, if applicable. Wrong answers illuminate misunderstanding.	Rigor and content seem appropriate for developing college-bound students. Content is "State test plus" in areas where state test is not college-preparatory. More complex than state tests (require additional critical thinking and application). More standards covered within the test and within the same question.	Comments and suggestions to improve question.
1				
2				
3				
4				
5				
6				
7				
8				

Interim Assessment Review copyright © 2010 by Paul Bambrick-Santoyo

Interim Assessment Item	The Right Content	The Right Format	The Right College-Ready Expectations	Comments
9				
10				
11				
12				
13				
14				
15				

OVERALL

Given this review, what are the key action steps to strengthen this assessment?

_____

_____

_____

_____

_____

NORTH STAR ASSESSMENT ANALYSIS SHEET AND INSTRUCTIONAL PLAN FOR TEACHER:

NSA Number and Subject: _____ Grade/Class: _____ Date _____

Standards Analysis	Analysis of Why Students Did Not Learn Standard	Instructional Plan—What Techniques Will You Use to Address These Standards
What standards warrant more time for whole-class instruction, re-teaching and review		
Whole class instruction:		

Small-Group Instruction:		Instructional Plan How or When Will You Structure Small-Group Instruction
What standards warrant more time for small-group instruction and review?		
. . .		

North Star Assessment Analysis Sheet and Instructional Plan copyright © 2010 by North Star Schools

CUMULATIVE AND TARGETED REVIEW OF STANDARDS

Write the standards you will address with each of the following

Spiral in Homework	Spiral in Do Now	Do Mini-Lesson	Do Now with Mini-Lesson	Spiral in Quizzes or Tests

Students of Major Concern	What They Need Most Help With	Instructional Plan—When or How Will They Get Tutored, Supported, Addressed
• • • • • •		

SIX-WEEK INSTRUCTIONAL PLAN FOR _____

WEEK 1—Date _____	WEEK 2—Date _____	WEEK 3—Date _____
Standards for Review	Standards for Review	Standards for Review
New Standards	New Standards	New Standards

WEEK 4—Date _____	WEEK 5—Date _____	WEEK 6—Date _____
Standards for Review	Standards for Review	Standards for Review
New Standards	New Standards	New Standards

ECS ASSESSMENT ANALYSIS SHEET AND INSTRUCTIONAL PLAN FOR TEACHER: *JACKSON/MILLER*

ECS Number and Subject: _ELA 3–2_   **Grade/Class:** _Cornell_   **Date:** _11/15/####_

CUMULATIVE REVIEW OF PROFICIENT STANDARDS—Write the standards you will address with each of the following			
Spiral in Homework	**Spiral in Do Now**	**Do Mini-Lesson**	**Spiral in Quizzes or Tests**
All reading standards	Capitalization and Punctuation	NA	All reading standards; sentences in context
Small-Group Instruction: What standards warrant more time for small-group instruction and review?		**Instructional Plan** How or When Will You Structure Small-Group Instruction	
• Fact versus Opinion			

Standards Analysis Whole-Class Instruction: What standards warrant more time for whole-class instruction, re-teaching and review?	Analysis of Why Students Did Not Learn the Standard	Instructional Plan—What Techniques Will You Use to Address These Standards
Sequencing (right after; middle event is OK)	SEQ #6, 12: Students didn't look *close enough* to the original event; they chose the second- or third-closest event after. Didn't highlight the *right after* concept enough.	Students will list every action that occurs between two events, concluding with how much can occur in a short period of time.
	SEQ #17: didn't read question closely enough. Confused two similar events (string to tooth and string to bedpost).	Practice "right after" in questioning: challenge students to find something that happens even closer to the action than what their peer says during the conversation.
Inference	INF #7 and 14: Students aced #7, so they can draw global conclusions. On #14, they couldn't make a specific inference about something missing. We haven't drawn such small, specific inferences in class.	In select passages, identify elements needed to make something happen that are not listed in the story explicitly (for example, you need a knife to make peanut butter and jelly sandwiches). Identify actions that had to have happened (but are not mentioned explicitly) for the character to be the current situation.
Supporting details	SD #18: Students can find events when asked, but can't find *evidence* to support an argument. We haven't done enough examples like these. They also struggle *writing* answers more than talking through them or identifying them.	Have students find evidence in the text for a character's feelings or personality. Make them point to the example and summarize it.
Character	CH: Students could easily identify a character's feelings (#24) but struggled with character (#20, especially when could be confused with *details* of the story or another character).	Students need much more practice writing down conclusions and supporting details.
Most important details	MID #21: Students don't know "most important," especially when given lots of information to choose from.	Practice more inferential character analysis: what can you conclude about their character? Use FOCUS inference book to help in this development.

Standards Analysis Whole-Class Instruction: What standards warrant more time for whole-class instruction, re-teaching and review?	Analysis of Why Students Did Not Learn the Standard	Instructional Plan—What Techniques Will You Use to Address These Standards
Vocabulary context	Students don't know techniques for finding meaning in words around the unknown word. This also trips them up when answering questions with an unknown (like "risk taker" today).	Students write lists of details and events from a passage they have read and then have to choose the most important and justify their answer. Generate similar lists as a group, and present the group with other lists of details and events. Teach strategies for determining meaning of an unknown word.
Students of Major Concern	What They Need Most Help With	Instructional Plan—When or How Will They Get Tutored, Supported, Addressed
Tryiq and Najee	Inference, sequence of events, character, supporting details, and writing in general.	Make these standards bigger part of their work with Ms. Ferrell and Ms. Arnold.
Zayyir, Dasir, Malik S., Lebarone, Jordan	Real problems with writing, even simple one- or two-sentence responses.	Need systemic approach to writing across the board, with specific support to this group (pending larger conversation about third-grade writing).

Notes

Introduction

1. Name changed to protect privacy of the student.

Chapter One

1. Many sources provide extensive discussion of interim assessments and their effectiveness. For a further in-depth look at the research, consult the following titles: "What is a 'Professional Learning Community'?" by Richard DuFour, *Educational Leadership*, May 2004 (*Marshall Memo* 38, #1); "Using Data/Getting Results: A Practical Guide for School Improvement in Mathematics" by Nancy Love, *Harvard Educational Review*, Spring 2004 (*Marshall Memo* 30, #3); "Seven Practices for Effective Learning" by Jay McTighe and Ken O'Connor, *Educational Leadership*, November 2005 (*Marshall Memo* 110, #1); "Teamwork on Assessments Creates Powerful Professional Development" by Jay McTighe and Marcella Emberger, *Journal of Staff Development*, Winter 2006 (*Marshall Memo* 117, #4); "The Mathematics Assessment Collaborative: Performance Testing to Improve Instruction" by David Foster and Pendred Noyce, *Phi Delta Kappan*, January 2004 (*Marshall Memo* 20, #1); *The Results Fieldbook* by Mike Schmoker (ASCD, 2001), pp. 8–25, 101–119, 120–132; *Accountability In Action* by Douglas Reeves (Advanced Learning Press, 2000), pp. 67–68, 189–195; *Learning by Doing: A Handbook*

for Professional Learning Communities at Work by Richard DuFour and others (Solution Tree, 2006).

2. See "Inside the Black Box: Raising Standards Through Classroom Assessment" by Paul Black and Dylan Wiliam, *Phi Delta Kappan*, October 1998; "Working Inside the Black Box: Assessment for Learning in the Classroom" by Paul Black, Christine Harrison, Clare Lee, Bethan Marshall, and Dylan Wiliam, *Phi Delta Kappan*, September 2004; "Classroom Assessment Minute by Minute, Day by Day" by Siobhan Leahy, Christine Lyon, Marnie Thompson, and Dylan Wiliam, *Educational Leadership*, November 2005; "From Formative Assessment to Assessment FOR Learning: A Path to Success in Standards-Based Schools" by Rick Stiggins, *Phi Delta Kappan*, December 2005; "Looking at Student Work for Teacher Learning, Teacher Community, and School Reform" by Judith Warren Little, Maryl Gearhart, Marnie Curry, and Judith Kafka, *Phi Delta Kappan*, November 2003; *Classroom Assessment That Works* by Robert Marzano, Debra Pickering, and Jane Pollock (ASCD, 2001), pp. 96–102; *The Art and Science of Teaching* by Robert Marzano (ASCD, 2007); *Educative Assessment* by Grant Wiggins (Jossey-Bass, 1998), pp. 43–69.

3. This book also includes an extensive bibliography of the books and articles that support this understanding of interim assessments. Please use those as a research foundation for the premises presented in this book.

4. *Rethinking Teacher Supervision and Evaluation: How to Work Smart, Build Collaboration, and Close the Achievement Gap* by Kim Marshall (Jossey-Bass, 2009), Chapter 5.

Chapter Three

1. "Classroom Assessment Minute by Minute, Day by Day" by Siobhan Leahy, Christine Lyon, Marnie Thompson, and Dylan Wiliam, *Educational Leadership*, November 2005; "High-Stakes Testing: Can Rapid Assessment Reduce the Pressure?" by Stuart Yeh, *Teachers College Record*, April 2006.

2. "What is a 'Professional Learning Community'?" by Richard DuFour, *Educational Leadership*, May 2004.

3. Originally highlighted as a part of Mike Schmoker's *The Results Fieldbook* (ASCD, 2001), pp. 101–119.

4. Rick Stiggins and Jan Chappuis have done extensive research on the importance of student involvement in the assessment process. Two of those articles are "Using Student-Involved Classroom Assessment to Close Achievement Gaps" by Rick Stiggins and Jan Chappuis, *Theory Into Practice*, Winter 2005, and "Assessment Through the Student's Eyes" by Rick Stiggins, *Educational Leadership*, May 2007.

Chapter Four

1. "Promoting a Collaborative Professional Culture in Three Elementary Schools That Have Beaten the Odds" by David Strahan, *Elementary School Journal*, November 2003; "Virginia's Excellent Adventure" by Kathy Christie, *Phi Delta Kappan*, April 2004; "Inside the Black Box of High-Performing High-Poverty Schools" by Patricia Kannapel and Stephen Clements, Prichard Committee for Academic Excellence, Lexington, Kentucky, 2005; "One Subject at a Time" by Catherine Gewertz, *Education Week*, February 2, 2005.
2. "Using Test Score Data to Focus Instruction" by Susan Trimble, Anne Gay, and Jan Matthews, *Middle School Journal*, March 2005.
3. "Informal Networks: The Company Behind the Chart" by David Krackhardt and Jeffrey Hanson, *Harvard Business Review*, July-August, 1993.

Chapter Six

1. Ed Sousa highlights the recent findings in brain research that support connecting with participants' emotions and having them use their experiences to apply concepts in creative ways. You can read more in his article: "Brain-Friendly Learning for Teachers," *Educational Leadership*, June 2009.

Bibliography

The following books and articles give extensive background to the field of interim assessments and data-driven instruction. This book builds on the learnings from these sources.

Interim and Benchmark Assessments

"Data in the Driver's Seat" by Paul Bambrick-Santoyo, *Educational Leadership*, December 2007/January 2008, pp. 43–46.

"What Is a 'Professional Learning Community'?" by Richard DuFour, *Educational Leadership*, May 2004.

Learning by Doing: *A Handbook for Professional Learning Communities at Work* by Richard DuFour et al. (Solution Tree, 2006).

"The Mathematics Assessment Collaborative: Performance Testing to Improve Instruction" by David Foster and Pendred Noyce, *Phi Delta Kappan*, January 2004.

"Using Data/Getting Results: A Practical Guide for School Improvement in Mathematics" by Nancy Love, *Harvard Educational Review*, Spring 2004.

"Teamwork on Assessments Creates Powerful Professional Development" by Jay McTighe and Marcella Emberger, *Journal of Staff Development*, Winter 2006.

"Seven Practices for Effective Learning" by Jay McTighe and Ken O'Connor, *Educational Leadership*, November 2005.

Accountability in Action by Douglas Reeves (Advanced Learning Press, 2000), pp. 67–68, 189–195.

The Results Fieldbook by Mike Schmoker (ASCD, 2001), pp. 8–25, 101–119, 120–132.

Dipstick or Formative Assessments

"Working Inside the Black Box: Assessment for Learning in the Classroom" by Paul Black, Christine Harrison, Clare Lee, Bethan Marshall, and Dylan Wiliam, *Phi Delta Kappan,* September 2004.

"Inside the Black Box: Raising Standards Through Classroom Assessment" by Paul Black and Dylan Wiliam, *Phi Delta Kappan,* October 1998.

"Looking at Student Work for Teacher Learning, Teacher Community, and School Reform" by Judith Warren Little, Maryl Gearhart, Marnie Curry, and Judith Kafka, *Phi Delta Kappan,* November 2003.

"Classroom Assessment Minute by Minute, Day by Day" by Siobhan Leahy, Christine Lyon, Marnie Thompson, and Dylan Wiliam, *Educational Leadership,* November 2005.

"Looking at Student Work for Teacher Learning, Teacher Community, and School Reform" by Judith Warren Little, Maryl Gearhart, Marnie Curry, and Judith Kafka, *Phi Delta Kappan,* November 2003.

Classroom Assessment That Works by Robert Marzano, Debra Pickering, and Jane Pollock (ASCD, 2001), pp. 96–102.

The Art and Science of Teaching by Robert Marzano (ASCD, 2007).

"From Formative Assessment to Assessment FOR Learning: A Path to Success in Standards-Based Schools" by Rick Stiggins, *Phi Delta Kappan,* December 2005.

Educative Assessment by Grant Wiggins (Jossey-Bass, 1998), pp. 43–69.

Getting Students Involved in Their Own Improvement

"Helping Students Understand Assessment" by Jan Chappuis, *Educational Leadership,* November 2005.

"Assessment Through the Student's Eyes" by Rick Stiggins, *Educational Leadership,* May 2007.

"Using Student-Involved Classroom Assessments to Close Achievement Gaps" by Rick Stiggins and Stephen Chappuis, *Theory Into Practice,* Winter 2005.

Mastery Learning

"A Historical Perspective on Closing the Achievement Gap" by Thomas Guskey, *NASSP Bulletin,* September 2005.

"Synthesis of Research on the Effects of Mastery Learning in Elementary and Secondary Classrooms" by Thomas Guskey and Sally Gates, *Educational Leadership,* May 1986.

Effective Schools

"Effective Schools for the Urban Poor" by Ronald Edmonds, *Educational Leadership*, October 1979.

"Effective Schools" by Lynn Olson, *Education Week*, January 15, 1986, special section.

Total Quality Management

"Transforming Schools Through Total Quality Management" by Mike Schmoker and Richard Wilson in *Phi Delta Kappan*, January 2003.

Building Culture and Overcoming Resistance

"Using Test Score Data to Focus Instruction" by Susan Trimble, Anne Gay, and Jan Matthews, *Middle School Journal*, March 2005.

Making Analysis and Action Stick

"Classroom Assessment Minute by Minute, Day by Day" by Siobhan Leahy, Christine Lyon, Marnie Thompson, and Dylan Wiliam, *Educational Leadership*, November 2005.

"High-Stakes Testing: Can Rapid Assessment Reduce the Pressure?" by Stuart Yeh, *Teachers College Record*, April 2006.

Building an Effective Data-Driven Culture

"The Relation Between Professional Climate and Student Learning Depends on the Way a School Treats Teachers" by Janet Angelis, *Middle School Journal*, May 2004.

"Virginia's Excellent Adventure" by Kathy Christie, *Phi Delta Kappan*, April 2004.

"No Choice But Success" by Dick Corbett, Bruce Wilson, and Belinda Williams, *Educational Leadership*, March 2005.

"One Subject at a Time" by Catherine Gewertz, *Education Week*, February 2, 2005.

"Inside the Black Box of High-Performing Schools" by Patricia Kannapel and Stephen Clements, Prichard Committee for Academic Excellence, Lexington, Kentucky.

"Promoting a Collaborative Professional Culture in Three Elementary Schools That Have Beaten the Odds" by David Strahan, *Elementary School Journal*, November 2003.

Leading Professional Development for Adults

"Brain-Friendly Learning for Teachers" by David Sousa, *Educational Leadership*, June 2009.

Index

frequently asked questions regarding, 137; at Greater Newark Charter School, 52; importance of, 6–8, 28, 34; lack of, xix, xxxiv–xxxv, 3, 129; in lesson plans, 78–80, 81; sample questions in, 6–7

D

E

F

G

H

High-stakes assessment: action plan for implementing assessment and, 28–34; calendar development and, 112–113; interim assessment writing or selection and, 13; interim assessments' alignment to, 16, 28, 31, 32; interim assessments' role in, 9; myths about, 21–23, 27

Holabird Academy, 173–174

Homework, 80, 84, 250

Homogenous group, 165

Hudnor, S., 30–31

Hurricane Katrina, 116–117

I

Ideology, 61, 96

Illinois ISAT Exam, 94–95, 108

In-class assessment, 29

Inspiring participants, 171–172

Instructional leader. *See* Leader, school

Instructional strategy: action plans for, 29, 75–85; best practices for, 245–250; collaboration for, 25; college-ready rigor in, 16–18; effects of, 11; interim assessments' role in, 8–9, 10; plan for, 276–279; for professional development, 148–169

Intentional group, 165

Interim assessment, xx; action plan for implementing, 28–34; alignment of high-stakes test with, 16, 28, 31, 32; benefits of, 8–9; calendar development and, 112; development of, 132–133; effects of, 11; examples of, 5, 25; versus formative assessment, 127; foundation of, 11–13; frequently asked questions about, 127–136; importance of, xxxi, 8, 12, 13; ineffective use of, xxxi, xxxiv; versus in-the-moment assessments, 9–11; postponement of, 135–136; preparation for, 56; purpose of, 33–34; resources about, 285; review of, 272–273; role of, in learning process, 11–12; selection of, 13–19, 25, 33–34; timing of, 11–12, 13, 28; widespread failure on, 133–134; writing of, 13–19, 33–34

Interim assessment analysis: action plan for implementation of, 65–66; data reports for, 41–44; effects of, 10; example of, 31; focus of, 136; form for, 41–44; foundation of, 41; frequently asked questions about, 136–140; at Greater Newark Charter School, 47–48, 51–52; at Holabird Academy, 174; methods for, 44–50; at North Star Academy, 37–40; in phases of data-driven instruction, 107; professional development in, 53–64, 193–212; at Samuel J. Green Middle School, 117; spreadsheet for, 25, 274–275; timing of, 50–52; tips for new teachers in, 137

Interim assessment analysis meeting: beginning of, 57, 63; communication tips for, 61–64; example of, 58–59; importance of, 53; leader's facilitation of, 53–54, 56–57, 61–64, 89, 100; one-on-one versus group style for, 54; preparation for, 54–57, 64; principles of, 60–64; professional development for, 56–57, 65, 206–212; protocol for, 91–96, 220–224, 244; rationale for, 53; tasks during, 57, 60–64; tips for success in, 256–257

In-the-moment assessment, 9–11

Ivy, T., 108–109

J

Jackson, J., 24

Jesuit Community Service, xviii

Jones, M., 180–183

Josephs, R., 37–38

Journal, 79

K

Kennedy, J., xl–xli, 88–89

Kingsbury Middle School, 130–131

Krackhardt, D., 110

Krey, L., 173–174

L

Language, 229

Lanier Middle School, 122–123

Large-group sharing: during professional development, 149, 163, 165–167; time management in, 169–171

Leader, school: action plans and, 85–96; in analysis meetings, 53–54, 56–57, 61–64, 89; assessment-implementation action plan for,

S

Samuel J. Green Middle School, 116–117

Sandburg, C., 18

Sanders, K., 123

Sanford, J., 94–95

Saphier, J., 29, 140, 165

SAT: interim assessment writing or selection and, 13; myths about, 21–23

Saturday Academy, 72

Scaffolding, 9, 166

Schmoker, M., 91, 220

School calendar. *See* Calendar, school

School leader. *See* Leader, school

Secretive assessment, xxxiv

Self-evaluation, 83–84, 249

Shared vision. *See* Culture; Vision

Sharing: during professional development, 149, 163, 165–167; time management of, 169–171

Shells, S., 102

Simulation, 162–163

The Skillful Teacher (Saphier), 29, 165

Small-group work, 164–165

S.M.A.R.T. goal, 142

Software, 15

South Bronx Classical school, 30–31

Sparling, C., 25

Spencer, R., 76–77

Spreadsheet, 25, 275–276

Springsteen Charter School, 160, 179–183

Staff turnover, 173–174

Standardized assessment: assessment-implementation action plan and, 29; myths about, 21–23; overuse of, 128–129; preparation for, 87; purpose of, 34

Standard-level analysis, 45–50, 136, 274

State standards, alignment with: examples of, xx; importance of, 6–8, 28, 34; results meeting protocol and, 93; sample questions demonstrating, 6–7; transparency and, 12

STEP (Strategic Teaching and Evaluation of Progress) assessment, 25, 26

Storytelling, 171–172

Strength, building on, 103

Student engagement: in action plan, 81–82, 96–99; example of, 95; importance of, 96–97; resources about, 286; templates for, 97–99

Supplemental assessment, 129

Support staff, 88

Suxo, L., 15

T

Targeted instruction, 8–9

Teach Like a Champion (Lemov), 166

Teacher: accountability of, 25; assessment-implementation action plan for, 28–29, 32; building buy-in of, 106–110, 111, 131, 141–142; data-driven culture and, 106–107, 119–120; first action steps of, 65, 100; in ineffective analysis meetings, 54–56; interim assessment analysis methods for, 44–50; justifying data-driven instruction to, 115, 117–118; as models of best practice, 115; new school assignments of, 137; observation of, 100; ownership of data-driven instruction by, xxxv, xxxvi, 19, 59; principals' observation of, xvii, 88–91; providing time for, 32; resistance from, 61–64, 105–106, 109; results meeting protocol for, 91–96; role of, in analysis meetings, 60

Teacher data team, 137

Teacher-owned analysis, 137

Teaching style, 141

Tennessee State Assessment, 122, 123, 130

TerraNova, 17, 24, 30

Test publisher, 16, 44

Test-in-hand analysis, 45–50

Test-taking skill, 87

Think ratio, 247

Third-party test, 16

Thurgood Marshall Academy Charter High School, 70–72

Time, for data-driven instruction: action plans in, 73, 85; analysis meetings and, 65, 66, 92; calendar development and, 112; data reports and, 44; effective use of, xxxvii, 88; interim assessment analysis and, 44, 50–52; lack of, xxxv–xxxvi; professional development considerations in, 149, 169–171; providing

How to Use the CD-ROM

SYSTEM REQUIREMENTS

PC with Microsoft Windows 2003 or later
Mac with Apple OS version 10.1 or later

USING THE CD-ROM WITH WINDOWS

To view the items located on the CD-ROM, follow these steps:

1. Insert the CD-ROM into your computer's CD-ROM drive.
2. A window appears with the following options:

   Contents: Allows you to view the files included on the CD-ROM.

   Software: Allows you to install useful software from the CD-ROM.

   Links: Displays a hyperlinked page of websites.

   Author: Displays a page with information about the author(s).

   Contact Us: Displays a page with information on contacting the publisher or author.

   Help: Displays a page with information on using the CD-ROM.

   Exit: Closes the interface window.

If you do not have autorun enabled, or if the autorun window does not appear, follow these steps to access the CD-ROM:

1. Click Start → Run.

2. In the dialog box that appears, type d:\start.exe, where d is the letter of your CD-ROM-ROM drive. This brings up the autorun window described in the preceding set of steps.

3. Choose the desired option from the menu. (See Step 2 in the preceding list for a description of these options.)

IN CASE OF TROUBLE

If you experience difficulty using the CD-ROM, please follow these steps:

1. Make sure your hardware and systems configurations conform to the systems requirements noted under "System Requirements" above.

2. Review the installation procedure for your type of hardware and operating system. It is possible to reinstall the software if necessary.

To speak with someone in Product Technical Support, call 800-762-2974 or 317-572-3994 Monday through Friday from 8:30 a.m. to 5:00 p.m. EST. You can also contact Product Technical Support and get support information through our website at www.wiley.com/techsupport.

Before calling or writing, please have the following information available:

- Type of computer and operating system.

- Any error messages displayed.

- Complete description of the problem.

- CD-ROM ID# from the front of the CD-ROM.

It is best if you are sitting at your computer when making the call.